Kabbalah: School of the Soul

Figure 1—RABBINIC SCHOOL
Here a group of scholars discusses the meaning of certain passages in the Bible while they celebrate the Passover. This festival is about the beginning of the journey out of the bondage of conditioning towards the goal of inner freedom. Such informal conversations with the Teacher, here at the head of the table, are as vital as any esoteric practices the students might follow. For example, the story of the initial reluctance of Moses to take up his destiny might be what is being discussed. This a major issue for anyone on the path, at some point. (Print from old Haggadah.)

Kabbalah: School of the Soul

Z'ev ben Shimon Halevi

KS Books Ltd
London
This edition published by:

www.kabbalahsocietybooks.com
E-mail: info@ksbooksltd.com

First published in 1985 by Gateway Books
Revised Edition in 2008 by Kabbalah Society
Copyright © Z'ev ben Shimon Halevi 1985, 2008, 2024

Every effort has been made to obtain permission to reproduce copyright material but there may be cases where we have been unable to trace the copyright holder. The publisher will be happy to correct any omissions in future printings.

The moral right of the author has been asserted.

All rights reserved.
No part of this publication may be reproduced, stored in a retrieval system or transmitted, in any form or by any means, without the prior permission in writing of the publisher, nor be circulated in any form of binding or cover other than that in which it is published and without a similar condition including this condition being imposed on the subsequent purchaser.

A CIP catalogue record for this book
is available from the British Library.

ISBN:978-1-917606-11-0

Design by Lion Dickinson

For Avraham Ibn Ezra
Scholar, Traveller and Kabbalist

By the same author:

Adam and The Kabbalistic Trees
A Kabbalistic Universe
The Way of Kabbalah
Introduction to The World of Kabbalah
The Kabbalist at Work
Kabbalah and Exodus
Psychology and Kabbalah
The Anointed–*a Kabbalistic novel*
The Kabbalistic Tree of Life
The Anatomy of Fate
Kabbalah and Astrology
The Path of a Kabbalist
Kabbalistic Contemplations

By Other Publishers:

Kabbalah—The Divine Plan (*HarperCollins*)
Kabbalah, Tradition of Hidden Knowledge (*Thames & Hudson*)
Astrology, The Celestial Mirror (*Thames & Hudson*)
As Above So Below (*Stuart & Watkins*)

Contents

	List of illustrations	ix
	Preface	xi
	Introduction	xiii
1.	Natural Setting	17
2.	Spiritual Organisation	22
3.	Chain of Teaching	27
4.	Situation	33
5.	Transmission	38
6.	Levels	44
7.	Ground Floor	50
8.	Pseudo Groups	54
9.	Group Tree	59
10.	Student Types	65
11.	Tutor Types	71
12.	Synthesis	76
13.	Starting Points	81
14.	Contacts	86
15.	Introduction	92
16.	Connection	97
17.	Tutor	101
18.	Initiation	107
19.	Circumstance	111
20.	Projection	116
21.	Inauguration	121
22.	Objective	126
23.	Early Meetings	130
24.	Honeymoon	136
25.	Selection	141
26.	Evil	147
27.	Theory	152
28.	Devotion	158
29.	Ritual	163

30.	Relationships	168
31.	Star Students	172
32.	Sacred Space	176
33.	Action Tree	181
34.	Inner Temple	186
35.	Seminar	192
36.	Gateway	197
37.	Dangers	202
38.	Crisis	208
39.	Reputation	213
40.	Organisation	218
41.	Dull Times	224
42.	Service	229
43.	Ordination	233
44.	Schools	239
45.	Introductory Course	245
46.	Production	250
47.	Retreat	255
48.	Conference	260
49.	Building the Temple	266
50.	Networking	272
51.	Hierarchy	277
52.	Timing	283
53.	Moment of Destiny	288
54.	Blossom and Decline	293
55.	Death and Rebirth	298
	Epilogue	303
	Index	305

Illustrations

1.	Rabbinic School	ii
2.	Tree of Life	x
3.	Separation	xii
4.	Four Worlds	xv
5.	Jacob's Ladder	xvi
6.	Descent and Ascent	18
7.	Correspondence	26
8.	Levels of Teaching	28
9.	Melchizedek	39
10.	Progression	45
11.	Group Tree	60
12.	Temperaments	66
13.	Seeker	89
14.	Teacher	102
15.	Options	112
16.	Projection	118
17.	Introduction	131
18.	Psyche in Detail	142
19.	Work	155
20.	Place	177
21.	Discipline	189
22.	Dangers	205
23.	Interaction	221
24.	Threshold	235
25.	Tradition	241
26.	Secrets	263
27.	Temple	269
28.	Situation	279
29.	Work	302

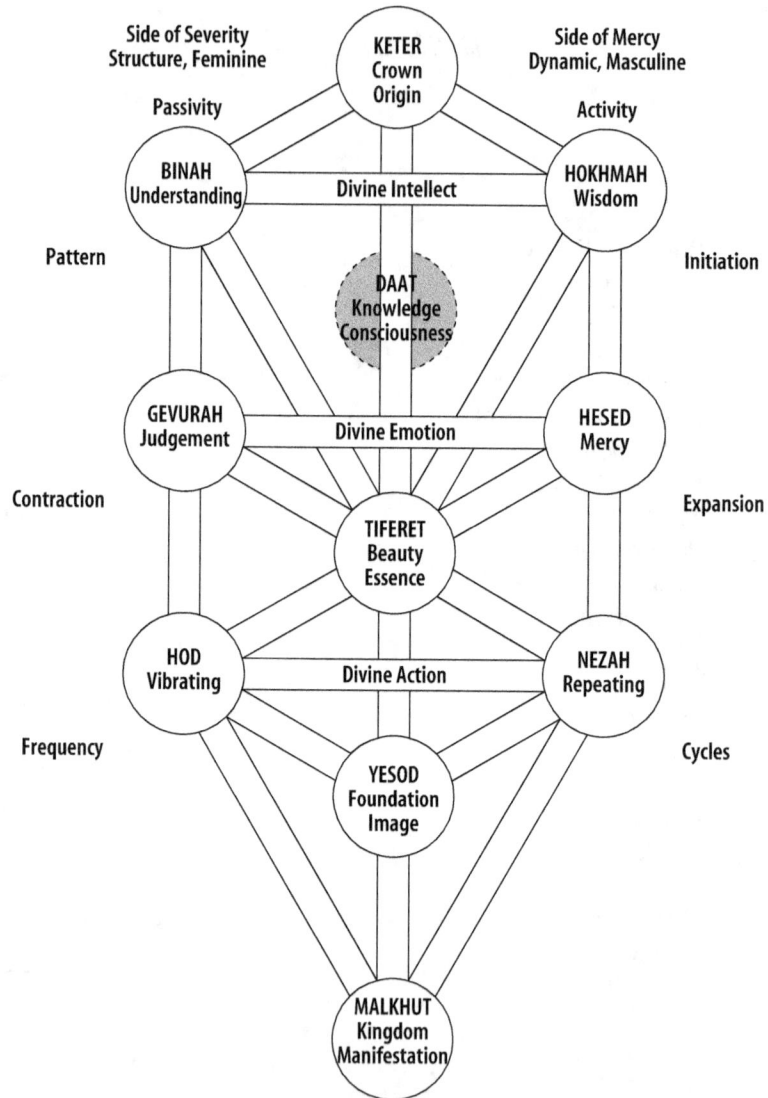

Figure 2 — TREE OF LIFE
This kabbalistic diagram is the basic metaphysical tool of the Tradition. It contains all the principles that govern Existence. Here the Hebrew terms, their translations and functions define the primordial World of Divinity. This is the first and highest realm of Emanation in which everything that can come into being is held in potential. The three lower Worlds that emerge from this place of Eternity are the vehicles by which God beholds God in the mirror of multiplicity to be seen in the different realities of Creation, Formation and Action. (Halevi definitions.)

Preface

In spiritual work an individual can only go so far. Beyond a certain point the Path becomes obscure because it enters the unknown. Here help is required. However, what is offered by circumstance is sometimes not what is needed and the inexperienced seeker cannot always tell the good from the bad. What can be said is that supportive companions are as vital as useful maps, well-tried techniques and a trustworthy guide, for the Way is beset with many trials to test and prevent the unready from moving out of their depth. A school of the soul is a convoy designed to take groups safely across this difficult country between the natural World and the Kingdom of the Spirit. Besides being a mode of training and transport, a school is a method by which people can form, under the direction of a tutor who is monitored by a master, a composite vessel that can encompass more than the sum of their knowledge or experience. Moreover, by the creation of such a vehicle, a company of committed people can not only enter the upper realms safely but also draw down the Holy Spirit so as to transform their activities into cosmic events that influence the world about them. This order of manifestation is the Work of every esoteric operation which is a link in the chain of Teaching. As part of a Line, a school of the soul not only belongs to an ancient tradition but is also a section in a worldwide network of spiritual organisations whose task it is to nourish the inner life of each generation, so that it may grow and bloom in the Garden of the Holy One.

London, Spring 5742

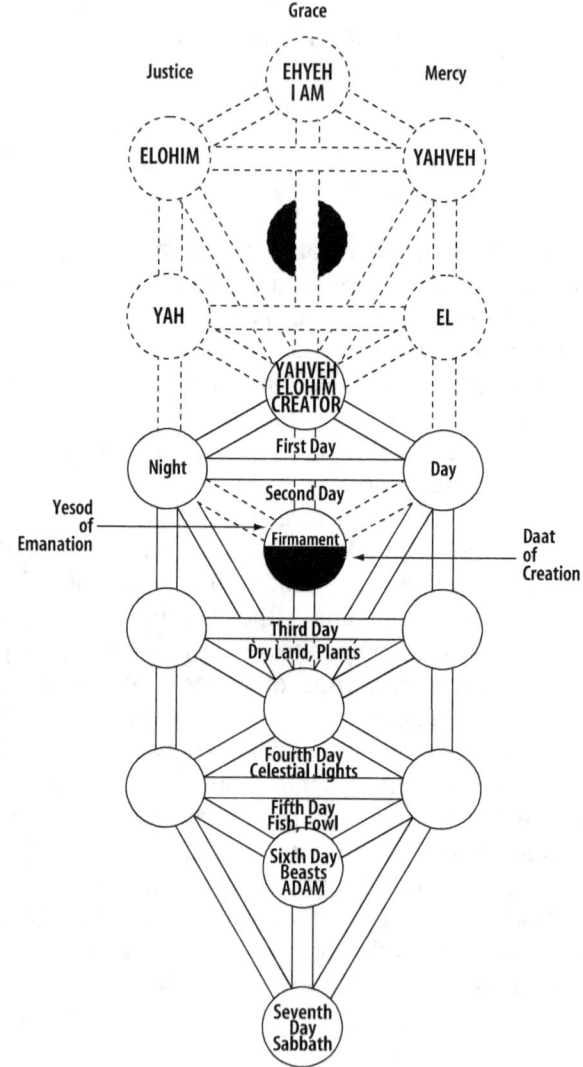

Figure 3—SEPARATION
Here the Divine Realm, with its Names of God, generates the World of the Spirit. This unfolds in the Seven Days of Creation. These levels are not material but essences of ideas of what will manifest in the lowest physical universe. First comes the notion of the four elements and their cosmic order with the plants representing the principle of Life. The Birds of the Air and Fish of the Sea, or Archangels and angels, emerge with the Beasts of the Field. These respectively symbolise the creatures of the three lower levels. Adam, the spiritual version of Adam Kadmon, the Divine Image of God above, appears just before the Creation process comes to rest. (Halevi interpretation.)

Introduction

In all previous books on Kabbalah, the emphasis has been on the theoretical side of the Tradition. *The Work of the Kabbalist* (now titled *The Kabbalist at Work*) began a new sequence written to meet the needs of those who wish to go further than just read about the subject. In that book the attitudes and techniques of individual work were set out so that a person could practise the traditional methods in a modern environment without losing contact with the essential principles of Kabbalah. In this book, the wider scale of a group developing into a school is examined, together with the problems involved. The creation of a school is explored in phases so that people can recognise the stage reached so far and what to expect.

One aim of this book is to help individuals set up their own group, if there is no one to lead them. In time a competent tutor will appear, either from an already existing school or, more likely, will emerge from the midst of an inner group that is created by those sufficiently committed to Kabbalah. While this is contrary to popular belief it is, nevertheless, a not-uncommon method by which a tradition is passed on. Besides the teacher-pupil transmission, Kabbalah can also come directly from above to a person who reaches that stage of initiation in which they are given instruction directly from what is called a *maggid* or inner teacher. There are many precedents for this phenomenon of heavenly instruction. The Baal Shem Tov of eighteenth-century Russia is one example. He received very little earthly training, yet his spiritual connection and teaching were clearly apparent and generated the Hassidic movement which brought holiness back into the Judaism of his area. For more humble mortals it is also possible to make such a contact with the living tradition. All that is required is diligence, intelligence, honesty and a method of becoming receptive so as to provide the time and space for what might descend from the Worlds above. This needs much preparation.

According to scholars, the first kabbalistic school, which arose in southern France, cannot trace its Line beyond a certain Rabbi Jacob HaNazir who lived in the twelfth century. It was said by his disciples that he was instructed by Elijah in a vision. This is a way of saying that their tutor had an interior *maggid* and inner connection with the upper Worlds. Evidence also indicates that he brought back the Teaching from Palestine. Either way, the conditions still had to be ripe for such a transmission to take place, that is, that the rabbinical group in the town of Lunel was ready and capable of receiving higher knowledge when it came. This was possible because they were well prepared by spiritual discipline and were receptive to what was given. Out of this esoteric contact rose the schools of Provence and Catalonia which led on to the radical reformulation of the oriental tradition into the medieval Spanish format of classical Kabbalah. The dissemination of Kabbalah from Spain thereafter not only contributed much to Judaism but to the general mystical life of Europe. Today the conditions are very similar to that pre-Renaissance period, except that we have scientific technology, rather than the logic of scholastic philosophy, to oppose spirituality. Moreover, we are on the edge of a new Reformation in which many people disillusioned with formal religion are seeking esoteric instruction. Kabbalah is one of the traditions that can meet the challenge of our time because it has always adapted its principles to the mode of the day. What follows is designed to be of use to anyone who wishes to be a Kabbalist in the service of the Divine.

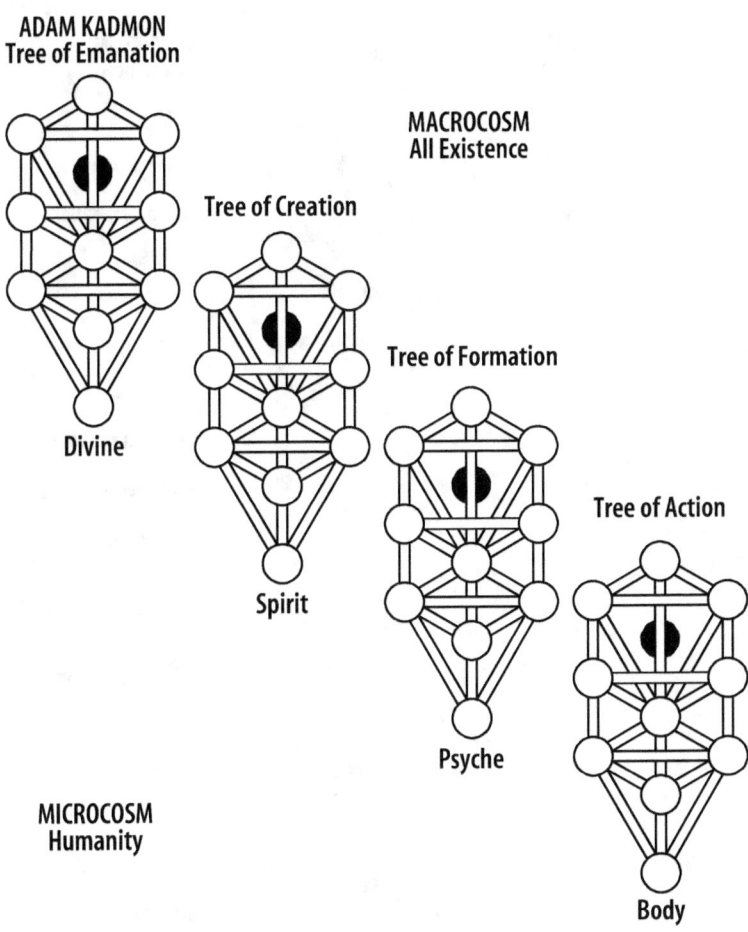

Figure 4—FOUR WORLDS
After the realm of Creation has been brought into being come those of Formation and Action. These correspond, in the microcosm of a human being, to the Divine, spiritual, psychological and physical aspects of an individual. As such they represent different levels. The body relates to the Earthly elements, the psyche to its Watery character, the spirit to Air and the Divine to Fire or the radiant spark deep within us all. As can be seen, while they are separate they do overlap so that, for example, the lower psyche is in contact with the body. At death they separate. (Esoteric version of Existence.)

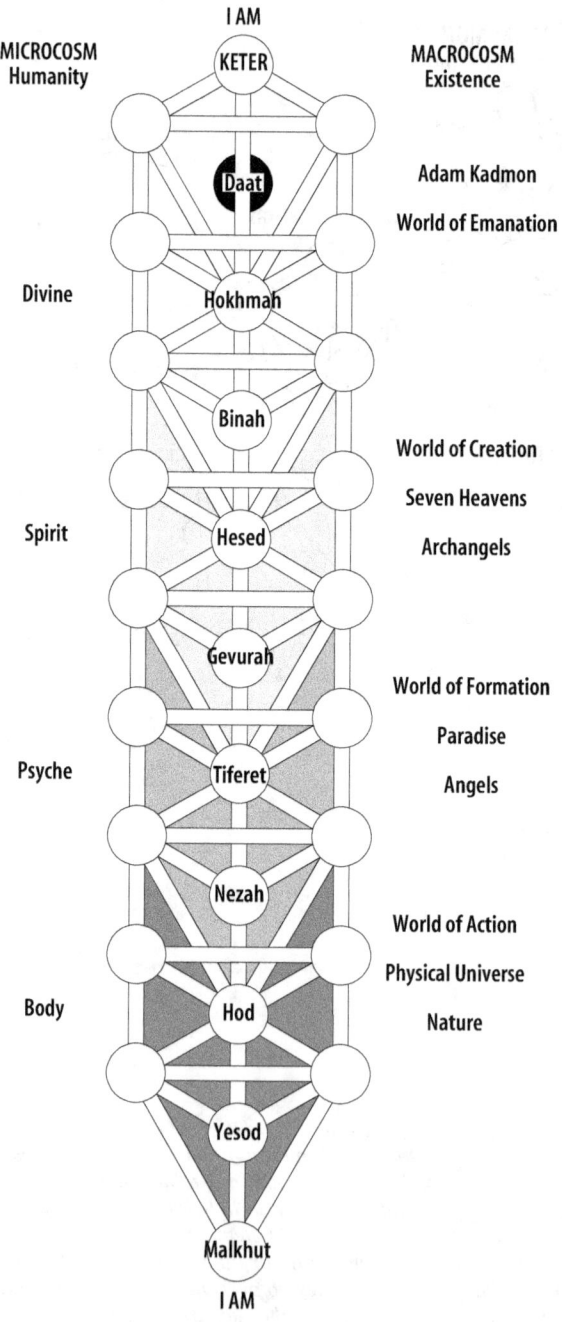

1. Natural Setting

According to Kabbalistic legend God, the Holy One, instructs an Academy on High upon the nature of Existence. This gathering is composed of the great human spirits who have attained the highest level of realisation during life on Earth and have merited direct instruction into the innermost meaning of the Torah. Moreover, tradition says that there is a chain of academies below this apex group in which a human being may study various areas of the Teaching. It is recorded that one great Rabbi, Shimon ben Yohai, used to visit the different *yeshivot* (as they are called) while in a mystic ascent, to see how each operated and what was its speciality. Some of these groups were named after their leaders, e.g. the Academy of Moses and the Academy of Aaron. This gives not only a hint of what each *yeshivah* studied, by the character of its tutor, but the fact that there are schools relating to particular Lines of development. No doubt every great spiritual tradition has its various schools and Lines, as they do on Earth, although the further up the hierarchy of Heaven one goes, the closer the Lines draw together, in principle, until one cannot tell the difference between Sufi and Buddhist, Hindu or Christian mystics. At these levels very little separates the magus from the gnostic, the mason from the shaman. Here the Teaching is the same, as the form dissolves into content and essential meaning.

One may ask why there are so many different religions if there is but one true Teaching, which, we observe in the history of mankind, is claimed exclusively by this or that sect as possessing the only version. The reason is witnessed by the fact that this dissension is only to be

---

Figure 5—JACOB'S LADDER (Left)
This is also called the Great Tree as it interlocks all the others into a single unified system. Such was the original Kabbalistic version of the Chain of Being, before it was almost forgotten. The central column contains all the sefirot, as they are called, that give access to Divine intervention at every level. Together they are symbolised by the Biblical forty years, or days and nights, which represent a complete process of transformation. This completion is vital in the development of an individual or nation as seen in the progress of the Israelites from a slave-minded rabble into an integrated people when they reached the Promised Land. (Oral tradition.)

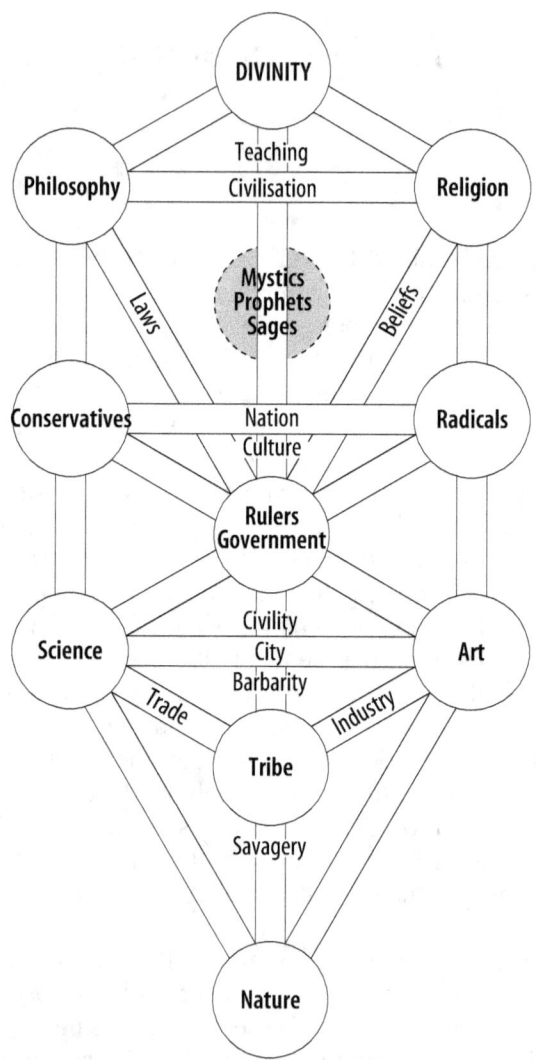

Figure 6—DESCENT AND ASCENT
Human beings, it is said, come from the Divine Adam Kadmon. They are the cells of consciousness that descend to take on spiritual, psychological and physical bodies. As the organs of perception for the Divine, they incarnate at the bottom of Jacob's Ladder. Here they begin the second journey of evolution. This is seen in this Tree of History as they develop as individuals and societies that define different phases. However, without highly advanced souls, most communities would remain at what are known as the vegetable and animal strata of humanity. Old souls are those who have been reincarnated many times but return on a third journey to teach in schools of the soul—or lead people astray, if they are evil. (History Tree, Halevi.)

found at the lower levels of comprehension where a multiplicity of views generated by physical and social conditions is an expression of a universal law: that the further one is from the source of realisation the more local and particular is the grasp of the total reality. A total view can only be found when one is in union with the Divine where no separation occurs. However, this is an ultimate state of evolution and between the first step and the last step of the spiritual path are many degrees and diversions. That is why so many different gates exist in the ordinary world. They are there to lead a seeker into contact with others on the Path.

With well-prepared companions many things become possible which could not be obtained on one's own. This book is about such spiritual collectives, how they bridge the evolutionary stages between the individual and the Absolute and operate at different levels. However, as this is a Kabbalistic approach, we must first observe the laws that appertain to the Ladder of Teaching and why it exists.

The totality of all that exists is contained in the One from which everything came. This Divine Unity is not only greater than anything contained within it but presents in itself the smallest separate unity. According to Kabbalah, the point of origin of all 'things' is symbolised by the Crown of Crowns which has attributed to it the Divine Name I AM THAT I AM. The meaning of this Holy statement is not only a declaration of intent but a description of the complete cycle of manifestation, from the going forth of Divine Will in the opening I AM to its return in the echo and repetition I AM. Between these two Holy Names, in the word 'that', is all there was, is, and shall be. This process of impulse and reflection radiates out from the Godhead to the furthest point of unfoldment in Existence where the principle of separation from the One into the multiplicity of the many creates, forms and makes myriads of beings and situations in a vast cosmic kaleidoscope of vibrations and particles. To the unknowing eye the universe is a profuse confusion of complications and random interactions; but to the knowing eye that observes patterns, the world is an ordered cosmos of structure and dynamic that is clearly moving through a distinct progression, be it seen in the turning of the seasons or in the relationship between Divinity and humanity. This order from the point of view of our study is to be noted in the unity and diversity of humanity in its various stages of evolution.

If we take mankind as a whole we will see that all human beings are essentially the same and recognise each other as distinct from any other species. Indeed, each individual can be said to contain, in miniature, all the attributes of a human being, whether they be male or female, because all elements are present in both sexes. It is only a question of emphasis. Here begins differentiation. However, besides the great sexual divide of the human race, there is the division of races. Some traditions split mankind into three types. Some Kabbalists, for example, take the symbols of the three sons of Noah as the people of action, devotion and contemplation—or those who work primarily through the body, heart or head. Other Kabbalists divide the human race into four according to the Holy Animals of Man, Eagle, Lion and Bull, that is the four spiritual types. Yet others divide the human race up into seven, according to their level of development. All these methods of division are valid. It depends what angle is being considered. However, these categories all have their limits because nothing in existence is in a pure state, so that while one could say that the civilisations of Africa, Asia and Europe might emphasise action, emotion and intellect respectively, there are many examples in all these general manifestations of human tendency that contain elements of the others, such as the European dancer, the Asian thinker or African poet.

The next general level of division might be seen as that of nations; that is, the spirit of a people which is a distinct entity within a race. The Scots, Welsh, Irish and English have long had to deal with this phenomenon and the Arab world, despite its nominal unity, is clearly a collection of diverse peoples with different values generated by location, climate and tribal custom. Such groups are definite organisms with characteristics all of their own. To the early European explorers all Africans looked alike, but with closer acquaintance there were clear and sometimes striking differences in temperament and attitudes between black nations. Indeed, the differentiation between peoples in India crystallised into the caste system which was originally designed to specify spiritual, not national duties.

Within the bodies of nations are the cells of various communities. These may be social or economic, class or geographical. Whatever they are, they relate to people who have certain things in common, be it heritage or profession, beliefs or even hobbies. Such communities may be located in one place or spread throughout a country. They can be found at every level, like football fan clubs, societies of water-colour painters or the Association for the Advancement of Science. The subdivision of these communities might be seen as families, so that, besides the obvious blood family we find, within the community centred round a church or synagogue, the local drama group, tennis club, horticultural society or just a circle of drinkers at a particular tavern. The chief characteristic of these groups is that they are composed of people who actually know each other personally, and share common values and often lives. In this family context, we find a clear set of rôles and an intimate reaction between individuals.

The individual is mankind in microcosm and, as such, is the smallest unit. However, the individual is a peculiar mixture of all greater levels in that each person has race, nation, community and family fused into their single and separate being. This means that each individual is like everyone, so that each person may be seen as a particular facet of all mankind. Here we have the end product of the process of descent through creation, formation and making to its turning point of individuation as the person begins the ascent of self-realisation.

By evolving out of the collective patterns, which are designed to help one survive and relate to the family, community and nation, individuation can begin. Many people think that individuality is acquired by being fashionably different or dominating one's fellows. It is not.

To be indeed unique requires a completely opposite approach, although this is often only recognised after succeeding or failing at life's most outward objectives. The first state of most seekers of real fulfilment is usually one of profound disappointment. It is at this point of despair that many individuals looking for Truth encounter someone in a spiritual tradition. Frequently, in their desolation and loneliness, they do not always realise that there is such a contact so close by. Mercifully, Providence creates a situation in which they are given the chance to recognise one of the 'companions', as people of the Path are sometimes called. If they do not miss the moment, they then begin the return journey to the Source by re-entering the orbit of a family; but this time a family group of quite a different order. This is the first stage of the corresponding levels of the inner hierarchy of groups, schools, Lines and Traditions that make up the spiritual infrastructure of mankind.

2. Spiritual Organisation

As there is a descending hierarchy of natural and social groupings of mankind, so there is an ascending set of associations that relate to the spiritual levels which rise up from the individual to Adam Kadmon who symbolises the archetypal human being. These inner groupings are as varied as their outer counterparts in that they are generated by every situation to be found in the human condition. Thus people of the spirit are to be discovered among the beggars of Cairo and amidst the affluent of San Francisco, the sophisticated circles in London and amongst the primitive Bushmen in the Kalahari Desert. Groups of such individuals may occur in the middle of an industrial city or in the remote countryside. Moreover, they are not always to be found in monasteries or dedicated communities. They may manifest as learned societies, business organisations or merely as an association of people living in a house that is run according to certain esoteric principles.

It has been said that one in a hundred people is interested in spiritual development but that only one in a hundred of these holds to the Path and carries it through to the end of his life. This means that only one in ten thousand people walking the Earth is involved in the esoteric life of the planet. Even so, this adds up to quite a number. Here, we begin to perceive that there must be some order in the selection process or the potential of this 'salt of the earth', as it has been called, will be lost. By this is meant that the apparently scattered array of such people must be monitored, screened and organised in some way. Obviously, such a vast operation cannot be carried out by individuals or, for that matter, by an earthly organisation, although the exterior practitioners of the world's great faiths have tried by various methods to imitate the process by converting and directing people into formal religious rôles. The approach of those in charge of the Way is, indeed, the very reverse, inasmuch as conditions are created that both test and resist anyone seeking the entrance to the Path so that only the trustworthy may enter.

How, then, is it done? What is the working system of an esoteric tradition? For clearly there is more to the various mystical schools than just gathering together to study and practise spirituality. Indeed, there is. A whole scheme of levels exists into which each tradition fits and performs its particular mission in the spiritual life of mankind. There are many ways of looking at the scheme. One is to perceive the chain of command, another to see how each school modifies its presentation according to need and location. Taking our model of the natural divisions of the human race, let us set it out in terms of correspondence so as to perceive its esoteric organisation.

The first unit is the individual who contains, in miniature, all the levels within. Such a person, we will assume, is no longer concerned with just physical survival or asserting an egotistical impression on society but wishes to explore the inner and upper Worlds so as to find a more complete fulfilment. These kinds of people seek for meaning, not only in their own lives but in the universe at large. They are not preoccupied just with their own little area of existence but wish to know why they are here on Earth and for what purpose. The first contact between a seeker and the Work, as it is sometimes called, is usually through their culture, either directly via family or at a distance through observation of the religious customs of their society. Very often the extent of such encounters is no more than taking part in a wedding or funeral. Those who attend religious services may sense that there is something deep implied by the ritual and scriptures but these experiences are undermined by the mechanical and soulless repetition of prayers and ceremonies. The only level that is touched, in many cases, is the tribal, even though the congregation may appear to be highly civilised. There are, of course, exceptions but this is usually contingent on the minister's inner connection, for there are rabbis, priests and imams who are mystics. Not every minister just marries and buries people.

The other primary contact with the realm of the spirit is through books which may be ancient writings or modern transcriptions of perennial philosophy. Some authors may be of the highest order and some a mixture of reality and fantasy. Certain texts can be a perfect window for that moment and others a closed door until the right time. The origin of works which have real substance is usually a tradition, although occasionally there is an individual like Jacob Boehme, the German visionary who, although uneducated, nevertheless produced a penetrating version of the Teaching. However, even he was subject to the cultural influence of his Christian grounding though he was not without direct help from the higher Worlds.

A Tradition is the vehicle by which the Teaching is transmitted in a particular form within a certain civilisation. Thus, we have Buddhist and Kabbalistic metaphysics, Greek Orthodox and Catholic rituals and a Hindu and Moslem liturgy. Very often the individual seeker, having rejected his or her own cultural background, finds a resonance in an alien tradition which does not carry the heavy loading of parental authority. This, for many, is the entry point into the second level of a spiritual family.

Groups correspond to the category of family. They are composed of a small number of people, ranging from four to forty members, just like a natural family in which everyone knows everybody else and has some kind of personal relationship, even if it is just being aware of sharing the same values and aim. A group, moreover, usually has a head—a father or mother figure—and several aunts, uncles or elders. A group also has the characteristics of a family in its celebrations and squabbles, moments of unity and tension, disarray and rally. People are people, even in spiritual Work, and the parent figurehead inevitably has foibles with the various positive and negative projections of children mixed in the group's interaction. But more of this in detail later as we wish, at this point, just to set out the general scheme.

Groups like families fit with other groups into a community which can be perceived as a school of groups. This level of organisation may be seen as a collection of spiritual families which follow a particular way of working. The outer connection may be no more than a shared source and method, like using the same text, or it may be an intimate alliance based upon having a common instructor who oversees a number of groups. Such schools can be recent innovations to meet the present or ancient establishments of orthodoxy. Some schools may possess buildings especially built for their purpose while others may meet in a selection of houses spread round a city or over the countryside. What makes a school, however, is that it exists and operates on a scale beyond the scope of a single group. A school, for example, can affect the life of a locality, like the monastic orders did in the Middle Ages. Here, we begin to recognise the increasing capacity and organisation of the spiritual hierarchy that watches over the world.

The level of a nation corresponds to a Line in spiritual terms. By this is meant that there is a certain emphasis in the form and its continuity. Thus several schools might carry a particular version of the Teaching to different parts of the world. Here we have, for example, the Hassidic mode of Kabbalah being lived out in New York and Jerusalem or the colleges of the Jesuits that educate Catholics in many countries. The chief characteristic of a Line is that it has, like a nation, a distinct nature that sets it apart from the other Lines, so that we may recognise certain Sufi orders by their methods. Indeed, we are told how a freemason may, by means of a handshake, tell if someone is in the same Line. A more obvious example of a Line is the Anglican Church which is precisely what it says. Its very English mode of worship may be as easily recognised in the United States of America as it is in Africa and Australasia. Not all Lines, however, are to be observed on the surface of life. Little is said or really known about the Rosicrucians who are a Line within the next level, that is, of a Tradition, in this case the occult.

Generally, Traditions develop within a civilisation. Christianity, for the most part, is a European phenomenon while Islam is Middle Eastern. This is because the interaction between race, place and spirit produces a particular civilisation in which the Teaching becomes externalised into an orthodoxy. Here esoteric themes become formal practices so that spiritual realities turn into doctrines of faith, personality cults and religious customs. All religions follow these patterns although each civilisation produces its own version. Traditions are usually based upon the lives of the great saints, sages and prophets who transmitted the Teaching for both mass and esoteric use in that particular part of the world. These impulses last millennia because the dynamic and structure of the Teaching is usually taken over by the secular clergy who hold the outer shell while the inner power is maintained by the mystics of the Tradition in the form of Lines, schools and groups, although this is rarely observed or acknowledged. Many priests and members of the laity are disturbed when Moses, Jesus and Mohammed are considered as mystics of the highest order.

The overall scheme is contained by mankind. The spiritual parallel is the Torah or Teaching given to Adam in order to reach full realisation. Here we have the complete chain of instruction for the imparting of knowledge about the nature of God, the universe and man and their mutual relationship. Thus, the spiritual hierarchy stretches from the individual up through group, school, Line and Tradition to the celestial colleges, that exist in another kind of time and space, up to the Academy on High taught by the Holy One. Seen as a totality, it is possible to perceive the whole scheme polarised between Adam Kadmon, the Primordial Man, and the individual human being with the various stages of development in the levels between. Having laid out the grand design, let us now examine what has been handed down to us about the history of the Teaching from the earliest times to our own, so as to see how it has flowed with the changing of conditions. In this way, we will prepare the background for our story of how a group goes through the process of becoming a school with a certain task and moment to blossom in time.

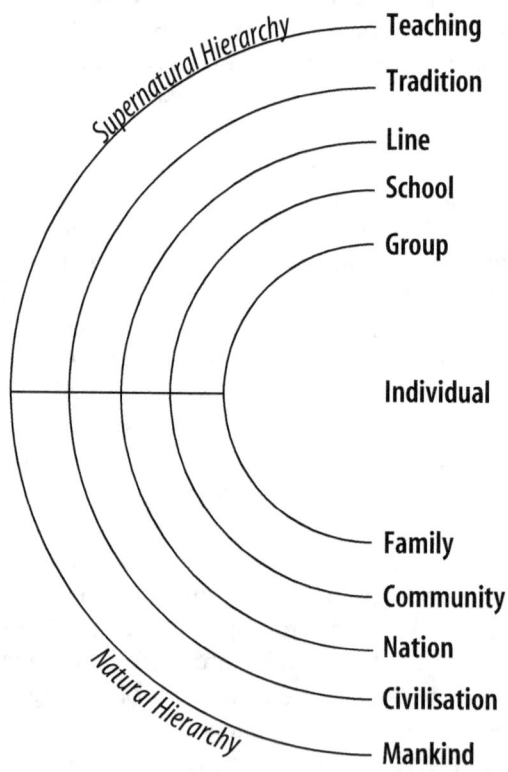

Figure 7—CORRESPONDENCE

This diagram sets out the law of 'as above, so below'. Here the levels mirror each other. The upper order represents a scale of organisations and development. As such, it is the body, mind and heart of civilisation. A society without revelations, religion and philosophy cannot go beyond the rule of tooth and claw. Fortunately, unethical and violent communities are eventually destroyed by their own karma. Many such brutal regimes have passed away without trace. In contrast, the high civilisations of ancient Greece and Judea are still an influence in the world. (Hierarchy, Halevi.)

3. Chain of Teaching

When Adam was given the Book of Secrets by the Archangel Raziel as he sat weeping outside Eden, there began a process by which mankind might regain access to the higher Worlds from which it had fallen. Some Kabbalists say that although the eating of the forbidden apple was an act of free will, it was in fact anticipated by the Omniscient Holy One in the way that a parent expects a child to break rules in order to learn about the universe in which it lives. By their action Adam and Eve opened up a consciousness of the World of Creation which made them aware of another dimension. This resulted in them being sent down into the physical World to prevent them from misusing the knowledge they had acquired, for they were still immature although now no longer innocent. The descent into matter was the first stage of a training in which they would expand their experience both upwards and downwards in the universe which is a capability no other creature, celestial or terrestrial, has. The Book of Raziel was given not just out of compassion but for a distinct purpose. It was to aid mankind to complete its destiny. It contained, we are told, an account of the laws that govern the universe and methods by which to find the way through the complexity of Existence and return in a state of maturity and responsibility to the Divine. This passage of innocence to experience was part of a great design in which mankind might come into full consciousness of the inner and outer aspects of Existence. Such an accomplishment would lead the human race to realise that the universe and itself were images of the same Face as God beheld God in the reflection of the great and small Adam: the Divine in manifestation.

The first individual to reach this state of total realisation was Enoch, the 'Initiated' one as his name implies. After living many years in holy seclusion while the rest of the human race learned to survive, Enoch was taken up out of his coat of skin into the Heavens where he was shown the wonders of the upper Worlds. When he returned to the Earth he was instructed to teach the ways of God so that mankind might start its evolution. He was the first man below to impart what

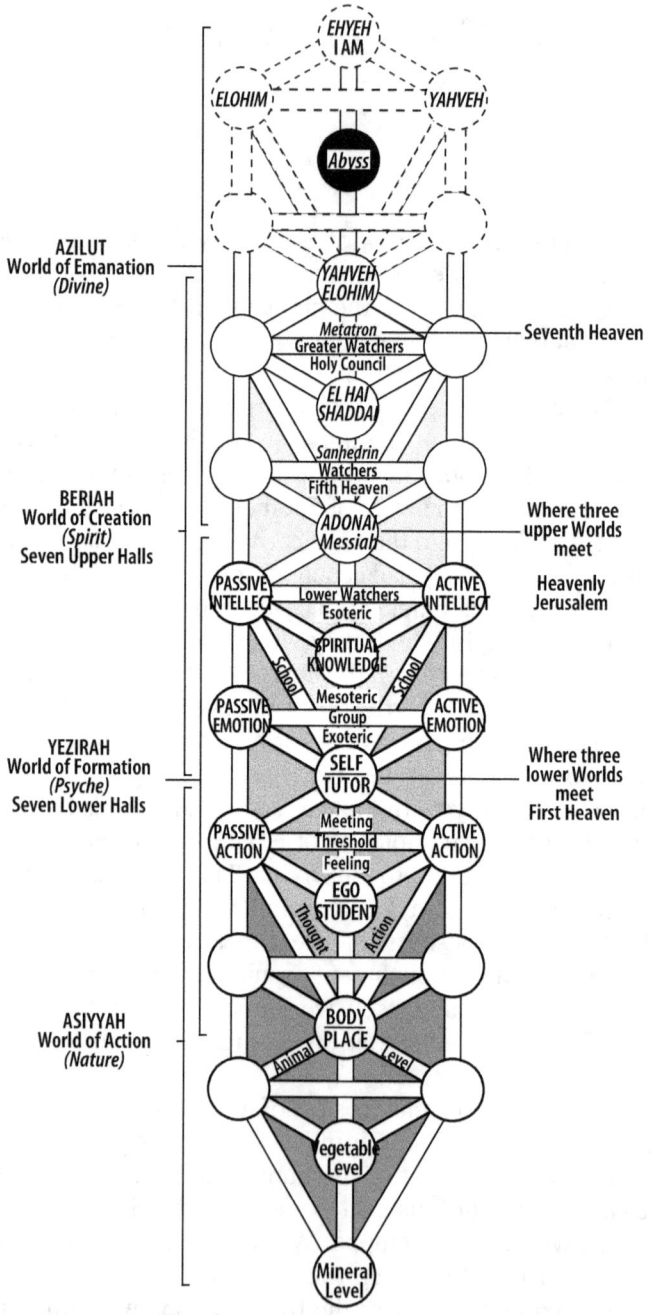

he had received from above to those who were seeking the Way of Return. Many people came to hear him, including kings and princes and, during the time that he was their guide, peace reigned in the lower World. Legend says that in the year that Adam died and was buried, Enoch retired from public life determined to devote himself to God. However, he was not allowed to do this as mankind needed his guidance and, indeed, the people implored him to stay in the world. After giving his last earthly instruction upon correct conduct according to Divine Law, he was eventually carried up once more into the heavens, only this time to take the place of the fallen Lucifer as the greatest Archangel Metatron who was to become responsible for the tuition of mankind over all the ages. In order to do this he did not taste death but was taken out of the normal cycle of birth and death to become transfigured into a Being of Fire, so as to become the first fully conscious cell of Adam Kadmon. Thus the primordial man began to realise Divine Consciousness within.

Enoch was the first true Teacher inasmuch as he became the head of a gathering devoted to esoteric study. As such he remains and is known by various names like Hermes Trismegistus, Thoth and Idris, according to the spiritual tradition. In Kabbalah he appears to the worthy Kabbalist as Elijah who instructs the initiate into the inner secrets of the Tradition. As the Great Scribe, Enoch is directly concerned with the whole operation of transmitting the Teaching in whatever form it may appear. Thus, we hear about the mysterious instructor who visited Jacob Boehme and the man who was seen by two students through the window of the Vilna Gaon but was not to be seen when they entered the room. These sightings indicate the intimate interest in individuals at crucial points of their spiritual development, as well as regard for the overall view of the esoteric chain of transmission. The intermediate levels of Tradition, Line, school and group are taken care of by others who have followed Enoch's trail-

---

Fig 8—LEVELS OF TEACHING
In this Ladder, different degrees of esoteric knowledge are closely defined. Above the level of ordinary experiences comes the exoteric, that is, the kind of spiritual information given out in the public domain. Then comes the mesoteric with schools of the soul. Above this are the schools of the spirit, the truly esoteric for the most advanced individuals. Beyond this are what are called the Academies on High for the discarnate masters and the Messiah who is the most spiritual person at present on Earth. They are sometimes called the Axis of the Age or the Buddha of the time. Above is the Great Holy Council presided over by Metatron, alias Enoch or Elijah when visiting the lower Worlds. (Halevi.)

blazing path, although there is good reason to believe that Abraham, who is the father of the Kabbalistic tradition, was in fact initiated by Enoch under the name of Melchizedek, the King of the righteous, outside Jerusalem.

In Western Asia and Europe there are several Traditions. These range from the Hindu, Persian, and Egyptian to the Celtic and Teutonic versions of the Teaching. Kabbalah is the Hebrew expression that became Christian under the Roman Empire and Islamic when blended with the Persian and Arabic Lines. Each of the Traditions has its own contact with Enoch and the spirit hierarchy that watches over those particular civilisations. Anyone standing in the middle of Stonehenge or walking through the Temple of Karnak at Luxor can sense, if they can shift to a higher gear of consciousness, that these were not just places of worship but institutions of instruction. Taking the flow just of the Judaic Tradition we find in the Bible and folklore embedded in the Talmud, together with such esoteric works as the *Sefer Yezirah,* traces of higher knowledge.

The scriptures give detailed accounts of the external mode of the Teaching through the designs of the tabernacle, ritual and laws; but these are meaningless without the hidden aspect of the Torah and this dual combination is sometimes symbolised by the tablets of the law. The oral tradition says that one tablet is to be studied during the day, that is in the open, and the other at night, that is in secret. The reason for this is that certain things cannot be understood without preparation and to receive them before one is ready is not only to have a partial comprehension but to impart a distorted view of them to others. An example of this is when a person thinks that reincarnation is simply a process of being reborn. There is much more to such a crucial event as rebirth, as many who have put off solving certain problems until the next life have found out. Esoteric or hidden knowledge is not for public consumption. Indeed, this book you are reading gives nothing away until the reader recognises what is written.

In the Bible the elders, priests and prophets symbolise 'those who know' which is the meaning of the word 'gnostic'. In fact, at a later period Kabbalists were called 'those who know the measure', that is, the laws of Existence. After the return from the first exile, the lines of transmission were to be found in the schools left behind in Babylonia as well as those re-established in Palestine. Later, as Jews began to set up colonies round the classical world, so groups were to be located in North Africa, Western Asia and Europe. During the Second Temple period the most important centres of the Inner Teaching were to be found in Jerusalem, either in the Temple area or in the study houses attached to the many synagogues in the Old City. Here we observe different Lines beginning to emerge as the priesthood, the Pharisees and the Essenes. There were others, such as the early Christians. Later, after the destruction of Herod's Temple by the Romans, the schools moved to Galilee. The great Rabbi ben Yochai was at the head of one such school. As these Lines declined, the groups hidden within the learned academies of Babylonia received their *Barakah* or Grace and became the chief transmitters of the tradition.

Little is known about the people involved in such activities but books like the *Sefer Yezirah* and various esoteric fragments describing the topography of the Heavens, such as the *Hekalot* literature, suggest a very active interest in mysticism amongst the rabbis of that period. As the Babylonian rabbinical academies waned, so various scholars turned to the West and travelled by the trade routes to Europe and North Africa where they found groups seeking higher knowledge. One particular Line, carried by the Kalonymus family, moved north through Italy and over the Alps into Germany to create a blend between oriental mysticism and German Jewish piety in the Middle Ages, while another Line entered Spain through Provence which had a particularly high cultural level in the twelfth century. Here various schools modified the Teaching to meet the threat of philosophy which was very much the preoccupation of the intelligentsia of the time. Groups, centred on various rabbis, exchanged letters and representatives and frequently visited each other to develop ideas. This was the period during which Kabbalah came to be known by that name. Besides the Jewish schools, there were the Christian and occult traditions which took up and adapted the Kabbalistic teaching to their own forms. These later developed into various Lines such as the Masons, who built the cathedrals, and the Rosicrucian Order.

To give an example of different Lines, the Spanish and German Lines of Kabbalah have quite distinct characteristics, in that the former is more intellectual and the latter more devotional. Within each stream various schools evolved, some concerned with meditation methods and others preoccupied in the metaphysics. Each school was naturally influenced by the temperament and interest of its leader and we see this phenomenon later in the various schools that arose in the Galilean town of Safed in the sixteenth century. Here the lucid thinker, Cordovero, led one school while his brilliant student, the charismatic

Luria, formed another which took quite a different direction. Deeply devotional schools working within the Lurian Line emerged in Germany and Poland while other groups in Holland and England developed a more secular approach. The philosopher Spinoza and the English mystic Fludd were products of these schools.

The flow of the Teaching does not always follow the orthodox way and in Kabbalah in particular there is a history of innovation and reformulation which has kept the Tradition alive despite opposition from the more conservative.

At the present time there are several Lines of Kabbalah operating around the world. The most conventional are the orthodox groups to be found in Jerusalem. Others, not always to be recognised as obviously in the Kabbalistic Line, exist in Western Europe and the Americas with embryo groups located in South Africa and Australia. Kabbalah today is not what it was a century ago. The world has been greatly changed by two wars and social and technological revolutions. Therefore, the Teaching must also change, although the more traditional schools still retain the old forms in Israel. At the moment there is a tremendous movement to form a global network between individuals and groups involved in the spirit. Never before have the various Traditions become so close. Thus Kabbalah, while retaining its own modes and methods, will relate to other traditions. However, before we can fully understand the implication of this operation, we must understand what makes a group the way it is and how it operates at the level of a human family, before seeing where it fits into the larger scheme as a distinct entity.

4. Situation

Groups, like families, are at once the same and yet quite different. They have the essential structure and dynamics of a related collection of people, which is modified by the general conditions of time and place, and the individual temperaments that make up the group. Kabbalah, or indeed any teaching concerned with the Spirit, has the added dimension of the upper Worlds so that there are not only the natural sympathies and antipathies between its members but the interactions of the various levels. For example, while the person leading the group may be an elder, he or she may not always be the teacher or the connection with the Tradition. Such a situation can occur at the beginning of a group's life when it is not yet established or at its end when it has become an empty shell of what was once a living organism. Moreover, as in all families there are those of different generations and stages of inner development so that, say, a younger member may be instructing an older person in some practice with which they are more familiar. These conditions, plus any other factors, give a group its particular character.

The most powerful influences on the form of a group are its physical and historical circumstances. These will have a bearing upon the nature of the Work being carried out. Clearly a primitive country will generate a simple culture that does not have an elaborate system of metaphysics, although it might develop a complex series of rituals and symbols such as can be found amongst the shamans of the Native Americans. Prehistoric cultures exhibit a high degree of this type of allegorical and practical knowledge concerning the nature of the universe and the forces operating between the visible and invisible Worlds. The system of the first temples and myths may not relate to our age but, to the discerning, they describe the structure and processes of Creation in the symbols used. The Red Indian differentiation between *Manitou*, the all-pervading God, and the spirits of the elements, plants and animals of nature is an example of the spiritual discernment of a people once thought by white people to be totally savage.

Where life was more organised, such as in early Mesopotamia and Egypt, the fusing of tribal interests into communities allowed a higher level of culture to emerge in the creation of the specialist occupations of a city society. Such a situation brought forth a professional priesthood which could spend more time on speculation and revelation, the prerequisites of conscious development. Out of this came the great temple complexes of Sumer and Memphis with their schools of priests who contemplated the ways of the universe, as well as serving the community and its gods. Ur of the Chaldees was such a place and into this most urbane city with avenues and gardens, university and library was born Abram, father of Kabbalah. However, when Abram reached maturity he found that he was not satisfied with the Urian view of many gods governing the universe. He perceived an overall unity which supervised the whole of Existence. On realising this, he was instructed by God to 'Get thee out of thy country and from thy kindred and from thy father's house unto a land that I will show thee'. That is, leave the confines of the natural World and begin the journey back towards the Holy Land. Most people think this is Canaan but it also means the World of the Spirit where Abraham was initiated by Melchizedek, the teacher king who, legend has it, ran an esoteric school in the city of Salem, later to be called Jerusalem.

A good teacher is vital to a group and even Moses, who had been educated in Egypt, had to be taught. His instructor was Jethro, his father-in-law, a rare priest of the time who also believed in the reality of a supreme God. Folklore tells us that Moses worked in the context of the family after initially being severely tested by Jethro to see if he was fit to join the group. After many years' training at being a shepherd in the desert, this highly cultivated man (remember he had been brought up as an aristocrat) had to "go down" into Egypt to rescue a demoralised people who had all but forgotten their ancestral God. Moses' training had been with flocks of sheep which prepared him well for his task. The circumstances and his personal background were exactly what was needed for the spiritual leadership of the twelve tribes. Those higher beings who prepare such people of destiny know just which schools and groups they should be sent to, although at the time Moses, no doubt, thought his life was adrift when he ran away from the comfort of Egypt and into the barrenness of the desert[1].

The Essenes of the Second Temple period were well organised as a school. Besides the various groups scattered around Judea, they built,

---

1. See the author's *Kabbalah and Exodus* (Kabbalah Society.)

according to some, the monastic complex at Qumran by the Dead Sea where they had dormitories, ablution chambers, a dining room, assembly hall and scriptorium. Self-sufficient, growing their own food, making their own pottery, doctoring themselves and even burying their own dead, they were a highly developed family with everyone knowing his or her place. Entrance into such a community was strictly controlled and their study and practices were in the simplest and purest form as a reaction against the over-elaborate methods of ritual and learning of the priesthood and Pharisees. Evidence indicates an astringent working method aimed at producing a particular kind of physical, psychological and spiritual purity. This was not the traditional way the Teaching had been taught up to that point, in that the Essenes withdrew from ordinary life and the historic process of which Judaism has always seen itself as part. But it must have met a specific need in Judea at the time for it was never re-established after the Romans had destroyed the site of Qumran.

The groups that operated within the rabbinic schools of Babylonia were quite different. They were conducted with the utmost secrecy. Set up behind the academic life of Sura and Pumbedita, between the first and tenth centuries, carefully selected people would study the techniques of inner development in order to perceive the higher Worlds. These practices had been carried out in Judea but, with the destruction of the Temple, many mystics had come to Babylonia to teach in the relatively secure and cultivated conditions of the Jews who lived under the Persian and later Arabic rule. Here many new esoteric formulations were made in the light of Greek, Arabic and Persian ideas. Occasionally one comes across some reference to such matters in Talmudic commentaries but generally any external speculation was confined to small and terse works like the highly obscure *Book of Formation*. Indeed, esoteric studies were discouraged by the rabbis, no doubt because they feared that the Teaching would be rapidly distorted and proliferate in the university where brilliant but young minds would be quickly overloaded with things even mature Kabbalists treat with great care and respect.

The conditions in medieval Toledo were not dissimilar but here there was a situation of yet closer multi-culture between East and West. In this cosmopolitan city Jews, Arabs, Berbers, Celts, Visigoths, French, Germans and Italians mixed with relative ease. At the intellectual levels people conversed in or read Arabic or Castilian, Hebrew, Latin and Greek. Schools of translation had been set up in the university and scholars came from all over the then known world to study the subjects particularly related to metaphysics and magic for which Toledo was famous. Many Moslem, Christian and Jewish mystics were, no doubt, more than just acquainted with each other. The book *Duties of the Heart*, written by a Jewish judge, became a standard work among the Diaspora although it contained many neo-Platonic and Sufi concepts. This was the cultural climate in which its author, Bahya ibn Paquda, lived. No doubt those who met in the equivalent of the student cafés discussed the meaning of life, as students have always done, and quite possibly someone sitting at a table scribbling eloquent Hebrew verses in the Arabic mode was on the look-out for likely candidates for the kabbalistic group that met near the palace of Samuel Halevi. Not all who study Kabbalah have been orthodox or rabbis. In the Spain of that time the level of education was probably the highest in Europe and it was certainly its spiritual capital.

Quite a different situation pertains to the groups that met in the Galilean hill town of Safed in the sixteenth century. Here was a gathering of exiles from Spain, set against the backdrop of an Arab but Turkish-ruled country. At that time there was little active culture in a land which had become decadent and desolate at all levels; and yet Kabbalists came to this little town from all over the Jewish world because, for two or three generations, there were spiritual schools at work there. Various groups met in the synagogues and study houses off the narrow winding streets of a town where the air was exceptionally clear. Interrupted only by the occasional earthquake and Arab riot, life was a continuous practice and study of kabbalistic principles. One group, for example, formed a spiritual society which lived in a constant state of confession and prayer while another group chose to withdraw into a quiet room after a heavy day's legal cogitation to listen to their teacher go into a semi-trance and speak about kabbalistic topics which he noted down in his diary. Many new prayers and rituals based upon kabbalistic notions were created in Safed that are still used in Jewish liturgy today. They are now regarded as quite traditional.

The conditions of the present time were partially generated by the 1939-45 Holocaust which all but wiped out the Hassidic line of Kabbalah. Whole schools were swept away and the thread of continuity has almost been lost. Fortunately the methods used are being preserved by the revival of the Hassidim in Israel and America but their way may only be studied by those who are orthodox Jews. Kabbalah, however, is greater than any sect and the Tradition is making itself manifest through various groups and schools. Some of these are based on already existing modes of transmission while some are new formulations that meet the spiritual hunger of people who want to work in the Way of Kabbalah. The last decades of the twentieth century and into the twenty-first see a great and spreading interest in esoterica internationally with many books being written about Kabbalah. However, Kabbalah can only be transmitted orally and so wherever the need is concentrated, interested people gather and attract an instructor to teach the system. Thus kabbalistic schools, some open and some closed, are beginning to cultivate and service groups in different parts of the world. Each group generated will have its own characteristics, according to the location and the people involved. Some will relate to the more traditional methods and others may be quite new in their approach. The school from which this book emanates, for example, blends ancient and modern terms. The result is just the same, if the inner connection is there.

This, of course, depends upon the leader of the group and his or her relation to the Teaching.

5. Transmission

According to legend, the source of Enoch's knowledge was the moment he was ordained by God. Having earned much by dint of his own effort to develop his body, soul and spirit, Enoch had merited the Grace that was given to him by the Divine. The ancient text describes how the Archangel Gabriel brought him up through the angelic hosts and set him before the Divine. Here he fell upon his face in awe but was picked up by Michael, the High Priest of Heaven, as the Holy One said, "Enoch be not afraid! Rise up and stand before My Face for ever." He was divested of his robe, that is, his grosser parts, anointed with holy oil and clothed in a celestial garment; and he ceased to tremble as he became one with the Spiritual World about him. He was then instructed to write down all that the Archangel of Wisdom was to read to him from all the books of the holy library and this, we are told, took thirty days and nights. By the end he knew all that there was to know about Heaven, Earth, angels and men that was suitable to be imparted. After this he was introduced by the Holy One into the secrets about all those matters that not even the archangels know of. The legend hints that these secrets were of how Creation was brought about, the purpose of evil, how long the universe will exist and what its end will be.

This ordination was the very first and is why Enoch bears the name 'The Initiated'. Thus began the chain of transmission that was to carry the Teaching on through all the generations. Clearly Enoch was unique in becoming the first fully realised human and it seems right that he should be ordained directly by the Divine as there was no other being in existence who could perform the operation. Much later we have Abraham's initiation by Melchizedek whom tradition also equates with Shem, the eldest son of Noah, himself the initiate who preserved the Teaching through the disaster of the Flood. According to another tradition the cave called *Shem va Ever*, in the Kabbalistic town of Safed, is the place where Shem, in later times, taught Jacob the Torah after he had run away from his home. Jacob in turn transmitted the knowledge to Joseph, his most gifted son, symbolising how the most

Figure 9—MELCHIZEDEK
This personage had neither father nor mother, indicating that he was not of the material World. It is said that this was yet another manifestation of Enoch whose name means 'the Initiate'. He is giving Abram bread and wine which symbolise the theory and practice of the esoteric Teaching. He then renamed Abram—Abraham, which, in translation, is 'Father of Many' people or schools of the soul. Indeed, out of this root came three monotheistic religions and many schools of the soul and spirit. It is said that Enoch can appear anywhere in time and space to instruct or protect masters, teachers or anyone worthy of his attention. (Bank's Bible.)

capable, not necessarily the eldest, receives the Blessing to continue the line. When Joseph died Levi, his brother, had a vision and received the *Barakah* from his grandfather, Isaac, according to his testament. Yet folklore says that the Line of transmission almost died out while the Israelites were slaves in Egypt. Only the tribe of Levi retained a dim remembrance of the Tradition and Moses, a member of this family, was selected to revive the connection. He was directly ordained by God on the Holy Mountain where he received detailed instruction upon the nature of the world, the purpose of human beings and their relationship to God. Legendary accounts of his ascent on Mount Sinai are very similar to the stories of the initiation of Enoch and Tradition adds that the angel of the Lord, sent before the Children of Israel in the desert to be a guide, was Metatron, the translated Enoch. Thus was the Line re-established and earthed in the ordination of Moses' brother, Aaron, as High Priest.

The priesthood carried on the outer form of the Teaching while Moses and the elders studied the inner content. Here, again,the symbolism of the Bible and its legends tells us something about the nature and function of schools in that some work with ritual and prayer, others in reflective contemplation. Moreover, the symbol of the elders indicates that a certain level of maturity has to be reached in order to be able to study the esoteric aspect of the Torah. The advantage of an ordained teacher to lead one through the difficulties of the Path is well illustrated by the Israelites' journey up out of Egypt, through the Sinai Desert and into the Land of Milk and Honey. However, the Books of *Judges* and *Samuel* reveal much about leadership and how one must not be misled by people who have power, like Samson, but a fatal weakness that destroys them; and how one must not trust an ego-centred King like Saul who, although anointed, nevertheless left the Path and became prone to fits of madness as such leaders do when they become jealous of their position. Ordination does not mean that spiritual knowledge cannot be abused. Such action can remove whatever Grace may have rested upon that person. For it will be remembered that King David, whose name means 'The Beloved', was not allowed to build the Temple on account of his many imperfections. Therefore always beware of teachers who, allowing for human error, do not do what they say to the point that it is a corruption of their teaching.

The prophets were an independent Line from the priesthood and kept it in check when it periodically became too rigid in form. They were masters who did not emerge from a father-son or teacher-pupil line of continuity but appeared spontaneously when the need arose. Here is the discreet side of the Tradition which is rarely seen while the orthodox carry on the outer aspect. In Kabbalah, there are many *maggidim* who come to teach, from where no one knows. Scholars find such characters difficult to cope with because there is little written evidence of their existence. In many cases Kabbalists do not know who is their teacher's teacher, either because they have never knowingly met the man or woman or because no connection is openly made for a variety of reasons, ranging from the social through political and professional, to a decision to set up an independent organisation, a new root or just be discreet. For example, there is no evidence of correspondence between William Blake, the mystic poet, and any Jewish scholar and yet a knowledge of Kabbalah from the inside is apparent in his work. Kabbalah is like the proverbial iceberg. Most of it is out of sight.

How, then, is knowledge transmitted to a teacher and on to a group? The most observable way is through the orthodox Lines of succession. Here it is interesting to note that, in Safed in its kabbalistic heyday, an attempt to reinstate an open and official ordination Line, broken with the destruction of the Temple, was foiled when the Chief Rabbi of Jerusalem refused to acknowledge the authority of the ceremony. So there is no pope-like succession in the Kabbalistic Tradition. What did happen was the passing on of the rôle of tutor to the most suitable candidate in each group although occasionally some students took it to themselves to be the transmitters of their master's teaching. The quality of their work, however, usually reveals a lower level of comprehension, in that it is often a superstitious understanding or poor imitation originating from a desire to bask in the reflected glory of the teacher's reputation. Very often the inner spark that illuminated the group is removed some time before the inevitable squabbles break out. Beware of schools that have petty power struggles. They are not in Kabbalah which is concerned with integration at all levels. Their task is either stillborn, as sometimes happens, or done, when the Light has gone.

A genuine teacher can emerge from an orthodox Line or appear out of nowhere. Such a person may have been trained in a recognisable school and have been secretly initiated by a hidden teacher. Because of this, some people may or may not speak about their background in detail. On the other hand, while some may prefer to keep such matters private, others will see it as a way of demonstrating principles at work. It depends on the time and place and the maturity of the students involved. The chief quality of a good teacher is the ability to teach which quite a number of people who think they have something to transmit do not have. Many so-called instructors think that to be obscure or mysterious is enough but time soon reveals, to the discerning, that these people are either interested in power or are deluded about their capacity. There are many such guru-type figures who draw to themselves people who wish to be carried away on a cloud of fantasy in order to avoid their worldly or personal problems.

A true instructor makes the workings of the upper Worlds intelligible and relates everything to life on Earth. Even the most esoteric Kabbalist, while speaking about the operations of Heaven, still refers to the way one makes such higher knowledge practical, otherwise there is no unification of Worlds. Moreover, good tutors of the Path never make promises they cannot fulfil or take a student or group beyond their capacity. These are the hallmarks of those who know how to operate within the limits of possibility while at the same time always extending the frontiers of knowledge and being.

Ultimately, whether a teacher comes from an identifiable Line or simply turns up without any credentials does not matter. What does is whether he or she has a connection with the Tradition. By this is meant that they are at that point of development where they have a real spiritual contact. This may be in the form of an earthly mentor or a direct relationship with a heavenly supervisor. It has been known, for example, for certain students with a psychic disposition to sense and even see a luminous figure standing behind a tutor during a meeting. This phenomenon is not unusual, as anyone who has to occupy the tutor's chair of a group inevitably has a guiding spirit who watches over the progress of the Work. Such a being may or may not be the personal mentor of the teacher. There are many accounts of such sightings but they should not be regarded as conclusive, not because they might be illusions but in that their presence is merely indicative of interest from above. As one rabbi remarked, 'When I was young, I used to see angels everywhere. Now I don't take notice of them'. One has to assess the teacher's merit in personal performance.

Ordination is an interior process. It may have an outer counterpart in some Lines of a Tradition but these can become, in time, merely empty ceremonies conferring status within a group, as has happened within some Masonic lodges. The genuine article is usually preceded by a series of examinations but these are, more often than not, tests in real life that corner and strain the person at his weak point in relation to the Work and the world. Only when a candidate for initiation has been proved trustworthy as regards integrity can he be allowed to enter the Tradition. Only when that individual has exhibited a deep commitment to the Work can he or she begin to transmit the Teaching. When this is accomplished, then quite spontaneously people start to come to that person and ask to be taught. A chosen teacher does not need to look for students or take over an existing group or school, as some ego-oriented gurus try to do. No! The circumstance is usually providential, in that there are seekers around who are ready and need what that person can offer, even if they have only finished the first stage of their training, for not all teachers are masters. There is a whole spectrum of instructors before one is ready to be taught by a Melchizedek. In Kabbalah, every step must be filled and experienced. Thus, no tutor can move until his or her place has been filled. In this way the Line of transmission is continued, not only through time but as an unbroken series of levels that reaches up from Earth to Heaven.

6. Levels

It has been said that there are three general levels of spiritual influence at work in the world. The first and lowest is that of ordinary life. Here the processes of Creation and evolution are roughly balanced, with a gradual progression being worked through as the universe at large evolves. The majority of mankind, who live within this sphere, progress very slowly in their development and pass many lifetimes learning just one or two lessons as they move at the speed of communities and history. This form of development is almost entirely external with circumstances and events acting as the teacher. Millions of men and women choose to grow this way because it requires no conscious effort and little responsibility for one's individuality. It is the way of mass evolution with its almost totally earth-oriented values and customs. One only has to note the progress of mankind in general over the last thirty thousand years to see that, despite our highly technical civilisation, most people are still at the local and tribal stage. Wars are still being fought over territory and dominance, and people on the whole continue to see religion as our ancestors did, as a social and superstitious belief based upon fear of the unknown and the worship of customs. This is the earth level of reality.

The second level of spiritual influence is that of indirect contact with the Work of Heaven. This may take the form of sacred books, the arts and buildings that speak of those higher Worlds. For example, one may detect spiritual knowledge present in certain dances, like the Mexican pole flyers or stories like Cinderella, or in the way particular people dress, like the wigs and gowns of British lawyers, though they may have lost contact with the original meaning. Works of art from many cultures indicate an intuitive sense of another reality, as in a painting of Paradise, a sculpture of an angel or a jewel made to represent different aspects of the zodiac. These objects carry a charge that no purely secular artifact has. They have a symbolic power that people recognise as being of a different dimension. The two candlesticks that are lit in Jewish homes on a Friday evening represent the Divine pillars of Mercy and Judgment, although few know this.

Figure 10—PROGRESSION
The stairs up to the Heavenly Jerusalem are in a particular order. The lower steps define the mineral, vegetable and animal levels of humanity. Those who do nothing about development become crystallised, like stones, while vegetable people are only concerned with survival and propagation. The animal level of mankind seeks to exploit and dominate, in contrast to the human level that wants to help others to evolve. Beyond them is the realm of angelics and the Divine. These are the levels in which a physical body is no longer required and where the most advanced human beings reside. The Heavenly Jerusalem is at the junction between Paradise and the two highest Worlds. (Medieval woodcut.)

The cup of Christian Communion carries its implication of connection with Divinity; but how many worshippers experience it? These objects and many others that have become faded symbols have their origin in the third level of a conscious spiritual tradition which is still alive but unseen.

Perhaps only a tenth of the priests and rabbis who perform the yearly cycle of religious ceremonies are conscious of their inner meaning. Generally speaking, most people are aware only up to the level of their own development. Thus an individual who is predominantly a person of action might experience the rituals as real but the metaphysical and devotional aspects as not having any particular significance. Likewise, the person of feeling will be deeply affected by prayer but may not register the ideas embedded in the text or regard the ritual beyond a routine form. Similarly, the contemplative type will perceive the theology of the faith but not be too concerned with the devotions and rituals, although these may be carried out with proficiency. To be aware and operate in all these areas simultaneously means that a person has been trained to work on the defective sides of the lower psyche and this can only be done by persistent effort under conscious direction. One cannot do this alone because it is all too easy to fool oneself, as many have, without the check of another, more evolved, mentor. Here is where the conscious level of spirituality makes itself manifest directly in the lower world in the form of an 'elder' who is a friend and member of a kabbalistic group. Here begins another set of levels.

An elder is anyone who knows more than you do. In this case, it is in degree of consciousness. A person may be brilliant at physical action, in evoking emotion or exploring ideas, but if he or she is unaware of their own state then they are no more than well-developed functions, even as a dog has a specialised nose or a giraffe a long neck. There are many clever thinkers whose inner lives are a confusion and even more practical doers and sensitive feelers whose balance is dominated by their gifts. The first step in Kabbalah is to recognise that there are different levels and that while a person may be acknowledged by the world as successful, he or she may be in fact a psychological imbecile or even a spiritual criminal. Many so-called great people, with hindsight, are seen to be no more than projected images of their time, like pop stars or political leaders who vanish when their moment of fame has gone and they are seen as inadequate human beings.

To begin to recognise one's own unconsciousness, or to recognise that there is a higher reality, is to begin to be dissatisfied with life as it is. In the course of a search for a solution a seeker after truth moves out of the first level of general evolution and into contact with the second. Here one reads about or picks up traces of higher knowledge in art and literature that can lead one on to direct contact with a living Tradition which will be met with initially in an individual and then in a group.

A group may be of a high or low order. It may be composed of two or three people who know that they must try to work consciously or it may be a complete organic unity with all seven levels of consciousness. The latter is rare and the seeker is more likely to encounter the former or those preparatory groups that are in the process of building up an inner structure (sometimes called a 'vessel') which can actually receive and transmit the knowledge and Grace descending from the higher Worlds. These groups, like people, come in degrees of evolution and organisation. The first measurement is the number of individuals that meet to work together consciously. This requires a physical commitment to a time and place. There are many such groups all around the world and, although the intent is there, very often because an elder is lacking they never get beyond wearing a cult uniform, repeating devotional formulae and arguing about metaphysics. Yet, if such a group gets beyond the ego-oriented stage of believing it is spiritual, it may enter the level of awakening in which it becomes aware that the ordinary state of consciousness leads nowhere but to illusion. Such a situation can only occur if an elder of the next level appears to guide the group out of what is called the *Katnut*, or lesser state, into the *Gadlut*, the greater state, and towards Self-consciousness.

A group that differentiates between these levels begins to perceive the world in quite a different way. It will, moreover, attract to itself help from above, for whoever is seated in the *Tiferet* place of the tutor (see Figure 8) will receive guidance, if he or she has not already this higher knowledge that cannot be obtained from books. Such a group begins to generate a Tree within its membership, bringing power and with it responsibility and temptation. We will describe this process in detail later; at present we are still setting out the general scheme of levels on which to hang the story.

The next level a group will reach on acquiring a tutor is that of beginning to develop a heart that relates all who are within its orbit, so that over time all past and present members may contact the soul of the group, no matter where they may be. This is because the accumulated experiences of the group consolidate into more than just a vessel and anyone who is aware of this is connected with the souls of others who are involved with the group. This level is related to fate. Indeed, many life-long relationships are made between people who meet at the group. To develop a group-soul takes a long time and those who enter the group after it has been established have to be able to attain that soul level in themselves before they can fully experience its presence. Sensitive visitors to groups can sometimes pick up this subtle organism although some might perceive it as the same phenomenon as the collective mind of a sports crowd. This is not so, for the group soul does not disperse after every meeting but persists, sometimes for many years, long after the group has dissolved or left that meeting place.

The level above this is that of the spirit. This is not concerned with the personal, like that of the soul, but is related to the cosmic aspect of Existence. Here the group relates to the larger picture of school, Line and Tradition. Usually only a minority of a group are aware of this dimension, although every member may touch it from time to time, through the offices of the tutor or by an act of Grace that descends upon a meeting. This level is the realm of the miraculous. Those who perceive this aspect are usually the core of a group which may have a majority of visitors, newcomers, passers-through and those in the early stages of initiation. The cosmic dimension of the Work is real to those who begin to acquire a vision of the wider implications of what the group is doing and act upon this vision. Such people live their lives on the transpersonal scale as well as at the personal. Here is where the group is seen to relate to a particular school and fits into a specific Line of a Tradition, such as propagating a meditation technique or disseminating certain ideas.

The topmost level of the group is the Divine. While every genuine group has this connection, most of its members will only be dimly aware that it exists except in theory or in a momentary flash that comes from time to time. Such episodes, alas, quickly fade despite the extraordinary afterglow of realisation. Little can be said about this kind of experience, as to describe it is to be misleading. What can be said is that the Holy Spirit appears to be very interested in such groups, for they are a contact point between individuals and the Divine which seeks to manifest into consciousness on every level of Existence. A kabbalistic group is for the training and tuning of consciousness. It is there to aid individual and collective integration.

In this way each group contributes a few cells towards the evolution of Adam Kadmon who, as the Image of God, gazes out on the universe and perceives in it a perfect reflection of the Holy One.

All the foregoing is an introduction to the background and elements that go towards creating a school. We have touched upon the origin of esoteric work and glimpsed its historic process develop through space and time. We will now begin to examine the situation in our own period and see how a school manifests according to local conditions and eternal laws. Having set out the general plan let us fill in the details, starting with the individual who is the foundation stone.

7. Ground Floor

No individual, no matter how learned, devout or skilled in esoteric matters, can go beyond a certain point of development alone. Even the Buddha and Joshua ben Miriam of Nazareth were part of a Tradition, although they may have broken away from the mainstream of their times. Both trained with teachers and groups and were steeped in the methods used. Even the person who reads no books, never goes to a religious service or does any spiritual practices is, nevertheless, influenced by the indirect esoteric values within the culture. This, however, is not enough and can only take a person to the outer door of a living Tradition.

In former times an individual who sought spiritual instruction could go to a recognisable school of the soul. The Jew had the rabbi's inner study group, the Christian the monastery and the Moslem the local Sufi circle. Today this situation does not exist. The orthodox way has lost much of its authority and the spiritual form its authenticity. While some find that they can operate within the conventional religious situation, because they have a deep belief in the essence of a Tradition, others require more. They wish to pursue a path of intimate knowledge of God and for them nothing less than a direct contact will do. Over many years they may study and practise the system and working methods of their own Tradition or even, as many do, seek a path in a Tradition which is alien to their culture, because it is not loaded with negative memories. Even then there will be a time when, if they do not relate to the collective culture of that Tradition, they will find the same problems of identity and reality. It is often at this point that people turn again to their origins; something deep within draws them back to their roots. This does not necessarily mean a return to the conventional but to an esoteric Line that operates within their culture and civilisation. They will seek contact with a school or group that takes them to the inner core of their own Tradition.

However, before this stage is reached several insights about groups are gained. The first is the realisation that one cannot develop alone. No amount of effort will take one beyond the range of ego. The person who has read every book on the subject but has no one to debate with soon becomes convinced that only they know the facts, because such information is gradually absorbed by the ego which forms a fixed set of unchallenged views. The individual who spends hours in prayer likewise may enter a state of what is called 'ego bliss' in which he or she is convinced that they have direct contact with God. This may be true but, unless he has a connection with the world outside, it can become a madness in which the person feels superior to everyone else who is involved with the mundane aspects of life. The physically oriented can likewise enter a state of ego holiness, spending years working on their bodies to make them perfect, regarding the mind and heart as secondary. All these situations have an unbalanced and obsessive element to them that affects even the most conscientious; after a while the chief characteristic of such individuals is that they do not wish to know about any other way of working. Very often only that part of their life is ordered while the rest, such as relationships and profession, are either neglected or become chaotic.

The seeker who recognises this insularity as a danger arrives at the point in which he or she realises that one must work with others in order to counterbalance any excessive tendency of the ego which invariably makes life suit its taste, in many cases avoiding conflict or seeking solitude. Working with others is not easy, especially if one thinks one knows, and it is a mark of maturity to concede that progress can only be made by submitting to a wider learning situation. At first this may be accomplished with someone with whom one shares similar views. This may be with a partner of some kind whom we shall assume is a peer. To work with another who is an inferior in this area is full of dangers that would reinforce the ego's dominance. Many people have started out with the best intentions and finished up either as a parent figure or a childish sibling of such a partner. The twosome situation is not a satisfactory arrangement. There occurs naturally a polarisation in which one partner must be the predominantly active and the other the passive. This creates tension over time and eventually a crisis that has little to do with the study or practices being carried out. It is possible to work in this way but only if one of the two is an elder and the other accepts the situation, like a dancing master teaching a student.

Working in a threesome is possible because the dynamic here is quite different. If all three members of this smallest of groups are equal then the polarities can alternate with the third rôle as intermediary.

This, of course, follows the law of the triad in which a flow is possible because the energy is not rigidly held in opposition. Three people working together on a text, devotion or ritual can produce a group presence. This is quite different from the relationship between two people which tends to be personal. Three can generate an intimacy but it is formal, in as much as it is a consciously agreed arrangement with a set of criteria that governs the situation. Thus, while one talks the others listen; or as one leads the prayer or ritual the others follow, each performing a rôle that can be switched from positive to negative to neutral. This facilitates movement in everyone. However even here, unless there is an elder if only by one degree, there can be only a limited amount of progress, for there is, as yet, no connection with a larger vessel upon whose capacity and experience they can draw.

A larger vessel does not mean just a bigger group, although this does help because it expands the scope of what is being studied and practised, but that a group can operate more effectively with the exoteric or outer aspect of spiritual work. This may mean examining traditional texts, holding meditation meetings or carrying out prescribed physical exercises designed to heighten consciousness. All these methods are available in the world at large. A larger group will certainly generate more power and give greater depth to those activities but there are also certain disadvantages if there is not a direct connection with a living Tradition.

After three, the next critical number of a group is seven. Here begins the leadership issue. Unless a chairperson is elected there will be periodic confusion, cross talk and a splitting up into separate factions. There has to be a directing focus, if only a formal one, for keeping of order or the issuing of instructions during meditation or exercises. If the group has as yet no elder or tutor, then it is good to have a chairpersonship rotated among the members. However, as often happens, some people do not feel up to the task and prefer others to do the job. This leaves it between those who take up such rôles as a duty and those who consciously or unconsciously seek power or just attention. Occasionally the natural leader of the group emerges quickly and people accept the impartiality or authority from a person who seems to be able to co-ordinate the group without disturbing its balance. Usually, this amicable state is arrived at only after a power struggle between several people, none of whom, in fact, being fit to chair the group because of their ego drives. The defeated often leave such an association and seek to fulfil their desire to rule elsewhere. Here we begin to perceive the advantage of a trained tutor being at the centre.

Very often the natural leader is the least assertive which is contrary to the normal social situation. Such a person usually emerges over a period of time as people recognise his inherent sanity and stability. His comments, which are perceived as pertinent and often sum up what the group requires rather than what any individual wants, are appreciated and generate the necessary respect. Such people, very often, are the most mature in soul although they may not be the eldest in years. They are also frequently the most balanced members of the group, in that they can set their own desires or ego to one side when advancing the consensus of the group. Natural leadership is a great asset eliminating, as it does, the wasted energy of group politics and concentrating all efforts in a general direction which gives the group a structure and energy that it could not otherwise have. If a good leader does not emerge in a group this size, then it either breaks up or becomes a dictatorship in which the weak and gullible are held while the more mature members oppose or leave; for we are still dealing with the animal level of groups that arise and dissolve.

In yet larger groups the dynamic increases and the structure begins to differentiate according to the laws of the herd, for as yet there is no real spiritual connection. Many so-called esoteric organisations are run this way. For example, there is often the powerful leader who is seen as master and the faithful close to the throne with the various degrees of lesser beings stratified in rank according to their commitment to the guru. In a real esoteric school the first loyalty is to the Truth, not to a person; but very often we find the personality of the leader is the draw, not the veracity of the Teaching. As a seeker becomes involved in larger groups so he or she should be aware of the criteria by which they are run because very often what began as a genuine gathering for the pursuit of wisdom becomes a personality-centred institution with all that goes with such organisations; its bureaucracy, its petty rules and its public relations department.

Having looked at the attempt to form a group without an initiated tutor and the problems that occur when an exoteric organism develops, let us examine some already existing groups that the seeker may encounter before finding the genuine article. These may be groups that have had knowledge at one time or have a leader who does know something of higher knowledge but is not transmitting it correctly.

8. *Pseudo Groups*

A pseudo group is an imitation of the real thing. It may have the outward appearance of being religiously conventional, or even have a good and genuine aim, but it does not have the inner connection. By this is meant that the esoteric criteria of the Tradition the group purports to follow are not truly met. To wear symbolic or orthodox dress or to go through the motions of formal and elaborate procedures does not mean that the Spirit will descend. Indeed, it is to be observed that the more paraphernalia there is, the less likely is there to be any reality to what is being done. Here we have the worship of outer form without the appreciation of the content. As one sage put it, 'They look at the coat and not the wearer'. However, at this stage a pseudo group may be all that is available and the seeker might do well to stay a while to learn what can be learned from the outer garment of a Tradition. Here is the beginning of spiritual discrimination.

The way you discern the genuine group from the pseudo and the false is to observe how everything is done, without projection or expectation and with as much impartiality as possible. This should be done with discretion, as committed members of the group will become hostile if any criticism is levelled against their methods or leadership. People who, deep down, are not quite sure of their beliefs will often defend and justify them fiercely because any probing assessment can be a threat to their supportive system. The spiritual rule here is that you should never cut another person's lifeline. It may not be the right method for you but it could be the saving of another at that point of their development. Participate politely and observe quietly, question with tact and explore as far as you can along that particular path until you go your way with courtesy.

To give an example, let us take a group concerned with action. Such a group may perform complex rituals or simple physical exercises. They may be taken from some ancient mode or a recently developed technique; the origin is not as important as whether the method is effective. There are many groups who stick absolutely to the old ways and become more involved in faithfully representing the past than living in the present. There are some groups, for instance, which still carry out the formalities of honouring their leader as it was done in the eighteenth century by dressing the part and even imitating the mannerisms of that period so that it is a parody of what it was meant to be. To practise certain physical positions because a particular master did does not necessarily lead to enlightenment. Indeed, it often results in much discomfort and preoccupation with hiding difficulties, lest one be thought incapable or unspiritual. Many people spend years putting effort into perfecting a ritual or body posture only to realise that someone else gets the same desired effect by conscious attention to whatever they are doing in ordinary action.

The belief that all devotional methods are effective is another area to be questioned. It is quite true that certain prayers, chants and mantras are very powerful and produce higher states of consciousness but this depends on who is carrying them out and with what intention. Many people believe that such devotion will bring them health and good fortune with no regard or interest for the higher aspects of reality they were designed to reveal. Some prayers are indeed intended as healing techniques and others to produce insights into oneself or the universe. Some devotions will bring one into contact with beings of another World and others close to the Divine. Many pseudo groups use these devotional formulae indiscriminately, often with the best of intentions, but do not realise that one chant is for the novice and another for the initiate. To repeat the Name of God mechanically will generate nothing but noise. This is taking the Holy One's Name in vain. Many ministers do just this. To speak a prayer fully aware of What or Who one is addressing is quite a different matter but this has to be taught by someone who knows and has the interior connection. Blind belief is not enough. This is why Kabbalah is called a Way of Knowledge.

To sit in on a pseudo intellectual group can be very impressive to the undiscriminating. One can hear profound ideas discussed with great learning, listen to people quote from this or that master and even hear original versions of old concepts. Many hours can be spent analysing just one phrase or inventing a new metaphysics that explains or fits some symbolic passage yet, at the end of it all, there is no real insight; there is obscurity and an aching skull. To know, technically, the Kabbalistic Tree and Jacob's Ladder of four Worlds is not enough. Ideas must be related to the rest of reality. A purely intellectual group, no matter how respectable a lineage or how bright its minds, without a conscious knowledge of what is being discussed is still a pseudo group. There have been many groups in the past that have added yet more theory to the complex metaphysics of Kabbalah without making it any clearer. Indeed, one student in Jerusalem was heard to say, 'We don't understand what we are studying but we read the books every afternoon. Maybe something will come through of what the great rabbi wrote'. This is not Kabbalah. Nothing conscious was received.

The fourth kind of group, after the ritual, devotional and contemplative approaches, is the one that has a connection with the upper Worlds but is in the early stages of inner evolution. This is a critical point in the development of an individual and of a group for, while knowledge and Grace begin to flow down, the level of handling them may not be sufficiently mature to hold the considerable power that becomes available. In the case of an individual there is usually someone around to check and guide the person through the ecstatic phase of the first contact with the upper Worlds. In the case of a group, the leader may not be up to the moment or may, as sometimes happens, turn it to personal advantage so that the power collected by the group is projected onto the chairperson who personifies their collective experience. This happened among the later Hassidim who saw their rabbis as wonderworkers who could appeal to Heaven on their behalf. Several rabbis caught up in this focus of ecstasy became charismatic figureheads and founded dynasties which today imprison their descendents in a straitjacket of religious tribalism.

Such a phenomenon might manifest in our time as the charismatic leader who depends upon the energy of his or her devotees. Such people have a certain degree of development but are not yet free of the ego image that they put out to match the needs of their followers for a parent figure. Individuals of this kind are usually physically well-endowed and are fascinating company, until one begins to perceive that it is not the person that is being seen but an image of what one and all the others project as the perfect example of how a practitioner of that particular way should look, talk and act. Very often the leader dresses in a particular way, usually in the costume of that Tradition, and uses phrases from the orthodox text, whatever that may be, so that people feel reassured that everything is genuine. Some followers in this situation become deeply devoted to the leader and earn favoured disciple status. Others use this opportunity to seek power for themselves over others or fulfil their own fantasies of being a guru. One will observe, for example, that there is a particular person always near the throne who models him or herself on the pattern of the leader, right down to the way the hair is combed and the hand is held.

The structure and dynamics of such organisations are still relatively primitive in terms of a group based upon the Kabbalistic Tree. However, this situation is of a higher order than a pseudo group, in that the awakening level has been touched. Contact with the higher Worlds can come through a leader who occasionally acts as the central focus. Unfortunately, for most of the time such a person can all too easily be the group's guru-oriented projection. The hallmark of these kinds of groups is that all the power is invested in the leader and that when he or she is absent the group becomes lifeless and without direction. While this is equally true of a preparatory group that is really working, there is not the personal magnetism factor or the paraphernalia that goes with the charismatic leader like the vizier, ministers, handmaids and other courtiers that surround the throne. Under the pressure of concentrated worship, any modesty of the guru may have eventually given way to deluded arrogance as the leader is caught up in the inflated rôle. Occasionally the collective decision is corrected by a providential exposure in which the leadership, thinking itself above the law, is found in a morally embarrassing situation that breaks the image. If this does not occur then people either leave after time as they outgrow the situation or stay until the leader's power and credibility wane, which they must, only to discover that they are human. There are, of course, always those who prefer their illusions and grow old with their guru in a gilded cage of exclusivity and fantasy.

Clearly the seeker must move beyond this fool's paradise. But such an experience should not be avoided. One can learn much from such people and even witness their redemption if they realise, in time, what is happening. It is not unknown for an honest leader to see the reality of the situation and warn followers of their fantasy before suddenly leaving a shocked court of committed admirers. This phenomenon is rare as it takes much integrity to relinquish the glamour of the rôle. How, one may ask, does a person get into such a situation? The answer is that very often this kind of leader has had some training in an esoteric group but has broken away, imagining that they know and could do better on their own. Because of this move, they lose the necessary check on an unbalanced progress forward under the impetus of the ego.

At this point we should set out the general kabbalistic theory of a group so as to acquire a frame of reference for the detail that will emerge as we explore the growth, structure and dynamics of collective work. This is the chief counterbalance to an over-rapid expansion and extension of experience.

9. Group Tree

The basic working tool of the Kabbalah is the Tree of Life (see Figure 11). This symbol, which was part of an esoteric scheme, emerged into the public domain in the early Middle Ages. The concept of Ten Divine Attributes had been brought from the Middle East by rabbis who left the declining schools of Babylonia for Europe in the ninth century. However, when the confrontation between religion and philosophy became a major issue the mystics took the side of revelation against reason by disclosing various esoteric themes that, until then, had been secret. By reformulating the system for their time they aided the wish to work through faith yet apply the rational to their religion. The Tree of Life emerged by degrees in Spain, each succeeding generation of Kabbalists adding to and refining the diagram so as to set out the simple yet subtle intricacy of Divine Law at work in the universe and man.

Since that period the Tree and the Ladder of the four Worlds of Emanation, Creation, Formation and Action have undergone many variations. Here it must be stated that there is no absolutely classic form of the diagrams because no system, however fine, can give a total picture of reality. What has been produced by different schools is their particular version of the situation. As it is in science, what is apparently concrete for one generation becomes outdated and redundant for the next. Newton's metaphysics were considered accurate for the understanding of his time but Einstein showed them to be very limited. The same is true of Kabbalah. The early and medieval periods produced remarkable views of Existence but they were relevant to the outlook of their ages. What follows is the continuum which is a blend of old and new kabbalistic ideas that makes Eternal principles comprehensible to our day.

The Tree of Life is based upon the relationship between the ten sefirot plus one non-sefirah. These Divine aspects are the manifestation of the Absolute in Existence. They are the mode by which the Holy One governs the Worlds of spirit, soul and physicality that emerge out of the primordial World of the radiant sefirot. The arrangement of the

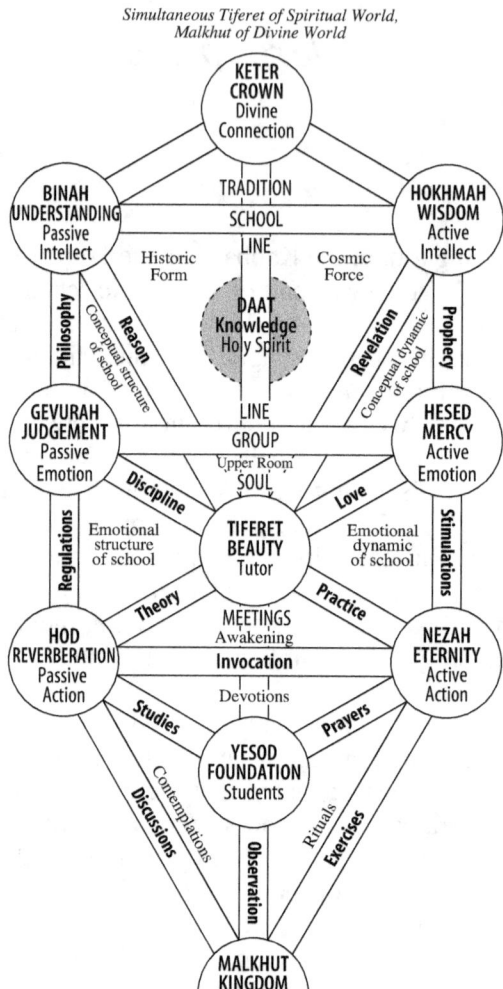

Figure 11 — GROUP TREE
Here the structures and dynamics of a group are put on the Tree. It shows the various activities and functions of a school of the soul. In the bottom triad are the three disciplines of Action, Devotion and Contemplation. The triad of Hod, Nezah and Tiferet is where theory and practice are brought together in a meeting. Above is the invisible chamber of the soul, which only those at this level can enter, while above that is the cosmic space in which the school exists, be it for the lifetime of a master, a millennium or as long as the Tradition lasts, presided over by the spirit of the founder. (Halevi.)

sefirot, based upon several fundamental laws, is the model for all that exists. The whole Tree is a unity; this is the primary law. There is also a polarity within this scheme, expressed allegorically by God's Mercy and Justice which are seen as active and passive, male and female, force and form and many other combinations that operate in pairs. The central pillar of equilibrium represents Divine Grace and this reconciles the two outer functional pillars that flank what is called the centre column of consciousness. The Tree is also divided into several horizontal levels. Keter, the Crown, represents the unifying principle and the point of origin and contact with the Divine. The two upper and outer sefirot, Hokhmah and Binah or Wisdom and Understanding, are seen to be the principles of Divine Intellect with the two below, Hesed and Gevurah or Mercy and Judgment, as the Divine Emotion. The two lowest and outer sefirot, Nezah and Hod or Eternity and Reverberation, represent the principles of Divine Action. Together the outer sefirot act as functional aspects like arms and legs, brain, heart and hands that serve the central axis of consciousness and will.

The central column defines various nodal points of synthesis. The topmost sefirah of Keter oversees all. The central sefirah Tiferet acts as the intermediary to every sefirah except the bottommost of Malkhut. The sefirah of Yesod, the Foundation, sits in the middle of the lower face, as the kite-like complex of the lower Tree is called. The lowest sefirah, Malkhut, the Kingdom, is the body of the Tree in as much as it is the place where everything above is manifest in materiality. This basic scheme is repeated in the three lower Worlds but at an increasingly dense level of reality, so that we have a chain of interpenetrating Worlds of pure light, cosmic dynamics, ever-changing forms and elemental substances and action. The particular Tree we are to examine is the second from the bottom, which is the psychological World that mediates between the natural realm of Earth below and that of Heaven above. At the highest level lies the Divine Tree whose base sefirah touches the Crown of the Tree of the psyche.

Each Tree not only has its own sefirotic scheme but also the triads made by the paths that join the sefirot. These triads contain the areas of action generated by the three sefirot that compose a given triad. Thus, for example, the three supernals, as they are called, at the top of any Tree make the triad of Divine connection in that World while the triad formed by the two emotional sefirot and the central one of Tiferet holds, in the psychological Tree, the heart or soul. The side triads are concerned with the more practical operations of the Tree;

structure on the left side and dynamics on the right. The central triads are related to states of consciousness, ranging from physical awareness, through mood and thought awareness to soul and spiritual consciousness. The non-sefirah of Daat or Knowledge is that place where the Divine can intervene or where human beings can enter into the World above and return.

When the anatomy of a group is set out on the Tree it reveals the various levels and how they operate. Firstly, a group relates particularly to the World that bridges the organic and elemental kingdoms and the upper part of Jacob's Ladder (see Figure 8). This Tree corresponds roughly to the psyche of an individual in that it has a physical aspect and an emotional and intellectual level. If it did not, then it would not be a kabbalistic group but simply a social gathering. Taking the bottom great triad of Hod, Nezah and Malkhut, with Yesod at its centre, we have the everyday working area of the group. Here are the meeting-place, the theory and practices and the various activities of contemplation, devotion and rituals of the group. Yesod is the ego or ordinary consciousness of the group, that is, simply the awareness of what is going on without being conscious of it. Members of the group, when in their everyday state, occupy this position like everyone else. Above is the awakening triad where the group should congregate in consciousness during a meeting, just below the central sefirah of the tutor who acts as the focal point of the Tree. The chairperson or tutor should watch over and guide those who go beyond to the triad of the soul which represents the inner core of the group. Only those who have that degree of self-consciousness can enter this place which is sometimes called the upper room. Here discrimination or Gevurah and love or Hesed work with Truth, Tiferet, to make a collective heart that can cross time and space to link members, living or dead, with the group.

The upper side triads contain the emotional experiences and concepts that emerge during the group's work. The left-hand side composes the structure upon which the group relies to support its efforts while the right-hand triads give it the dynamics. Thus the left emotional triad will hold discipline while the left conceptual triad the ideas that have been formulated during meetings. The right-hand conceptual triad would contain those notions that stimulate thought, like rebirth, while the emotional complexes of the right would generate a vital interest in growth and change. Initially these triads will be filled with traditional material but, as the group matures, they will be filled with the group's own experiences which will give it a distinct character of its own, just as these triads do in an individual.

The great triad of Binah, Hokhmah and Tiferet defines the spiritual aspect of the group which will only become manifest if the group reaches a sufficiently high level of consciousness, going beyond the group soul and entering into the cosmic dimension of Kabbalah.

This may take many years although certain individuals, like the group leader, may already have access to this area. In the triad concerned is the sefirah of the Holy Spirit at Daat and it is from here that the Teaching comes. The two upper and outer sefirot of Binah and Hokhmah represent Tradition and Revelation and these help facilitate the flow of Grace which can descend from the Divine triad, headed by the Crown, to the tutor at Tiferet and through to the group below, so that sometimes even a visitor can perceive the presence of a living connection with the Celestial Academy.

The overall scheme, like the ecology of a newly planted forest, takes many stages to fill out to its full capacity. A group may have the potential to attain a high status on Jacob's Ladder but many things can slow down its progress, disrupt or even destroy it. Some of these factors will be discussed later. Now, however, we have the kabbalistic plan of the group and its composition. This enables us to see how it fits into the bigger design of things.

A group, represented by the soul, is part of a school which may be seen as the spiritual triad while the particular Line relates to the path between Tiferet and Daat. The upper section of this column connects with the Tradition. The side triads of the Tree, holding the experience of the group, school and Line, give it its collective and cultural character while the Crown at the topmost point of the Tree parallels the Teaching to that which is beyond any traditional form in its Divine essence. (See Figure 8).

Groups are not ready-made, even though the design of them is potentially present the moment any serious work is begun. Meetings, no matter how well intentioned, cannot become a kabbalistic group until people subdue their egos and relate everything to the Tree, whether or not one has an elder or an experienced tutor in the chair. In this way there is an objectivity in the Work that is above personal opinion. This objectivity is vital in a group that has, as yet, no leader but wishes to maintain its aim in learning how to raise the consciousness of its members. Such an operation requires great diligence and much humility on the part of everyone but, if it is held long enough, the call will be heard in Heaven and Providence will step in. This may be in the form of a visitor or a letter that will bring about a contact with someone from the Tradition. It does happen. As the saying goes, 'When the pupil is ready, the teacher appears'. So it is for people looking for an instructor and for a tutor waiting for students to come.

10. Student Types

Before a person can become a pupil certain preliminary stages have to be gone through, for the experience and knowledge of a tutor would be wasted upon an individual who could not make full use of the instruction given. Many people think or feel, once they have discovered the esoteric, that they should expect and have a right to the greatest teacher. While it is true to say that in a moment of Grace one might comprehend the higher truths, it does not follow that that state of lucidity can be sustained. Indeed, if it could, many would go mad as they became detached from the earth and from ordinary life. There must be a firm line of connection and stability between the upper and lower Worlds before one is allowed to be taught by a master. This is one reason why drugs are considered dangerous by most spiritual schools. They give an insight into other dimensions but, unless there is considerable experience and discipline to hold the aspirant steady, profound confusion can occur. Moreover, the distortions of an undeveloped or sick psyche can trigger a neurotic condition which can defer the possibility of gradual but secure development.

The first step after recognising that there is more to life than the physical and social levels is to seek for something deeper. This is acquired initially through reading or contact with esoteric ideas. Having realised that there is such a thing as higher knowledge, people are drawn to those Traditions to which they feel akin. Within these Lines certain types can be observed, no matter what discipline it is. For example, the twelve zodiacal temperaments indicate the general kind of psychology a student possesses. These correspond to the twelve tribes and the twelve disciples. They symbolise the various aspects of the human race. If any group were fortunate enough to be composed of the twelve signs, then it would indeed be a unique situation for an all-round comprehension and transmission of higher knowledge and influence. One suspects that the most efficacious groups down the ages had just such a combination. Alas, it rarely occurs.

Examining the types as individuals we will find that each can contribute a facet to the whole but, until they work in concert, they

Figure 12 — TEMPERAMENTS
The twelve tribes of Israel, like the twelve disciples of Joshua ben Miriam of Nazareth, represent the twelve types of people. They parallel the Zodiac which dates back to the time and city of Abram, Ur of the Chaldees. For example, Judah corresponds to Aries, the warlike tribe, while the tribe of Dan relates to Capricorn. The name Dan has its root in the principle of Justice, a Capricornian trait. Together they make up the composite temperaments of humanity, each one with a particular fate and destiny. So it is with individuals, each of which have their own path and type of school. (Medieval woodcut.)

remain individuals or sub-factions within a group. Thus the Earth signs of Capricorn, Taurus and Virgo will see the Teaching in a practical way and the Water signs of Pisces, Cancer and Scorpio in a more emotional vein. The Air signs of Libra, Aquarius and Gemini will be more intellectual in their approach and the Fire signs of Sagittarius, Aries and Leo more inspirational.

These definitions of approach are, of course, only general because no one is a pure Sun sign but a combination of several factors, including the Ascendant that governs the body type, the Moon whose zodiacal position determines the nature of the ego, and the planets which influence how the various psychological functions operate. But what can be said is that each general type, subject to modifications by the other factors, will seek certain ways of working and versions of the Teaching. Thus the Virgo will follow the more analytic method while the Aries will seek a way of action. The Aquarian will be inclined to intellectual group work, in contrast to the Pisces who will seek people with whom to meditate. Added to the zodiacal dimension will be the factor that all Fixed signs will tend to hold a position while the Cardinal ones will seek to change the Teaching and Mutable signs adapt to it. Thus, the Gemini will explore many disciplines while the Taurean will remain stolid in one idea, as the Cancerian tries to turn a meeting into a family affair. All these types will be met in groups, each seeing it from their own point of view until they begin to shift their level from the personal, which is in fact general in as much as they are types, into the true individual, that is from the ego of Yesod to the Self of Tiferet.

Seen strictly kabbalistically, various types of student may be viewed in terms of the sefirot. They correspond closely to the nature of the planets, Sun, Moon and Earth and indicate particular stages of development although, at this point of realisation, none is superior to the others as all are as yet unintegrated and remain, for the most part, in a Yesodic state of spiritual sleep. Taking Malkhut at the bottom of the Tree, we have those who only see the Teaching in terms of practicality. They regard anything remote from ordinary life as useless. 'Divinity is in a stone', they declare. They are correct but, like all points of view, this is lopsided. They have to learn that the unmanifest is just as important as that which appears to the senses.

The Yesodic type tends to look for images of the Teaching and charismatic personalities. They will wear symbols and act out what they think is the right way to be a Kabbalist or whatever path they are following. Very often they have psychic abilities which they and others mistake for spirituality and not infrequently they seek the leadership of a group on the basis that they are extremely sensitive to the group's mood. Under discipline they become receptive to the highest influences and can impart a feeling of the upper Worlds that is not apparent to all. But this gift has to be monitored or like Miriam, the sister of Moses, they can consider themselves as prophets in their own right. As students in the early stage of the Work they are extremely susceptible to first impressions which can be translated into an image rather than reality.

The Hod type is easily recognised by the amount of information he carries. Every book on the subject has been read, especially those that have a peripheral relevance, like Kabbalah and criticism. Intelligent but inclined to be facile, the Hodian student has tried everything and has stayed with Kabbalah because its scope is so wide, although its depths may be explored some other time. Such people are normally great talkers and spend much time telling the early groups about all the other versions of the Teaching. They do, however, contribute much to the wider implications of what is being studied and prevent the group from being too parochial, as can happen when no real knowledge is yet forthcoming. The Hodian will keep the group amused and informed of current esoteric events and sometimes startle everyone by a jewel of an observation that only a Hodian would be fast enough to note, like seeing the curtain of physical reality drawn back, if only for a moment.

The type related to Nezah is sensual, seeing things in terms of practice and rhythm, beauty and repetition. Such people will be inclined towards prayer and ritual, active participation and direct experience. They will not be too interested in the theory but will articulate well in action or art. They will tend to have strong likes and dislikes but will work extremely hard if they can find a way of expression. Less reflective than most, they give a dynamic to a group that needs guts. They will occasionally become lazy in that they can just repeat themselves but they will always seek a harmony that mitigates too much cleverness or conflict. They are the doers and feelers who add the drive to a situation although they can be sometimes a little obsessional. Once committed they generally stay the course and act as the flywheel to a group, holding its momentum if only by repetition of ritual actions. They are the dancers, singers and artists of a group.

The Gevuric type manifests as the strict disciplinarian. They apply this tendency equally to themselves and to others. Often pedantic, they are frequently in argument and will not shift the debate away from a rigid view of principle. Usually purists, they will see the Teaching from a more traditional standpoint, expecting others to bow to the rules or not be considered serious students. They are scrupulous and will defend a point for or against anyone. Although intolerant, they do maintain standards in a group and will curtail any woolliness that emerges. Working by the book or a set of criteria, they will tighten the bonds and focus the power that is generated. They will also be hard on any backslider. Astringent and limited, they provide the backbone to a situation when things become a little too chaotic in the changes that occur in a group from time to time. They are the soldiers and lawyers of the group.

The Hesedic type is the vital counterbalance to the Gevuric. They bring love and tolerance. Benevolent, they give much although sometimes they allow more than they should. Powerful but easy going, these people have a deep sense of the religious and add an expansive element to the group. Often amusing, they contribute a benign atmosphere that can become potent if they are brought into focus. A group without such a person lacks affirming emotion and the ability to allow others to be themselves. The Hesedic type mitigates and supports by their generosity, although sometimes such actions can block the occasional summary rebuke necessary to correct a discrepancy that is pushing a group out of balance. Here we begin to see how the types relate and work together.

The Binah type is the philosopher and lawgiver. Such people bring reason to the group. Sometimes this is a rather hard line, based either upon experience or upon principles that can be deadening if not softened by humaneness. Heavy and powerful, the Binah type holds an overall view of what a group needs which can be a little too detached sometimes, although this detachment is necessary if things are to be seen in their larger context. Occasionally this type will open up a cosmic vista and at other times narrow it down to a simple but profound law. The balance has to be right. At some moments the beauty of the system is revealed by the Binah type of intelligence; at others it can be presented as an inflexible prison which occurs when the person is only operating from that particular sefirah. Fortunately, this happens only occasionally.

The counterbalance to the Binah is the Hokhmah type whose sudden flash of inspiration illuminates the system with living light. While such a gift is great, however, it can become a menace to the person and to the group if not contained and put in its right place. To have a visionary in a group can be disconcerting because no one can be sure of the veracity of such visions. They could be just illusions. This is why all the types have to be present in a group in order to correct each others' tendencies. Prophecy is a miraculous gift but, without the check of reason, the discrimination of judgement and all the other qualities of the sefirotic types, there would be chaos and disintegration. It is as well that the Hokhmah type is rare.

Here we have a brief outline of the purest form of each type, leaving out the central sefirah of Tiferet, the Teacher, which will be examined in a chapter of its own.

11. Tutor Types

In terms of the Tree, the rôle of Teacher occupies the Tiferet position in the group. This is because it is at the nodal point between the upper and lower faces of the Tree and has access to most of the sefirot and triads which give it a unique insight and capability. Theoretically, whoever occupies this position is in contact with the three lower Worlds of Action, Formation and Creation, that is, the physical, psychological and spiritual levels. Besides this, the Teacher is the pivot of the group and can perceive and influence the fluctuations and imbalances of the group's Tree. It is a highly responsible position and, as the word 'responsible' implies, carries with it the task of being sensitive to the needs of every aspect of a given situation. The Tiferet seat cannot be occupied by someone living in the ego. If this occurs then they cease to be the connection between the upper and lower Worlds and the group has no influx of higher knowledge. To have a person of perfect equilibrium and development is obviously rare. Not every group leader is a Rabbi Shimon ben Yohai who took the Great Assembly in the *Zohar*. Most of us have not only to be content with a less than perfect tutor but grateful that we have someone who at least has some degree of experience.

The rôle of tutor is to facilitate the operation of the group. This means not only chairing all the discussions but leading the devotions and directing the physical exercises. The tutor must also act as co-ordinator of whatever is going on in the group in general and be able to deal with the personal and particular. The tutor must know the theory of Kabbalah well and practise the art of being. *Kabal* means 'able to receive'. This requires a high degree of commitment. There is no such thing as a part-time Kabbalist. You either are, or are not, a Kabbalist. This has to be so in the case of the tutor because, at certain points, one is not only responsible for the group as its captain but for the individual souls placed, for a time, in one's care. Any deviation from the impeccable can cause much damage and, if persisted in, degenerate into corruption which, in spiritual work, is extremely dangerous for a group and for the individuals within it. Therefore the tutor, no matter how difficult he or she may find their private problems, must act with great care within the group context.

The most common form of tutorship is that of the person given the task of training newcomers into the science and art of Kabbalah. These are group leaders who have received enough training to be able to impart what they know with some authority; which means that they have imbibed enough for it to have begun to affect their daily lives and be evident in their being. Often such people do not believe they have the ability to lead and are surprised when they are selected to start a new group. Being the tutor may have, to some, a certain glamour but it is only sustained by diligent work and much effort. After taking a group for a while, the new tutor begins to learn more than he or she teaches because by sitting in the Tiferet position one is connected with the Grace that descends from the Daat or place of Knowledge of the group as it acts as the intermediary between Tiferet and Keter, the Crown.

As we are still dealing with the psychological levels, so the character of the group is bound to be affected by the type of person occupying the chair. Thus, if we follow the rising sequence of the Tree, there is the Malkhutian, earthy, practical tutor who relates everything to ordinary life, the Yesodic character who teaches through symbols or personal examples and the Hodian type who transmits the Teaching by clever cross-references, wit and eloquent insights. The Nezahian personality demonstrates principles by feelings, harmony and strong reaction. The Gevuric tutor goes by the rules and imposes a strict regime in order to bring out the Teaching in a particularly pure form. The Hesed type generates love within the group that allows the Teaching to manifest in worship and good will. The Binah type has a group which appears to be concerned with the more metaphysical aspect of the Teaching, with protracted discussions over historic or cosmic topics, while the Hokhmah group leader will have uneven sessions of inspiration, crisis, dull patches and illumination when everything and everybody is periodically shaken.

All the above types express only general tendencies but, after visiting various meetings, one may begin to perceive how a group takes on the character of its tutor. Which does not mean to say that the tutor sets out to achieve this but that a law operates in which those who wish to work in that particular way will be attracted to that particular tutor. Those who are not in sympathy soon leave and seek someone who can teach them in their own language. This is the inner meaning of the scriptural comment: each person to their own tongue. Every person has a predominant sefirah and will either seek out a tutor who transmits in a way they can understand or find someone who can cultivate the particular sefirah they need to balance or strengthen. An example of this is the intellectual who seeks the scholarly tutor or, conversely, the person of action who comes to the same group because they need to bring their thinking faculty up to a standard. Thus a group may be composed primarily of the same types as the tutor with several other types present who balance and extend the group's capacity as well as their own. The tutor has to be able to accommodate them all, if possible.

This stretching of the tutor is vital for growth. If the tutor does not also expand then material is only repeated and the group stagnates. Individuals who surpass the tutor then depart, leaving behind those who cannot do without the security of a dull but safe haven. This happens when there is something wrong for the tutor, perhaps some inner crisis that he or she cannot rise above; tutors, like students, are still susceptible to trauma. For this reason charismatic projection upon tutors should be discouraged or students will see them only as figureheads and not as people who also have to struggle and work. Growth is equally vital for the tutor if the group is to enlarge the scope of its consciousness, clearly seen in its relationship to the three Worlds that meet in the Tiferet of the group which is where the tutor sits.

The first level is that of the natural World. Here the Keter or Crown of that cosmos touches the place of the tutor. This manifests in the fact that the tutor should be able to handle everyday matters. Traditionally it was expressed in the form that a person should be healthy, could make a living, was married and mature; that is, be able to make their way in the world without excessive effort. Such ease indicated skill in operating in the realm of Action and Elements. The qualification of marriage was partially a physical one, showing that the tutor was at least biologically normal, according to the standards of that time, and socially integrated in the sense of having an intimate relationship with someone other than oneself for, in the kabbalistic tradition, one's partner acts as the complementary mirror. The solitary approach to inner development has no checks on it and can therefore lead to psychological sidetracks and deviant tendencies. The issue of relationships also belongs to the psychological level, in that one can operate within a circle, like a family and a group. Here, sensitivity to others is crucial, for a tutor cannot operate correctly if he or she only sees what is their own view. Working with the psychological World is a very subtle business.

The realm of Yezirah or Formation is the World in which much of the group work takes place and thus the place of the tutor is located at its centre. From here, at the simultaneous peak of the physical Tree, the tutor can view the natural World while perceiving the operations of the group from the arena of the soul which is at the heart of the group. Although it is possible to have a leader who is just a physical person, like a successful businessman who knows nothing else or an astute psychologist who knows the way people function, it is not possible to have a kabbalistic group without the spiritual connection with the third World that touches the Tiferet of the meetings (see Figure 11). Here we have the uniqueness of any esoteric gathering. There has to be someone who can bring all three lower Worlds into the linking position of the chair.

Now, while many tutors cannot sustain a status of inner connection for long in their ordinary life, it is a miraculous fact that while seated in the chair and conducting a meeting, such a state is possible. Anyone who can hold the ego under discipline can occupy and experience this position, as many who have been an acting chairperson have found. Some who have not been quite ready for it have discovered that it is an awesome place to sit for the energy that is focused there is more than that given by the chair of an ordinary social meeting. Many people realise, after sitting in that 'Siege Perilous' position, that it is not quite as glamourous as they thought for it carries heavy responsibilities and few can bear them without a deep commitment to Kabbalah.

Ideally, a tutor should be conscious of the three Worlds simultaneously. Usually, however, a person can be aware of only one or two Worlds at a time because the range of attention is at first not wide enough, although this will come with time. Often, for instance, a tutor is aware only of the group dynamics or, perhaps, of someone in distress while at the same time sensing that the room is too stuffy or hot. Sometimes a profound presence of the Spirit suddenly dissolves all sensory awareness as the group shifts levels and the tutor has to bring the meeting back to Earth.

A tutor's job is like that of a ship's captain. He or she has to monitor every level and make instant and long term decisions from the bridge at the centre of the group Tree. Here is the focus of the receiving and imparting of knowledge, as the tutor holds the connection between the group in the lower two Trees and the upper ones of Heaven and the Divine. It is not an easy position in which to be.

12. Synthesis

So far we have filled in the theory of the group Tree on the side pillars and the lower face. This is the visible level made up of students and tutor who constitute the human connection between the heavenly and earthly Worlds. Nothing can flow either way, however, until the group is in proper order and operative which means that there is more to a meeting than just a collection of people interested in Kabbalah, led by someone who knows a little more than the rest. There has to be a communion between above and below. A group may have all the facilities of a place, a good tutor and keen students but, unless Heaven wishes to join in the work, nothing will happen. Many groups have been set up with elaborate rituals, long devotional sessions and deep discussions about the nature of Existence, despite which nothing but social activity has resulted, no matter how arduous, devoted and learned the exercises have been. Either there is no inner receptivity in the group or the right time for communion has not come.

The primary agent of connection between the upper and lower Worlds is made through the tutor who acts as the Tiferet of the group. As the focus for whatever is happening, a tutor should be sensitive to every shift and fluctuation within the group's Tree. A good tutor must be aware of the slightest digression and increase of consciousness, flowing down of knowledge and descent of Grace. A tutor, moreover, has to resonate the note generated by the group and seek to tune out any discords and hold it at its harmonic of collective awareness. This includes dealing with those who are hostile to what is going on because they are at a resistant stage, which happens from time to time, or with someone who is fundamentally opposed to what the group is doing but has not yet left. There is periodically at least one member of the group in this state.

The tutor's task is to bring together the upper and lower faces of the Tree and to synthesise the various paths and triads, so that they begin to co-ordinate at least at the centre of the group.

At the start of a new group this is a most difficult operation because perhaps only a few people at the initial meetings have any kind of collective discipline. Fortunately, in such an ancient tradition as Kabbalah, there are procedures based upon principles such as the one to be set out and this gives a kabbalistic group a clear set of guidelines as well as support from the upper Worlds, should the group and tutor be ready for it.

As has been said, there is a hierarchy of spiritual levels. The uppermost is in direct contact with the Divine at the Crown of the Creative World which corresponds to the Tiferet of the World of Emanation. This is the place of the seventh heaven and the habitat of Metatron who is responsible for the transmission of higher knowledge. Below come the various other levels in seven degrees of spirituality that take in the lower face of the Divine World of Azilut and the upper face of the psychological Tree. This means that the Malkhut of the Spiritual Tree corresponds to the Tiferet of Yezirah or the psyche. Thus an individual and, in this case, a group can, with kabbalistic work, gain access to the higher Worlds while still being grounded in the Earth. The Tiferet of the group is the contact point and whoever is in the chair is in range of the realms of the psyche, spirit, and Divinity. Such a position makes it possible for a group to make a connection with any Celestial Assembly that may consider the group as a potential outlet for higher knowledge into the natural World. This can only occur, however, if the group is correctly constituted, well tested and run. Working up to this level takes much time, which should always be made clear to members of a new group or to latecomers who want instant action. In the early stages of a group what is received is by Grace and not because of the merit of its members.

The implication of the above is that the upper levels are already organised. This is indeed so and we see evidence of it in the Traditions, Lines and schools that form the hierarchy above a group. We also see how a Tradition, when established on the Earth, can last for millennia and a Line for hundreds of years while a school can exist for several generations because these organisations are not rooted in the World of Action, where everything is in motion, but operate from the upper Worlds that are not subject to the ordinary laws of nature. They exist in a different reality, in contrast to a group which is an ephemeral phenomenon that meets perhaps once a week on Earth. Here we begin to perceive the reverse of what the senses lead us to believe, in that what appears to be truly enduring does not belong to the world of solid materiality but resides in a time and space which is quite different from our normal experience.

When a new kabbalistic group is formed, it is the result of a lot of preparation. It does not come about by accident. Nor do the people who enter it get there by fluke. Everything is arranged from above for a distinct purpose. Indeed, as a group gets under way so the 'Dark Ones', referred to as the 'Opposition' in this book, take the trouble to oppose its progress as this is all part of an ongoing struggle between good and evil in the universe. The game has already been long in existence between these two factors, although it might seem coincidental that certain people who turn up at meetings seem intent on destroying the group. Sometimes this conflict is external and sometimes within an individual who has not quite yet decided which side to work with. More of this later; here we wish to examine the synthesising rather than the disruptive principle.

Set out on Jacob's Ladder, we can see how the upper part of the group Tree matches the lower part of the World of Beriah or Spirit. We can also see that the highest sefirot of the group touch the lowest sefirot of the Azilutic World and so there is a direct connection with the Divine. This will not become operational, however, except for an act of Grace coming through the Keter of the group or the intervention of Heaven as it brings the lower part of the spiritual Tree into active engagement with the upper face of the group's Tree.

The way this operates theoretically is that when a group has done enough work on the structure and dynamics of the lower part of its Tree, then there is a receptacle for the Spirit to enter and into which to flow. This occurs when the soul triad or heart of the group is well established as a result of much effort by its members who, with the tutor as the focus at Tiferet, begin to operate the interleaving upper and lower faces of the psychological and spiritual Tree (see Figure 11). Upon this happening the Malkhut of Beriah is joined to the Tiferet of Yezirah and the Keter of Asiyyah or Action. Thus the Daat or place of knowledge in the group Tree gains access to the Yesod or Foundation of Beriah, the Spirit. When that occurs there is a simultaneous match between the psychological Binah and the spiritual Hod, the psychological Hokhmah and the spiritual Nezah and the Keter of Yezirah comes into union with the Tiferet of Beriah, perhaps even with the Malkhut of the Divine. In such a moment there is a flow up and down between all four Worlds. Anyone who has been present at such a happening has a sense of profound alignment with everything and remembers it for life. Sometimes such moments manifest as a vertical shaft of light in the midst of the meeting.

But, before events of this order can become a not-uncommon occurrence, many things have to happen in a group. Firstly, there has to be a sufficient number of committed members and this takes time. Then a deep relationship, based on mutual trust between tutor and student, has to be established as the theory of Kabbalah is learned and its practices are absorbed by the group and the individual. A completely new language has to be created so that everyone understands precisely what is being communicated. This requires a long period of casting aside old ideas and prejudices as well as the undergoing of ego changes which precipitate many social and personal crises. Such situations are not easy. There are many mutually enjoyed occasions, however, so that a pool of common memories starts to be built up in the emotional triads of the group as well as in the two triads concerned with concepts. Over time a common identity has to be formed and with it comes the ability to operate as a group. This creates what is called 'the upper room of the soul' of the group that can be entered at will. Such a place is only accessible to those who are aware of it and can sustain their consciousness there. All this takes many years in which people will come and go, some in a friendly way, others in hostility, for various reasons to be discussed. Sometimes there will be dramatic crises that threaten to break up the group and at others there will be the quiet undermining of complacency. There is never a time when a group can take itself for granted.

As we can see there has to be a form and a dynamic interaction between the various factors of group work. This develops the infrastructure to what is above and what is below. The group must also relate to what is going on in the outside world, once it has established itself and has passed beyond being just a spiritual nursery. It has been said that an esoteric group is the kindergarten for the young, a haven for the weak, a hospital for the sick and a gymnasium for the strong. Everyone who joins such a group has all four of these elements in them, so that each person brings to it their life experience which can be shared in order to help or heal the others. What makes the difference between a kabbalistic group and a gathering with just high ideals is that it seeks a practical connection with the upper levels, so as to make itself available to carry out whatever Work is needed in that time and place. Such an operation is often unobtrusive to the world at large. A Kabbalist working in race relations, in art or in science can help to alter the course of history by introducing the spiritual dimension into a crucial council meeting, a seminal book on psychology or a socially important invention. Such contributions might not be spectacular but this is how many spiritual traditions work. Jesus and Mohammed were individuals who have affected millions but this could not have occurred without the thousands of unseen people who prepared the ground in a myriad ways that made their cultures receptive to higher knowledge. This is the wider task of schools.

Having set out the bones of a group let us now begin to clothe them with the details of flesh and blood so that we may perhaps experience, in human terms, what kabbalistic schools are like and how they start.

13. Starting Points

All group work begins and ends with the individual. It starts with Adam who represents the unified image of all that exists, becomes a human being who presents in miniature all those physical, psychological and spiritual qualities and resolves again in Adam when the cycle of Creation and Evolution terminates in the full awareness of all these levels in the Divine. The stage with which we are particularly concerned is the point of conscious return. This is when a person has gone through all the processes of coming into manifestation, has descended into the mineral, vegetable and animal kingdoms and begun to emerge as an incarnate human being, that is, an earthly creature that can know that it knows. In other words, the person is no longer subject to elemental conditions, the dominance of his appetites or subject to its drives. A human is a being that recognises different levels and can choose one in which it wishes to live.

Most people have not reached this stage of development and are ruled by their overriding desire for physical security, preoccupation with food or a pursuit of status. It is only in rare or occasional moments that they reflect upon the nature of the universe and mankind's place and purpose in it. When a person does begin to do this, to the point that all other matters become less important, then there starts the process of individuation. It is at this stage that they begin to look for others who ask the same questions or perhaps even know the answers. It may take many years and a number of situations and crises to arrive at such a contact. Here are some composite examples based upon the three types of approach.

'M' was a man of action. Born into a subtropical climate and a culture that placed great stress on religious ritual, all seemed set for him. He grew up in an easy-going society and was married at an early age to one of the beauties of a socially accepted family. On the face of it, all was well. He had time to work and play and even ponder why he had been born, although this was only a passing consideration because life was good, or so it seemed because, after a honeymoon period, things began to go wrong. This was precipitated when the couple moved to another country and the support constraints of the society they had left were removed. Suddenly they began to discover that they had little in common besides their culture. An alien society and its different values produced attraction and tensions and 'M's' wife left him for a more exciting existence and another man. 'M' was desolate. During this period of grief and deep self-questioning he met another woman whom he somehow recognised as familiar even though she was of a completely different race and culture. She had had the same experience. Through her he met others of her circle which turned out to be the periphery of an esoteric group, although he did not become aware of this for some time. When he began to realise that, even within an apparently social circumstance, there was a quiet discipline he started to suspect he was on the edge of something quite different from any situations he had encountered before. Answers to old and pertinent questions were suddenly forthcoming. Later he was invited to join the group and became a committed member.

'Y' was a woman born into a clerical family. She was brought up surrounded by devotion and this developed her capacity for love. Like all adolescents she rebelled against her parents and their lifestyle for, although she recognised their values, these tenets were not for her. She followed the usual path of women from such staid backgrounds and went completely wild. What she sought in her affairs, however, was not sensual release and experience but genuine love. She was strongly selective in her partners, choosing only those who had a certain quality of emotion. These ranged from young men who still retained some ideal about love but were too immature, to older companions who knew about love but were too widely experienced to remain faithful for long. She devoted all her love to one man for several years, seeking to awaken his stunted heart by means of her love and prayer, for she had not abandoned her religious belief, although she no longer practised its outer form. During this time, her friends sustained her faith. Among these were one or two connected with esoteric work. These in particular helped her maintain an essential equilibrium through a very dark time. Perceiving the wider picture from her contact with these people, she left the man and came into a group which deepened her understanding of the nature of love and how her relationship could only continue if the man wished to grow. He did not and she was given, by Grace, a partner who did so that full use was made of her great capacity to love in a marriage and family of her own.

'Z' was an intellectual soldier by profession. Trained as an engineer, he joined the military because it was part of the family tradition and offered much reward for a bright young man. After serving as a junior officer he was soon selected for higher rank. Charming and intelligent, he was destined for favour. Quick and charismatic, his soldiers admired and trusted him and he spent several years coasting along on his brilliance. Then came war. Suddenly the war games became real. The calculations for the artillery were no longer a matter for intellectual conjecture. People died each time his computations were correct. This, together with the sights of the battlefield, was too much and in the post-war period there was much brooding upon why he was in the army. One day, while driving a jeep across some rough country, he had a vision, because of which he decided to leave a promising career in the army, much to the dismay of his men, superiors and family. He wandered the world, going to this and that country for what appeared to be the most random of reasons. He arrived in England to seek out a girl he had once met and somehow found himself at a party where there was a discussion on astrology. His birth chart was read and he was astounded at how much could be ascertained from such little data as his time and place of birth. This opened up a whole new world to his intellect. Soon he began to probe deeper into esoteric subjects until he made his connection with a person who took him to a group where many of his questions were answered.

The above stories are typical of many who find themselves in a preparatory group. People may arrive from the far ends of the Earth or step in from next door. Some may come from conventional homes and others from the most unusual backgrounds. One person might be in a marriage where their partner has no interest at all in esoterica and another might be a fugitive from a family that indulged in every kind of occult hocus pocus. What brings them mostly together is the unconscious pursuit of Truth, love of the Good and the need to act correctly. Sometimes it may be only one of these desires which can make a person search the world over for an answer to their yearning. While many people do not know what they are looking for, they instantly recognise, on coming into contact with it, that this is what they want. Sometimes, it must be said, they cannot cope with what they see and run away because they are not yet ready to take on the changes such an acknowledgment would bring. Many people pass by the door of their salvation for years, half-knowing and yet denying that it is there. This is because they have yet to come to a point when they recognise that they cannot act on their own. Such a moment requires great humility—or deep disappointment and inner anguish—and these states are not arrived at without a certain degree of suffering.

When a person first realises that he or she is not quite like the rest of humanity, there arises a sense of inferiority and superiority leading to a distaste for the world and a taking into the ego of the fragments of wisdom imbibed from various sources. This creates a certain heavily defended arrogance. There are many such people wandering the world who know they are different and yet cannot accept that they can learn from anyone. They have read all the books and even do certain spiritual practices. They carry a conviction of superiority but cannot risk it in the arena of life or test it against an elder in accomplishment. They avoid the ordinary and evade any direct contact with higher knowledge. It sometimes takes many years for them to realise that they can go no further without help for, very often, pride forbids them to admit they are stuck. They will talk about the spiritual life at length or demonstrate that they know all there is to know. While this may impress the naive and bore the uninitiated, it does not fool those who do know and very often such people are the most difficult to reach and release from their predicament. Usually, if the situation has not become too crystallised, some personal crisis dissolves or destroys their gilded cage and, in the dismay and loss of their supposed higher status, there emerges the possibility of progress beyond an ego imitation of real development.

Disappointment in some personal ritual or devotional practice or the failure of certain private concepts is usually the spur that takes people further. It shakes them out of their self-containment, erodes their hubristic individuality and reveals that personal efforts must be followed up by work with others, so that there is not only a collective support but the interaction with people on the same path. To work alone creates the illusion that one is a centre and, while this is right, even a pivotal point has no place unless it is in relationship with others. No one knows his stature or position, except in contrast to something smaller or larger. One cannot tell where one is on the Ladder of Existence in isolation. Moreover, one is no use to the universe unless one is part of a whole and this requires knowing who is one's inferior or superior and who one's neighbour. Such a recognition means that one is not afraid to be open, to be nothing or something, according to the need of the moment, and this takes true humility. That is one reason why a real esoteric contact is difficult to detect. This is apart from the fact that true initiates will not readily let it be known what they are. One only perceives the connection when receptive to that level. This is the only time an inner contact can be made.

14. Contacts

Contacts with any truly esoteric tradition are not easily made. One may walk the streets of Jerusalem or Konya, London or San Francisco and see many people who dress and act as if they were an esoteric seeker but the chances are that they are either imitating what they believe a walker of the Path may be like or merely following the custom or the fashion of their particular society. One observes that many of those who wear the traditional dress of some esoteric order or sect are, more often than not, more concerned with status or making a living or both. Moreover, quite a number of the people who gather around ashrams, lodges, tombs or saints and sacred sites and dress and speak in the style of that place, are often deluding themselves, and others, that they have authority. Authority is not so easily acquired or given. It has to come at the right time and in a moment of initiation.

Initiation means to begin something. To be an initiate means to commit oneself to a particular path of action, devotion or contemplation. One does not arrive at such a point easily. It is the result of either many years of gradual preparation or, over the short term, a period of intense joy or suffering. Such an experience usually puts one in a state where there seems to be no way out of a personal predicament in which nothing worse or better can happen. At such moments the upper Worlds intervene. In Kabbalah this is called 'The Supervision of Heaven' which watches over people just coming up to the critical point when a breakthrough can occur, either because they are at the end of their tether or because they have become open. Both of these conditions can be what is called a state of *Kabal* or being receptive, the moment when they are most able to perceive what can be made available to them.

Take the case of the woman who had sacrificed love for a career. She worked many years perfecting her talents as an artist but was still unrecognised when she reached the peak of her capability. She continued to practise her art with great conscientiousness but each year that passed took away the likelihood of her ever being able to gain recognition. She turned to conventional religion but found no solace there because the minister could not explain the meaning of her seemingly hard fate. He offered her his belief but she wanted real knowledge. Her whole religious foundation faltered because she could not accept the suffering she was experiencing as a pointless rejection of her gift from God. One day she went into an esoteric bookshop and asked for a particular book. The perceptive assistant, seeing that she was deeply in crisis, suggested that she contact someone who might be able to tell her more. The trail was followed up and a long acquaintanceship ensued, mostly over the telephone, which led the woman out of her crisis and towards understanding why she had such a life. During this time her contact person made only a passing mention of a group and the woman has yet to ask to enter. She still believes she is going it alone although in fact she has been placed under supervision by a chain of providential circumstances. Note that the candidate is still unaware of the opportunity, even though hints have been given. No obvious initiative on the part of the contact is taken. This would be quite counter-productive.

In some situations, however, the reverse might be the case. Take the man who came to a point of choice in his life. On the one hand he was offered a comfortable career with financial security but little fulfilment, on the other an extremely creative interest which was to take him into an inwardly productive but financially unrewarding way of life. After receiving a series of setbacks to his creative projects he began to slip towards the secure job. He started to over-eat and drink and became cynical about life until suddenly realising that he was inwardly dying. In desperation he telephoned someone he had known for years and explained the dilemma. That person, who was in Kabbalah and recognised the test facing the man, told him bluntly that he was in a graver position than he perhaps realised, adding, 'You have the choice to risk and grow or sleep until you are dead'. The man retorted that he had responsibilities. The reply came, to whom and to what? A withering soul was not the way to take care of a family. In the long run, misfortune would overtake them all as he lost contact with himself, then his wife and children. It was pointed out, by given examples, how Heaven takes care of those who place themselves under its care. There can be no hedging of bets. Either one lives according to spiritual values or earthly ones and their respective effects on the quality of life. The man has yet to make the decision; but at least he now knows what the issues are and where they will lead because his contact placed him in a position to be able to perceive two entirely different sets of laws that can govern a life.

Such crises can precipitate a meeting with someone in Kabbalah. The contact may be a person known for many years or someone known for a very short time. In the former situation the contact is well acquainted with the person, knowing their psyche, state of spirit and worldly problems. Here the contact may wait a decade while the situation matures and even then hold silence until exactly the right moment. This is what happened in the situation of a woman who clung on to her dreams long after they had been shattered by reality. Nothing could be said to her until, in hindsight, she saw them for what they were and opened up her heart to the possibility of something else that might lead to inner development. In the case of the short acquaintance, it often happens that the contact comes into the life of the candidate just at the crucial period when everything is up to question or when the person has reached the culmination point where some outside help is needed to seal the circle, as in the example of the man who, having studied esoteric books for most of his life, suddenly realised with horror that he had wasted many years and that he had to practise what he knew theoretically or he would go to his grave no more than a bookworm. It so happened that he had recently become friendly with a person who seemed to know as much as he did, even though he was not so well read. Moreover, the individual appeared to anticipate his observations and answer his questions, if only in an oblique way. Then one day it dawned on him that the man was the connection he had been reading about and had not recognised until now. From that point on he began to move.

Some contacts are truly miraculous in that they do not fit into the normal sequence of timing. They may occur anywhere at any time, on an aircraft, at a party, in a far-away place, as well as close to home. Take the case of the guest at a traditional wedding. He was muttering some despairing remarks about tribal customs to himself, saying that he never met anyone spiritual at such gatherings, when he heard the person next to him say, almost imperceptibly, that there were others present if he had eyes to see. The man then took another look at the speaker and there began a conversation about matters of mutual interest that took them late into the night. He never saw the man again but he knew the meeting had been providentially arranged for him to prove a point. In another example, a woman travelled many thousands of miles from Israel to find herself, through a series of coincidences (or so they seemed) at a kabbalistic meeting. She was deeply affected for, after searching for twenty years in the East for such a group, she found it in the last place she had expected it: in the West.

Figure 13—SEEKER
Those who seek the Path will find traces of the Torah or Teaching in every culture. The story of Aladdin and the four caves of copper, silver, gold and the miraculous lamp speaks of the four Worlds and enlightenment. So too does Cinderella, the symbol of the soul who, despite all opposition, marries the Prince of the Spirit. Here the mature seeker, signified by a beard, follows through the darkness of ignorance, with the aid of the spectacles of clarity, the lamp of theory and the staff of practice, the footprints of Truth to the door of a school of the soul. (Renaissance woodcut.)

From the point of view of the contacts themselves, the situation is quite different. Anyone who is involved with Kabbalah is a potential contact for someone, because all are involved in the chain of transmission. This does not mean, however, that anyone who shows interest in esoteric matters is a suitable candidate. The contact has to exercise a great deal of discrimination. He or she must assess at what stage the person is and in what state. For instance, many people who talk about esoteric matters may be quite oblivious of the fact that someone in the Work is present. That is why the less said by the contact the better. If a really genuine candidate presents his or herself, then the contact goes on to maximum alert. Over the hours or years, as the case may be, the conversation is gently led towards culmination. Integrity is checked by delicate but probing questions. Vanity is tested, so too is humility. Limits of knowledge are explored and so is experience. Many profess to know much in order to impress and some people quote the obscure sayings and ideas of the deep and great with apparent conviction. Being a contact requires much skill because to blow one's cover at the wrong time can create problems, like never being trusted again by someone who feels that he or she has been duped or manipulated by a sinister lunatic. Such a mistake could be crucial and create a major stumbling block, if it does not put off the person for life. This was one of the original reasons why the Masons and Kabbalists have always been so discreet.

Being a contact means that one is a link to something else. This does not mean other people or a teacher but to a group or school and, indeed, to a whole Tradition. Much consideration has to be given, therefore, as to with whom one makes an open contact. Besides those who would take up the opportunity for the right reasons, there are people who, out of curiosity, would love to get into an esoteric society to see what goes on. There are also individuals who seek such an intimate circle because they are lonely. Kabbalistic group work is not for them, nor is it for those seeking spiritual novelty; and there are many who wander around doing just this. A new and inexperienced contact can mistake enthusiasm for the strange or unusual for a real interest in spirituality, as their own zeal blinds them to the subtle ambition of some individuals for higher knowledge for the wrong motivation. Such people must not be allowed access to a group for they can be dangerous, to those without protection, if they take a fragment of the system and use it to infatuate the innocent and gullible. At this juncture one must be careful; it is here that the principle of Evil seeks to intrude into the situation and to distract those seeking the Gate to the Path. Because of this factor, the contact must be particularly watchful for sometimes the 'opposition' places one of its own, often unconscious, agents in the position of being invited into a group. Only those who have, in the judgement of the contact, the right motivation should be allowed to enter the next stage which is why a traditional delaying procedure is used to select the sheep from the goats. While this method is not quite so apparently strict in our day it is, nevertheless, applied at the more advanced stages. However, we are here still at the stage of introduction.

15. Introduction

The moment of contact is sometimes the turning point in a person's life which is why it must be handled with enormous care. Suddenly a new dimension is opened, a completely different way of looking at life. This can have the most far-reaching effect for good or for bad, depending on the way it is presented by the contact and received by the recipient. While the moment itself may be a flash of recognition of what is being revealed, the preparation for it is spread over a long time. Some people have taken almost a lifetime to reach such a moment while others may have had to pass through an intense experience into which many lessons have been compressed. Thus, when the contact comes to the point of revelation, there must be a fairly certain chance of its being received correctly.

If people are told about the reality of other Worlds before they are ready, it can set them back many years. This cannot be impressed enough on the contact person. Many zealous people in the honeymoon stage of the Work are keen to impart what they have learned and the operation becomes one of projection and conversion rather than indicating and introducing the candidate to the esoteric view of Existence. Take the case of a young woman who was questioning the meaning of her life and why she was so unlucky. She was interrogated by a man who possessed some psychic skill but little understanding of people and who thought he could help her by bringing her under a discipline. What he succeeded in doing was arousing her antagonism to authority figures and a very sensitive soul was driven away from the possibility of solving her problem for many years.

The introduction of higher knowledge must be done extremely carefully. To some, for example, the notion of reincarnation is unacceptable, as is the idea of angelic beings. To be told that the physical World is the least important is a threat to the sense-oriented and is not strictly true either. Many unprepared people have been put off by being informed that their lives are an illusion and that they are dominated by their desires; and not a few have been repulsed by the sales talk of the contact that his or her teacher is an all-knowing wonder-worker. Many would-be contact makers have lost their chance to impart what they have received because they were more involved with what they could give rather than with what the candidate needed. This is one of the first tests of many to come to prove that one really knows what Kabbalah is about.

Consider the following analogue. The contact is a bottle of champagne. It is full and under the pressure of fermentation. The candidate may be a glass that is empty, half-full or even up to the brim with all sorts of experiences and ideas. First the contact has to assess whether the candidate is ready to take what he has to offer. If the person is empty that may be possible but it could obliterate what individuality that person has, as sometimes happens when someone takes on totally a set of ideas and practices that give them much-needed identity. This could be disastrous. Such people need to be given a little at a time, so that they can absorb it at their pace and make it truly their own. Inexperienced contacts who are bursting with effervescence must restrain themselves before such apparently easy converts because when the initial enthusiasm has run its course the reverse sets in and the prospective candidate retreats rapidly with an overdose of spiritual fermentation and a broken connection that may take a long time to repair, if it ever is.

The situation of the half-full candidate is quite a different problem. Such a person may have a jumble of mixed ideas or a half-digested comprehension of spiritual matters that have no coherent order. This can generate critical misunderstanding when presented with certain concepts like, 'Do what you think is right' (even if it causes suffering for others) or 'I can avoid karma by detachment from life'. Individuals who do this can be psychotic in that they have distorted spiritual ideas to enhance their personal fantasy. Such people are often impressive because they exploit one aspect of their psyche to a high degree but at the cost of the other parts of themselves. The religious maniac is like this. In contrast, there is the half-filled person who is extremely confused, in as much as he has a sense of spirituality but not an overall scheme to which to relate his experience. Now it has been said that one must have a little gold to make more gold and some knowledge of esoteric themes is very useful, providing it has not become crystallised into a set of rigid beliefs. This situation is most common among educated candidates. These people, provided that they are in a receptive state, are capable of integrating what they are given.

The full-glass person is the most difficult with whom to make contact.

Usually they believe that they know everything and so there is little possibility of gaining access to them. This kind of individual is often found amongst the learned, especially those who study esoterica either as a profession or as a committed hobby. As might be expected, many priests and rabbis are found in this category, as are (I might add) writers and those who have made a life study of a particular system. This does not mean to say that all practitioners of this kind are inaccessible but only those who worship a system for its own sake or depend on it as a way of support. Generally, people of this type do not seek help but some, who have come to realise that the edifice they worship has no connection with Earth or Heaven, come to a major crisis. This takes the form in which they have to face that all their knowledge leads them nowhere. We see this in the case of the Oxford don who, despite his vast library of profound books, sees no point in reading any more; or the athlete who, having won all the medals he can, finds nothing else to do after all his time has been devoted to winning. These people, while being full to the brim, perceive an emptiness in their lives and can, at the right moment, be introduced to another dimension. Most full glasses are unapproachable even to the well-meant pressure of the subtle and knowledgeable zealot who can only make them retreat yet more deeply into the drowning depths of their achievement.

The mode of approach by a contact must be designed for the conditions of the moment. There is no preconceived procedure other than to respond to the situation as it truly is. One must not project anything into it that would mar the flow of Heaven to Earth for we are not dealing with a simple case of putting someone right, according to our ideas, but in acting in accordance with a higher principle than that of ego. The prerequisite of all such encounters between a candidate and a contact is that the contact lives in the moment. As soon as the spoken or, sometimes, unspoken need reveals itself in a candidate, the contact should become acutely alert. This means to look and listen to every nuance of word and gesture so as to determine how genuine is the signal being given out. If it seems right, after being tested by suggestion and implication, then the appropriate idea can be introduced. This may be related to the topic being discussed or that which is apparently emerging from the conversation. It could be a sensitive painter seeking a spiritual meaning in art or a man in a bar looking at the cosmic significance of politics. Such conversations can occur during a love affair, when the heart is being opened, or at a funeral when death is in the air. The touchstone is a deeper concern or probing into a more profound view of things.

The meeting is made in the instant when the candidate realises that the contact is not speaking personally but from another level that puts the discussion into a grander context. Suddenly there is a flow in which the contact makes the connection with upper Worlds for the candidate. Very often there is a distinct change in atmosphere and mood and the whole interchange shifts dimension, in as much as the candidate actually experiences a lift in consciousness. This is due to the fact that the contact acts as a link through their group or school to the vast resources of a Tradition. Whatever is said, provided that it is transmitted without interference from the ego, passes directly through the Self of the contact and into the Self of the candidate who, if she is in the right state, immediately recognises what is being said as a self-evident truth. This does not mean that it is merely a convincing argument or an eloquent elucidation but direct recognition of the reality behind what is being transmitted. Such a communication may not always be articulated. It may be demonstrated in a gesture or by a glance that awakens the candidate to that other reality. The Buddha only had to look at certain people for them to realise their true situation and, indeed, this can occur even with the most humble and unsophisticated contacts, if they are centred correctly in themselves.

What is being transmitted always has a cosmic dimension in that, while it is deeply pertinent to that individual, it also extends what is going on to a further horizon. If not carefully handled this can frighten the candidate who may, as in one case, become aware of their own spiritual mentor standing in the room. Such an astounding experience makes some people leap back into the physical world, like Jack scrambling down the beanstalk after seeing the upper World. He then cut the connection by chopping the beanstalk down so as to stop the greater World entering ego's kingdom. If skillfully managed, the candidate should be left with the question of what to do with such an experience and where to go from there. This is the moment when the contact begins to realise that to make such a connection for a person means taking on the responsibility of bringing them safely into the Work, if they want to come. For while some individuals seek to have a mystical insight, only a few want to follow it up. Here the contact must be cautious and only invite the candidate to the group if an interest in serious work on spiritual development is expressed intensely enough. As one great Kabbalist said, 'Many are called but few are chosen'. This means 'choosing' oneself which is something that only the candidate can do.

16. Connection

The stages by which a person actually comes to asking for help are many. Some people, according to temperament, will grab at the first thing offered while others will delay so long as to lose the opportunity presenting itself. Others do not recognise what they have before them for a long time while there are those who know but are reluctant to act. Yet others see but are too proud to reveal their need and others, while recognising what is being offered, turn away because it means change and they prefer to suffer with the familiar. Different people at different stages, in different states and in different circumstances produce a wide variety of situations in which they can leap the gap between ignorance and knowledge.

Ignorance in this context means to 'ignore' what is known because anyone who has reached this stage of questioning already knows a great deal. One cannot arrive at pondering about the meaning of Existence from a position of innocence. A person must have had some experience of life to seek a solution to this or that question, be it intensely personal like 'Why am I always missing everything?' to 'What is the nature of God?' The innocent are still in a state of unknowing, like children, and the world situation, cosmic crises and the issues of good and evil have not yet touched them. Such matters affect only those who have become aware of the drama of Creation or have encountered the struggle of morality in the soul. These are the people for whom contacts are watching out, so as to help them on their way.

We have seen that the moment of contact may be crucial for many reasons. A person, for example, looking for some answers can meet a contact who has them and yet spend the whole evening talking about his own opinions which may, indeed, be very interesting but not the point of that encounter. All the contact can do, in this case, is sit and watch for a gap in the talk that may never come, at least between these two people. Indeed, it may be many years before such an individual is in the position again of having someone listen to him who knows what he wants. Such chances are often lost by the apparently brilliant and successful; for the clever are usually remarkably stupid when it comes to esoteric matters. The problem for the contact is how to draw out the unspoken question of what can be done about his spiritual state or how to comprehend the world and know God. Some people might set up a social situation, like a supper loaded with people from the group who talk discreetly or openly about the spiritual work in general terms. This is sometimes the perfect solution to generate interest and can result in a minor revelation when the person realises that she is not alone after all and that there are others who do not live just by worldly standards but follow a path of inner development. There are times, however, when, despite all the careful preparation and work, everything goes wrong, as in the case of the party at which the candidate got drunk so as to avoid any real conversation. This was his choice and had to be respected, for no one must ever be forced into the spiritual work.

Assuming that the candidate is really interested in inner development, the contact provides and leads the conversation, perhaps over many months or for just an hour, towards the moment when, as is said in Kabbalah, 'the veil of Heaven is drawn back'. In an instant the situation is totally changed and candidate and contact are joined in a moment of Grace. Such an event is memorable even to those who, afterwards, back away and want to forget the whole thing ever happened, as sometimes occurs. What takes place is the illumination of the Self of that person who afterwards sees with extraordinary clarity what their life situation is and what the options are. In the case of an individual at a crossroads, it may be the turning point in a journey of despair or a faltering at the peak of success. It may be the perception of the midpoint in a crisis or recognition of a non-event. Insights like these reveal a totally different way of looking at reality; suddenly the implications of the moment are glimpsed in great depth and solutions that were not observable in the normal state of awareness are seen to emerge from the most unlikely quarters, like realising that a situation would not collapse if one were left to pursue a true Path.

Having helped to open the door to Heaven, the contact then has to wait to see what the follow-up reaction will be, since not everyone wants to take up the opportunity offered. Many are tempted to run because such a realisation means the transformation of a whole way of life. The contact may have to wait a moment or many months for the experience, which perhaps only lasted a second, to sink in and have its full effect on the candidate. This is also because there are some people who instantly wish to take up their cross (to use a Christian term), only to find that it is too heavy. While Kabbalah is a fascinating occupation for the body, soul and spirit, it is no light labour and carries with it responsibilities of which most people are completely unaware. Very often, therefore, after the breakthrough there will be a pause for a long or a short period, depending on the person, giving the candidate a chance to reflect, reconsider and react to the experience and recontact, if so wished, the person who introduced him or her to this new dimension. This is an example of the kind of responsibility meant. It is quite a liability to be the point of entry into Kabbalah. Such an obligation is called, in Kabbalah, being a *Sandik* or godparent who initiates the candidate into the tradition.

As a safeguard against error, which can occur on either side, Tradition lays down certain procedures to be carried out in doubtful cases. After the crucial meeting, barriers are set up to make things difficult for the candidate. A barrier may be a time lapse or a social device, such as the contact's not being available or being referred elsewhere, so that the candidate has to make a definite effort to maintain the connection. This is not only to test the tenacity of the original experience but to allow both sides to see how committed is the person in the pursuit of Truth. Some groups set a very difficult course for their prospective members. In one case a person had to travel late at night between various railway stations in order to pick up a trail that eventually led him to a certain address. In another example, however, very little was done besides telling the candidate to look up a certain name in the telephone book; it depends on the circumstances. Here it must be added that any abuse of this procedure on the part of the contact or the group indicates that they are no longer in the spirit of the Tradition and that what they belong to is a decadent institution. This warning is to protect the seeker.

Having established a connection, the candidate now becomes eligible to be introduced into a group. This may be a simple matter, in the case of a small and intimate company, but not quite so straightforward in a fully operational school. People come to Kabbalah for many reasons. Some, for example, may need to be healed, for many who are interested in the Way are often damaged by life and require help. Of these a certain number may actually be sick but this is a risk that sometimes has to be taken, if the person is willing to come under discipline. Such people cannot be allowed to participate in certain exercises in case their particular weakness is triggered and they become disturbed.

Much skill is required in selecting and directing people into the right group. On the other hand, there is the problem of those who are excessively clever or stupid, both of whom may have a genuine interest in self-development and service. There are always people to be taken care of and accommodated by those who have been in a group for some time already. The periodic introduction of new blood is a good thing but sometimes the wrong combination does produce a disruption and a temporary lowering of the level of consciousness. Even groups, however, have to cope with life as it is and hold their own.

We have spoken so far of an already existing school in which the Tree, its structure and infrastructure is already at work, a situation which takes many years to materialise. Often a large number of people will pass through a group before it matures, their common experience helping to build up a reservoir of patterned energy to form the foundations of an esoteric vessel. To comprehend this process, let us study the situation from the beginning, so as to see how a group is conceived, born and grows to become a school. Let us presume that the Tradition is about to expand its range of activities and that someone has been sent out by the Line to start a school that meets the need of a particular time and place. Such events occur in each generation. We begin with a person, whom we shall call 'X', whose brief is to form an entirely new group of people dedicated to healing and developing themselves, in order to help to unify the Worlds and to aid God to behold God.

17. Tutor

'X' has been given a commission. His tutor of many years has told him that he must now leave the present group and go out and form one of his own to carry on the Line and widen the range of school with which the group is associated. This brief seems simple enough and many less experienced people would be excited by the prospect. But this is not so for those who know what is involved. Some who are new to the Work would relish the opportunity to direct, teach, and carry out the various operations of a group. For them there is the attraction of being at the centre with its power to influence a situation. Even the well informed are tempted by this. On the face of it, to run a group looks like a fascinating and straightforward operation. The theory of Kabbalah is well structured and the various practices are laid out. A group can be disciplined, if there is a common intent, and there are precedents for the problems that occur from time to time. The rules as to what a group can and cannot do are simple. For example, the invocation made at the beginning of each meeting may not be said if less than seven people are present. This and other regulations are plain but, as any group leader knows, nothing quite follows the book.

'X' has been prepared for this moment over a long time. Indeed, since he entered the old group as a candidate he has been in training for just this task, although he may not have realised it. After learning the theory of the sefirotic Tree and the carrying out of the various exercises, he would have spent many years deepening his comprehension and perfecting his performance both in the group and out in life. During this time, which might stretch over a decade, he has grown in being and knowledge and this has been observed by his elders who have earmarked him to be a tutor, for not everyone who stays the course is selected to take a group. Some people can be in Kabbalah for twenty years and still not grasp the principles of the Tree and some, although they know the theory thoroughly, have no idea how to communicate it to others. While occasionally such people might be asked to take the group as an exercise in mutual

Figure 14—TEACHER
One's first tutor has to be a person who knows something you do not know about development. They may be a month or a lifetime ahead. Either way, one can learn from them if they have to have the ability to illuminate the student. Some people seek a great Master but they would not comprehend what was being taught. There is a tutor for every stage and one who understands your particular circumstance. Here a rabbi who knows the culture of his students opens, in their terms, a window of illumination appropriate for their phase of evolution. (19th century print.)

communications, the responsibility of the forming of a new outfit requires special skills and temperament.

The most important quality that the elders will look for is reliability. A person may be quick or slow, sharp or even tempered, subtle or plain. This is not so important as consistency. This does not mean doggedness or rigidity, tenacity or even being single-minded but the ability always to be aware of what is the purpose of Kabbalah. Many groups have withered before they have even budded because the potential tutor believed the authority of the chair came before the Teaching. Many of the world's great religions have suffered from the blight of dogma and power and there is no difference in the miniature community of an esoteric group. The constancy referred to here is the ability to adapt to changing conditions and yet to maintain the aim of the operation. An example of this might be when the theoretical study of the Tree has to be dropped and a completely new way of working is formulated that illustrates its principles. A creative capacity is required that can turn any situation to kabbalistic advantage. Such a gift would have been discerned and developed while 'X' was a student in the old group by giving him certain projects, like producing a lecture on temples.

Another quality needed for a group leader is a certain amount of experience. According to the traditional formula, a person had to be at least thirty or even forty years old. By this is meant that they should be mature. It was also reckoned that a person should be married and learned. These conditions were drafted in a time and place very different from the modern Western world. People no longer live in a medieval or Middle Eastern society where everybody had a distinct rôle. Today everything is in flux socially and so we refer now to principles. Thus the marriage issue is seen as being able to hold a real relationship and 'learning' as simply being intelligently informed about life in general. One must also remember that many people today are better educated and have finer libraries than many ancient scholars possessed. The overriding criterion which is found in one text on how to teach Kabbalah is that 'one may speak of such things to a person who knows of him/herself'; that is, already possesses an inner knowledge and awareness of higher matters. The life experience of a potential tutor has to be sufficiently wide that he is able to handle not only his own problems but also those of others who may have very different backgrounds and attitudes.

The fact that a person comes from a particular place or class should not, in this Work, have a major bearing although it will clearly influence the approach. The person from San Francisco will not have the same cultural values as another from London or Jerusalem. Nevertheless, when it comes to Kabbalah certain values have universal importance: intellectual integrity, emotional courage and correct action. Such inner criteria must be part of a prospective tutor's being for he or she has to try to demonstrate what is being taught, even while under external or internal pressure. Instinctively an individual may not find it convenient to carry out these principles and so many tests are devised to determine whether a prospective tutor can be relied on in sustaining routine operations and dealing with emergencies. For an instance, the brilliant but unstable student may panic in a crisis and lose a good group or the plodding but good dumb-bell bore people away with his pedantry. Such people do have their place and moment to serve, be it the single lecture which demonstrates a specific aspect of Kabbalah or the readiness to drive someone to the airport. One such student helped the Work more than most by ferrying her tutor about. She also learnt more by simply being there, so every person has his job and spiritual remuneration.

Having been given the commission, 'X' has now to take action. He can, of course, refuse the commission outright or simply let it be stillborn. This may happen when the person suddenly realises that he has let himself in for an enormous commitment. One does not take on a group for a few weeks. It is the work of several years and sometimes of well over a decade, if not more. Group leadership is not a thing to be taken on lightly and then dropped; up to a certain point the tutor is responsible for the spiritual welfare of students, especially those who are just starting on the Path. If these people are let down during the introductory period, then they are very often lost for many years, if not for that lifetime. Some might argue that such people may not have been ready for the Work but this does not detract from the tutor's responsibility. To act as the bridge between the inner and outer worlds is no mean task. It requires a thorough comprehension of what is involved.

Very often, although not always, there is a parting ceremony between the new tutor and his or her mentor. This may take the form of a formal ritual in which the younger is made an elder and acknowledged as such by others of equal rank of development; or it may be a simple but poignant conversation in which the *Barakah* or blessing is passed from the senior to the junior. This can be seen as a kind of confirmation but it is more than this. It is closer to an ordination in which the flow that has come down from a long chain of tutors is passed on, like a cloak, to the next in line. Many esoteric traditions have such ceremonies, although they are not always quite as one imagines. Most of what we see or read about is the shadow of what was once a profound ceremony that has become, over the centuries, the outer shell of symbolism. The real thing may happen well out of sight or right out in the open. One case was a man waiting alone in a rented room who was given something by a complete stranger who entered and left. The object symbolised his particular strength and weakness. This gift had been carefully selected by his elders to impress upon his soul and spirit what his tasks and temptations were. These personal talismans can range from a symbolic garment of the Order, with a small bell to wake others up but not deafen them, to a sharp knife for dispensing Manna without cutting oneself. One man was given an arrow to point the Way, not shoot out of it, at his lectures.

Having completed his apprenticeship, 'X' becomes a journeyman. Here begins the phase in which he starts to work semi-independently. Having learnt the basics of the Tradition, he can now carry out a project of his own, although under indirect supervision. Thus, while responsible for running the group, he can nonetheless refer to an elder should he require advice. 'X' may run a group for the rest of his life as a journeyman because he only becomes a master if a completely new direction is required by the Tradition; and this task is not given to just anyone. Such a rôle bears enormous responsibility. To be a master requires a high degree of spiritual originality, in that the person is directly in touch with the World of Creation and generates an entirely new formulation of the Teaching. This usually occurs when there is a profound need to revive the Tradition. Only certain schools are given this commission while most others simply help in the unfolding expression of a great impulse. The spiritual creativity of the Gerona School and its influence on Spanish Kabbalah is an example. When the force had been spent and the Teaching had again become a formal study and dead ritual, then it was time for the next creative impulse and the arrival of a master like the Baal Shem Tov of the Hassidim.

However, in our case we are not examining such a seminal situation but looking at a midpoint stage where traditional ideas are simply being related to contemporary conditions. 'X' now has to consider how he will present the Teaching in terms of his gifts. His job, however, is not to innovate but to make accessible the existing material that has been passed down. In order to do this he must have people to instruct, a problem that has not, up till now, been his concern. Here is where Providence steps in with that remarkable timing which so often occurs at such moments: suddenly individuals start to come from many directions seeking spiritual counsel.

18. Initiation

As often happens at a major turning point in life, many things occur simultaneously. It is as if the long-awaited monsoon has come and everything undergoes a transformation. Situations that have remained static or repetitive suddenly start to give way or to collapse. Relationships dissolve and jobs disappear with new occupations and, sometimes, partnerships emerging as if out of nowhere. People who have formed the stable backdrop to a life fade away as they, or the person at the centre of the monsoon, no longer fit into the old scheme. Places alter and do not have the same meaning or function as they did, as events change the geography of the person's world who is undergoing an inner shift at their centre of gravity.

For 'X', our new tutor, the change may be slow, barely noticed by any except those who know what he is going through; or there may be a dramatic transformation in which home and profession are shaken from top to bottom. In one woman's case, for example, she found that she was being made by circumstances either to break a major rule in her life or miss the chance of real growth. In another instance, the individual found himself offered a position with the power to do all that he wanted, provided he sold his integrity. The alternative was to leave an excellent job prospect and enter a situation in which he did not know where the next penny was coming from. He chose to keep his freedom and integrity and, a little later, came an even better opportunity. Very often such a turning point is a test or initiation which reveals just how much trust a person places upon his inner values. It is often also the first serious initiation, being not about a theoretical issue or a minor practical problem but one in which the stakes are the highest.

The classic beginning of such an initiation is usually, but not always, to feel uneasy as if there were something impending. This may happen some months ahead of the turning point. Then comes the first real sign of change as things begin to slow down or go wrong. To the untrained eye, such events are unfortunate and precipitate a stiff resistance to change or a gradual giving way. The reason is that no matter what one might attempt, if it is a fatal event nothing can be done except accept or fight on until defeated because, no matter how stubborn one might be, circumstances always win. For the initiate things are different because he or she should view the situation from a higher vantage point than most; so that while things may be perceived as disastrous to the ego, they are not regarded so by the Self which always sees the larger picture. As a situation crumbles so the initiate is expected to step back, up into an essentially impregnable position for, although the psyche might be shaken and the world about may be swept away, the initiate is not supposed to be overthrown. The initiate may suffer despair and anguish, experience anger and hurt but the inner Self is not meant to be touched by things that would destroy most people's confidence. Strangely enough, the crisis phase is the easiest stage to bear for one can often react well to dramatic events. The hardest period is the interim when nothing seems to happen for a long time and there is nothing present to support the person, except self-discipline and belief in the Grace of God, for one is often left, at such times, entirely on one's own.

This epoch, which may last years, months or days, is called by some traditions the 'dark night of the soul', in which the person is tested and strengthened, in as much as the situation is designed to develop the initiate and make him or her ready to cope with Work that is about to be given. This may seem hard but it should be remembered that few people are really prepared to take on the responsibility of training others and so it is vital that they be able to carry the load. Initiates must be proved capable, to themselves and to those in charge of such operations. Help eventually comes in various forms, just as the breaking-point is approached. It might turn up as money when it is needed or a relationship necessary for growth. It could arrive in a mundane situation, such as a critical house sale going through remarkably quickly or someone turning up with a vacant seat for a vital journey. Many of these significant incidents could go unnoticed but the initiate Kabbalist takes nothing for granted, least of all the unexpected and especially that which seems so appropriate. This is the hallmark of the hand of Heaven.

Confidence in the purposes of Heaven is a crucial test in kabbalistic Work, for so long as one relies only on one's own judgement and effort minimal help will be offered from above. This is a law and many who have hedged their bets by taking out earthly insurances have been allowed to labour hard in their lack of belief until they perceive that one cannot have faith and not trust. To be able to wait for the storm to pass requires much patience but, if Kabbalah has become part of one's being, then there is much to be learned from these dark times. During the period of being nowhere, faults and assets come to the surface which can be corrected or used to advantage in later crises. Many hours can be spent in reflection and in observing the interaction of the Worlds at work in one's life. Other peoples' reactions are extremely revealing at such times as real friends and hidden enemies emerge to support or criticise. Various traits of character are shown up as loyalties are strained by the initiation of the person. Some people, for example, have been sorely tested by severe good luck, such as the woman who was left a great legacy which she swore she would devote to spiritual work but in fact kept exclusively to herself and her own development. She lost a remarkable opportunity to contribute what she had not even earned to a group project and missed the chance of a lifetime. Or take the case of the man who was given his father's school to run and turned it into a little empire with himself as Pharaoh. Both these people have yet to grasp why they were never allowed beyond the limit of the outer court of the Temple.

The first sign of the end of the initiation reveals itself in external events such as the offer of a new job or a reconciliation within a relationship. It might manifest, for some, in a symbolic occurrence like a journey to a great sage's tomb or the return of an old friend who observes the transformation which has occurred that only those who have been away a long time would be able to see. Shortly after the turning point, other things begin to happen one after the other or simultaneously. Elements of one's life that seemed to have no connection begin to relate. People who know each other in different spheres of activity become acquainted. New connections are made and there begins to flow a certain power in everything about one. Again, nothing is without significance and one starts to recognise that the hand of Heaven is gently accelerating the situation. Indeed, one gradually perceives how everything in one's life is being adjusted and monitored so that all merges together to constitute a completely new formula for one's existence.

'X', our prospective tutor, would have been left almost entirely on his own by his teacher during such an initiation because he has to pass through it by himself. When he has come through, many things begin to happen. At first there will be a new-found strength and intensity of purpose. This will start to be called upon by the people coming to him for help and advice. To begin with it will seem like a series of coincidences but, as the days go by and the stream of callers increases, so it will dawn upon him that they are being sent to him by Heaven and that he is now in a focal position. Such a realisation is sometimes awesome and it has been known for people to bolt at this point because the responsibility for taking on a group is too much. The prospect of decades of people asking questions about the direction of their lives, what should they do about this or that spiritual problem, as well as the enormous effort involved in building up and running a group, places the highest demand upon the initiate's commitment. If the initiate backs away, then not only will that opportunity perhaps never return but the chance to impart what has been given will be lost to those coming to him for many years, in some cases for that lifetime.

Such a situation is not discarded lightly. When a large number of people turn up asking the same kind of question, then the initiate has to recognise that there is a deep need in the local sector of the Work and that he or she is there to meet it. They have, as said in some schools of inner development, 'got their posting'. Providence, in this case, has placed him exactly where his skill and capabilities are most useful. This is borne out by the fact that those who might work with 'X' get to hear about him in all sorts of strange ways. Very often a whole group of loosely related people will turn up over a few months as one person speaks to another about 'X'. Very soon, rather like the incandescent gas of a planet in formation, an amorphous group begins to circle 'X'. By this time he should recognise the signs and commence to make plans for a meeting. This will precipitate another shift in level as the process of his transformation touches down to the lowest sefirah of the Tree of his personal evolution. He must now make the upward turn, taking with him those who will help in the construction of the vehicle for a new group. The first stage of the return is largely determined by the circumstances of time and place which provide the ground base of Malkhut.

19. Circumstance

There is a notion that in every spiritual Tradition there is a classical form of presentation and manifestation. However, if one looks at the history of esoteric schools it will be seen that this is far from true and that circumstances determine the form of the Teaching and how it is taught. At one time, for example, the equivalent of Kabbalah was practised in the desert amid the culture of a nomadic people, so that language was the principal form of transmission. Later, during a period of stable high culture, a great Temple was built embodying all the principles of the Torah in its architecture and rituals. Later still, when the Second Temple was destroyed, the Teaching was passed on in the back rooms of the universities of Babylonia and later, again, reformulated in the study centres of France and Spain. Times change and each new generation has to adapt to the conditions of geography, political and economic circumstances and cultural level. The Hassidim of eighteenth century Russia were not a sophisticated sector of Kabbalah. They did not have the learned or philosophical background of the northern rabbinical academies or the southern Spanish schools and so they translated the Teaching into direct action, which gave rise to the essentially ritualistic movement of Hassidism that survives to this day.

Now, while one may walk through certain districts of London, New York and Jerusalem and perceive that Kabbalah is still being studied in the old ways, these methods are not for everyone who wishes to follow the Path of Kabbalah. There are many lines to this ancient Tradition that range from the most ultra-orthodox through a liberal approach to a very gentile application of the principles, such as is found in occultism and Christian Kabbalah. Although some orthodox people might see anything without its Jewish dimension as being not Kabbalah, they should remember that the Torah is universal and separate the religious outer garment from the Teaching. If they cannot, then they are trapped in the World of Formation which merely provides the cultural form for the spiritual content. Let us take an example from another tradition. Anyone who witnesses the Dervish turning at the

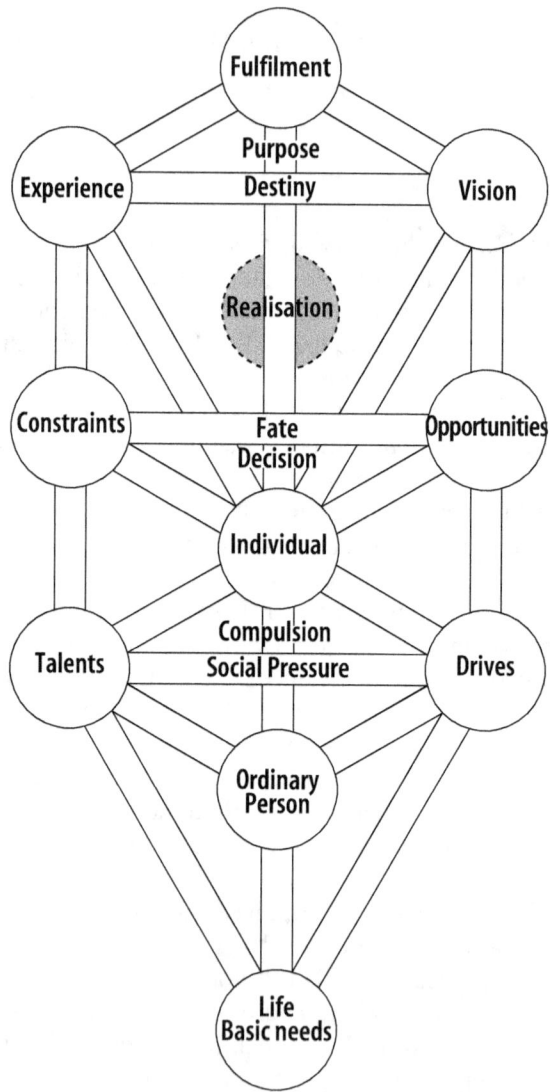

Figure 15 — OPTIONS
When an individual is incarnated, they bring in with them what they learned in the last and other lives. This manifests as talents and drives. However, one must first learn the vegetable level skills of survival in the everyday World and develop the animal will to succeed. Then comes the choice to be a real individual and live out one's fate. Most people do not. This is the option of free will which operates at the level of the soul. Above this is the dimension of the Spirit and realisation of one's destiny, that is for what one was 'called forth, created, formed and made'. (Halevi.)

Sufi Centre at Konya in Turkey with perception will recognise the same Teaching as Kabbalah. The pattern may be Islamic and Turkish but the meaning is the same; so are all true expressions of the Torah in any genuine Tradition. The format is merely the result of the local conditions of time and place.

During the medieval period, philosophy and art were the modes of expression and so we have the great metaphysical systems of Sufism, Kabbalah and the great cathedrals of Christendom. In certain places, at particular times, there arose specific formulae, like the Dervish turning which was designed by a Master of Rumi's stature to demonstrate, in movement, the still centre about which each Dervish revolves in his life as he progresses from birth to death. The Kabbalists of sixteenth-century Safed in the Galilee devised another format in the mode of a brotherhood with a strict set of rules and a new set of prayers. While these are still used, it does not mean that they are the last word in kabbalistic creation. This goes on in every generation, otherwise the living impulse will atrophy and die. Therefore, there is always a leading edge in Kabbalah that relates to the present and its unique conditions.

Up to 1914 there existed in eastern Europe and the Middle East a certain number of esoteric schools of every Tradition. War and economic transformation have changed the situation in these places and there is now to be found only a remnant of these schools that date back to medieval times. As far as can be ascertained, the spiritual Traditions have moved to the West which is now the most vital area of the planet from this point of view. While it may be said that westerners are naïve in these matters, they are also innovative and we observe the same creative processes by which ancient principles are adapted to contemporary conditions as were at work in ninth century Baghdad and thirteenth century Toledo. Each place generates its own mode according to the combination of circumstance and Providence.

Taking our example, let us assume that 'X' lives in a western city. We may accept this because it is a characteristic that Kabbalah usually thrives where there is a lot of activity. Safed may be a small town by modern standards but it was a very busy market and academic centre at its height. Thus, likewise 'X' finds, although he may have come originally from a remote place, that his kabbalistic path will lead him into a centre of civilisation. By this is meant that all the levels of a complete society will be present around him. These range from the personal and residential to manufacturing and trading, financial, academic and artistic; the presence of government and religion give the national and cultural flavour. All these factors go to make up great cities which draw so many people in search of something else besides wealth, ambition and entertainment. New York, Paris and London have all these levels, so have San Francisco and Amsterdam. Here are to be found many groups of schools, some false and some genuine but all involved with self-development. The isolated groups in the heart of the countryside are usually the result of a source in the city. This is because large numbers of people are required to generate a group for, as said, only one in a thousand will seek and then take up spiritual Work seriously.

Of the people who hear about 'X' and come to him, only a fraction will stay although some may remain for several years before going. They, like the others, will be attracted to 'X' for a variety of reasons. Some will be looking for a substitute parent and others for mystery. Some will be drawn by the possibility of magical power, because Kabbalah has a reputation for such things, and others will come because it is the thing to do—and there are fashions even in esoterica. A few individuals will come because they genuinely wish to find out what Kabbalah is about. Occasionally, someone will turn up who is really looking to develop themselves and, even more rare, the person who actually knows what Kabbalah is about and wishes to help. 'X' will see all these people one at a time, so as to ascertain why they want to study Kabbalah. After a while a sufficient number will have been gathered together to form into a rudimentary group.

This situation creates the problem of where and under what conditions, for some people prefer to tutor in a neutral space, like a hired classroom, while others like to operate at home or in a carefully arranged room. All these conditions will be determined by the temperament of the tutor, the type of people drawn to him and their social and economic circumstances and the mood of the time. Every group has a unique beginning that will generate distinct characteristics. Thus, a group started in the Bronx of New York City will be very different from a group founded in the university city of Oxford, not only because of the locality and the people but because, at that point in time, there will be quite a different need to be met. Those who remember the Sixties of the last century will know that there was a feeling of a 'breakout' in the air that was modified in the Seventies and changed again in the Eighties. Now, while an esoteric group is concerned with Eternal principles it will not be born and grow if it does not take into account the quality of the decade. Many groups have died at birth because they were out of step with the epoch. To continue ancient traditions is, indeed, one of the tasks of a group but if it merely imitates the past it remains an anachronism and allows no new growth.

If we step back for a moment and view the situation from another scale, we will see that the group that is beginning to form round 'X' is the result not only of a need of a number of people but part of a larger movement occurring in that city. This, in turn, is a fraction of a trend in a country, such as Holland, which is in a different spiritual state from, say, Spain which has its needs met in another way. This swell of interest in esoterica is a portion of a wave that is building up in western Europe which, in turn, has an effect on and is affected by what is going on in North America and *vice versa*. This phenomenon is observable in all the major countries of the West where people are studying and practising all sorts of spiritual disciplines that have, up till recent times, been hidden. On a global scale we see a shift of religiosity from the Orient to the Occident. Thus, while fundamentalists fight over rites in church, synagogue and mosque, the more sensitive wish to know what lies behind the ancient Teachings that are at the core of the world's great religions. Those who want to delve even deeper will seek out the esoteric aspects of a tradition and follow up various trails that eventually lead them to people like 'X' who are just about ready to start transmitting what they have been taught.

All these conditions, great and small, converge to create the particular circumstance surrounding the formation of a new group. Thus, at a certain point the dynamics of the situation will produce a time and a place for the first meeting. Needless to say, while all the prospective students will look forward to the group meeting with great anticipation, 'X' will be full of apprehension. This is a fact that is not always appreciated by students who only see 'X' as the teacher. One must always remember the rôle is filled by a human being, however wise and experienced. The phenomena of expectation and projection are the first problems a tutor has to face in a new group.

20. Projection

When people encounter knowledge of the higher Worlds there are several distinct reactions. The most common is to back away and obliterate any connection that might alter their current view of life because even uninformed and uninterested people sense the power of such knowledge. They will change the subject or become excessively trivial so as to avoid being affected by it. Very often, people will distort its meaning in order to reduce its potency and devalue its significance. They will regard it as superstitious nonsense or irrelevant to this world. Such people are best left as they are and should in no way be encouraged to enter the field, for they will only use what they perceive in their limited way as ammunition for denial. Their time will come and it is best that Providence introduces them to higher knowledge by way of life experience rather than argument.

At the other end of reaction is the recognition of the miraculous and of the coming into contact with something that has always been known deep within one's being. It is like the recognition of knowledge that has been forgotten and, indeed, Tradition says that everyone knows up to the moment of birth about the higher Worlds but soon forgets as the body slowly embeds the spirit and psyche in matter. Some people find that they remember considering such topics as angels, the Messiah and God as young children but somehow lost the thread of their pondering until the moment they came in contact with certain books or, in this case, a person who could see clearly what they perceived only dimly. The connection with an individual who could instruct them in such matters is like meeting one's master and many regard their prospective tutor as such, if they have little or no experience of esoteric work.

Those who have passed in and out of the guru phase of their search, and have come through without losing sight of the fact that the Work comes first, will see 'X' for what he is; and this may be any type of person for we have deliberately not specified 'X''s particular character. The old campaigners will, quite rightly, accept his nature and the possibility that he knows more than they and is therefore their elder. They will both draw from and support the new tutor in his work because they will know from previous encounters with various instructors that each one has his limit and all are essentially human. If a tutor is not, then he or she should be regarded with much suspicion because not a few so-called teachers may be charlatans, self-deluded mentors, conscious villains or even under possession of some archetype or entity. More on this later. For a prospective group to have one or two sympathetic sceptics is useful both to the tutor and to those who hang upon every word the tutor says. 'X' will be very grateful at times for the quiet sane comment that earths the over-heated devotee when he is not available. Such seasoned people make up the non-commissioned officers of a group and will hold the perimeter line of discipline. Some of these may be officer cadets in training themselves for group-taking at a later date.

Most people coming to the first meeting will be full of high expectation and many will, almost immediately, begin to project an image upon 'X' without his encouragement. He will be seen as the all-wise Teacher who has a direct connection with the line of masters. This fantasy is based on fragments of information gleaned from books and hearsay about the Tradition of Kabbalah. It is also rooted in the deep need for a parental guide that most people desire at this point in their development. Some people of course may, indeed, be looking for a real father substitute—there is always the psychological factor—but more often than not the spiritual element is mixed in, so that there is an amalgam of genuine appreciation for a person who knows something of higher knowledge and projected superstition that enhances a tutor's rôle far beyond his real capacity.

This phenomenon is recorded throughout the history of every spiritual Tradition. Moreover, any who have been present at a remarkable event know that such an episode becomes even more remarkable when it is reported by those who did not really understand what was happening and especially by those who were not even there, so that by the time it has reached the second or third generation, what was an interesting conversation has become, with a few added fictions and much literary embroidery, a miraculous episode. People love the miraculous but what is never realised is that the most important miracles take place unnoticed. The tutor is very vulnerable. Many gifted but essentially earthly instructors have been elevated, by their more naïve disciples, into heavenly beings during their lives and most certainly after death. When this occurs a group becomes a cult, holding the form sacred and not the content.

Figure 16—PROJECTION
One of the temptations of a charismatic teacher and his students is to believe that they are more that they really are. Here Shabbetai Zvi, a 17th century rabbi who was convinced he was the Messiah, is worshipped by his followers. This Lucific test is one every teacher must face as they gain the power to influence those who seek a parent figure or to belong to a family or tribal movement. When a school of the soul becomes corrupt in this way, it becomes exclusive and deluded that it alone has the Teaching. One of the signs is the clone syndrome in which conformity of conduct, attitudes and even dress takes precedence over individual integrity. (17th century engraving.)

An historic example of this was the projection placed upon many Hassidic rabbis by their congregations. Now, while many of the first leaders of this school were remarkable, later disciples could not tell the difference between their levels of being and so quite mediocre people were often called masters because they were related by blood to the spiritual line. This occurs in all Traditions and is a sign that the school has passed its most creative period. Many Hassidic stories illustrate the dangers of projection, as well as the wisdom of their rabbi, like the tale of the two students boasting about whose rabbi had the most kabbalistic power. One ardent follower claimed his rabbi was the greatest because he could create a dry passage through a rain storm. The other dismissed this as amateur; his rabbi could arrange for it still to be Friday afternoon where he walked while it was the Sabbath Eve everywhere else, so that he did not exceed the distance prescribed for the Sabbath. Whilst his tale is typical of Jewish humour it also sets out a warning.

The character of a tutor will often be the hook for the type of projection. Thus the intelligent will be seen as all knowing, the kind as the epitome of love and the person of action capable of the most remarkable physical feats. Now, while this may seem ridiculous on the cold page of a book, the living atmosphere of the early stages of a group generates, on the basis of high expectation, the most extraordinary situations. Outwardly ordinary people with stable backgrounds can become quite unhinged because they believe they must give up all to advance spiritually. It has been known, for instance, for people who have lived essentially conventional lives to sell their homes and give the proceeds to their guru whom they see as the all-provider. It is also not uncommon for women to fall deeply in love with a male tutor and offer him everything, even though he is blatantly a knowledgeable villain, because they see in him the phantom lover they cannot find in mortal men.

As will be appreciated, a tutor's rôle is not an easy one. Not only has he, or she for that matter, got to contend with the projections of certain students but also with the temptations that arise from being in such a position. A tutor is human and without question has all the desires and hopes of the flesh and ego. Many a first-time tutor has been swept away by the projection of immature or sick students and not a few have fallen into the arms of their greatest weaknesses which have been loosely defined as the temptations of wealth, sex and power. The ability to deal with projection is one of the acid tests of integrity, and one of the ways in which one may judge whether a tutor is reliable or not. For example, some people taking groups hold their position by virtue of the projection of students and little else, because what they originally had to give has gone and they repeat only what they once knew until people become bored, or alerted to what is really happening, and leave. Alas, there are always those who seek sensation and mystery, as well as teachers who will solve all their problems, and so such groups continue to attract numbers until the flame that was lit long ago finally flickers out, leaving the pseudo-guru burnt out and his followers bereaved, unless they are able to move on into maturity.

So it is not without reason that the first meeting is convened by 'X' with some apprehension. Energy will be present but, at that point, little or no structure beyond the rudimentary relations between students and tutor. The Teaching is available but only in potential. The various theories, diagrams, devotional exercises and rituals have to be learned and realised, studied and practised. And this takes time; many people expect to be given all these things in a very short period and some even believe they will be able to master Kabbalah in a few weeks. The tutor knows it will be a long haul, longer even than some of the more experienced students can imagine. However, at this stage more practical things have to be taken into account. Such as what are the numbers likely to be? Do they have enough space? Is it accessible to most people and which day is the best one for meeting? All such matters have to be sorted out provisionally so that the Malkhut of the group is well established. This phase is vital because once the place and time have been set, it will become an important landmark in many people's week, giving them a stable spiritual haven and rhythm in their lives. Once these things have been organised, then a suitable date can be fixed to inaugurate the formal beginning of the new group.

21. Inauguration

To arrange the right place and time in setting up a kabbalistic group is more than just organising a convenient situation and hour. Besides the practical considerations there is the long term view that takes into account things not normally thought of, because one is dealing with more than the worldly level. All elements have to be considered; from the ordinary minutiae, such as having enough cups for coffee, to the large-scale implication of the operation in relation to a global exercise, such as what is sometimes called the 'Noon Fellowship' in which groups come in spiritual contact with each other all round the world as midday passes through their country. Our group, at this stage, has no capability at this level as yet, because it is, at this point, just gestating in that the people gathering round 'X' are still individuals and have no relation to each other. They are not yet a cohesive unit. This can only happen when the group is brought into being by a ceremony of inauguration.

The moment of birth of a group has to be carefully chosen. Now, while all the people involved will draw together over a specific period, it does not mean that they will by necessity become a group. As in the birth of a child, things can go wrong and it can abort or become a stillborn. The crucial factor is the tutor who acts as the co-ordinator to the people circling about the as yet amorphous idea of a group. If the tutor does not want to take on the task, then nothing can bring this about. After a little while, the energy focused upon the tutor will lose its force and cohesion. It will then disperse and the moment will have been lost as the people drift away from the wasted opportunity. This does occur occasionally when a prospective tutor loses his or her nerve or does something incorrect that invalidates the right and privilege to instruct a group. Perhaps some last temptation is succumbed to; like a sudden inflation of the ego that believes it alone is the reason for attracting all these people and not Providence. It does happen.

Conversely, if the prospective tutor takes on the responsibility for a group, then all the procedures leading up to its inauguration have to be gone through. Firstly, a place has to be found in which to meet.

This site may be permanent or temporary. It might be in a private house or in a public building that has been hired for the purpose. It may be in someone's home or in a room especially set aside for group work. The history of Kabbalah indicates that many different kinds of venue were used, from the side chambers of the Temple in Jerusalem to the open fields outside Safed, from the inner rooms of the Talmudic academies to the study house of a Hassidic community. In the non-Judaic line of Kabbalah, academic libraries and miniature temples have been used as well as personal apartments and back rooms. There is no classical format for a place of meeting except that it can be made into a Holy Space during the time it is used.

The frequency of meetings depends upon conditions and the inclination of the group. Some people like to meet every day but this requires a particular and locally-oriented way of life, such as was to be found in the old villages and towns of Poland. Others prefer to meet once a month and this may be all that is possible in a widely spread group, such as might be found in the country or a large territory, such as Australia. The usual frequency of meeting is once a week and here the day is determined by several factors, such as how many can be assembled on a particular evening, because there are always some who would like to come but cannot make it then due to other commitments. This is sometimes quite a test of seriousness. Many people, for example, soon find that a certain night is inconvenient for some reason and, indeed, very often they are the people who wanted that night in particular. Such demanding people are usually the first to drop out. The real seeker simply adjusts life around the group and will travel almost any distance to be there because it is important, while the less committed will find any excuse not to turn up, even though they may live just around the corner. After taking a consensus of opinion, the tutor then makes a decision on which day of the week the meeting will take place. This will be the weekly pattern for three monthly terms of spring, summer and autumn. The reason for this system is to give people time for rest and reflection, take their holidays and learn to value the group when it is not physically meeting. Having settled the organisational aspect of the group, the choosing of a date for the initial meeting becomes crucial.

Up to the Renaissance nothing important was begun at random. Every enterprise—the laying of a foundation stone of a building, the setting sail of a ship or the moment of a marriage—was carefully considered. This was because it was recognised that there were propitious times in which to do or refrain from doing anything. This understanding goes back to esoteric sources which perceived that in the interplay between different Worlds there were periods of harmony and disharmony and times when it could go either way. These subtle tides, moreover, not only had their ebbs and flows but a distinct set of characteristics at certain times of the day, month, and year which were favourable to certain objectives and unfavourable to others. Thus, it was observed that the period just before the Sun reached its noon meridian was a good time to begin something that was to have a long-term practical effect in the world while it was noted that events related to when the Sun was in the sign of Libra had a distinct bearing upon the issue of partnerships. In some cultures the position of the Moon was taken into account so that nothing was done during its last unfavourable phase while something might be very favourably begun on the New Moon.

Kabbalistically, the inauguration of any enterprise brings it through from the realms of Creation and Formation into the mundane, so that its material crystallisation in the World of Action carries the charge and character present in that moment of manifestation. This principle is taken into account in the formal start of group. Generally speaking, if the tutor does not know exactly what time to select, then he will be advised by his or her elders, if not by Providence which usually gives very clear signs when the group should be begun. Very often the whole operation slowly focuses down to a particular date, because a series and combination of events tunes it in onto that particular day. Once this has been identified and set, then the ceremony of inauguration can be designed. Such a ritual can be simple or complex, according to taste or the need of the prospective group. The essential element is to be quite sure what is the objective of the inauguration ceremony. This will not only determine the nature of the ceremony but the quality of the group as long as it exists; which may be for a few months or a hundred years, for no one but the visionary can know what is intended for such a vehicle. If we look at history, there are many examples of little groups of obscure people in remote places, like the Galilee, which have grown into schools and then Lines that have transformed whole civilisations. Such events are rare but always possible if the time is propitious and Heaven intends to use the vehicle created in that way.

Having set the day, the hour and place of meeting, all who are involved should be informed that they must prepare themselves for the ceremony. This may be done according to the tutor's judgement. Some might request that everyone bathes and comes in fresh clothes. Others might be more or less demanding. The important thing to remember is that some special effort should be made, like the Israelites did in Exodus just before they came up before the Holy Mountain of Sinai to receive the Torah. Symbolically and practically, this is exactly the same situation for, when the people gather together for the first time as a group, they will receive something they cannot be given as individuals. This is because a group, being a larger vehicle, can accommodate more, at this point, that any one person. Thus, the inaugural meeting should be marked as the moment the group comes into existence as the gathering is fused into a greater whole.

Speaking practically about the ceremony, everyone should arrive at least fifteen minutes before the appointed hour and sit in complete silence and stillness. The tutor may be already seated in the chair or silently welcome people at the door. The form does not matter. What does matter is that an atmosphere that something special is about to occur is created. This is deepened when the tutor takes up the position of focus before the group, once the doors have been closed and everyone is in his place. After a solemn silence, in which people become aware of the rising of consciousness, the tutor invokes the Tree of Life by speaking out each sefirotic name, thus:

Malkhut — Kingdom

Yesod — Foundation

Hod — Reverberation   *Nezah* — Eternity

Tiferet — Beauty

Gevurah — Judgement   *Hesed* — Mercy

Daat — Knowledge

Binah — Understanding   *Hokhmah* — Wisdom

Keter — The Crown

After a pause, the tutor then goes on to call upon the Divine Names of the central column of the Tree of Emanation or *Azilut*, thus:

> ADONAI: Lord
>
> Thou art
>
> EL HAI SHADDAI: The Living Almighty
>
> Thou art
>
> HAKODESH: the Holy One
>
> Thou art
>
> **EHEYEH ASHER EHEYEH: I AM THAT I AM**

The tutor then says:

'If it be Thy Will, let thy Holy Spirit descend upon us this day that we may know Thy Presence'.

The tutor then lights two prepared candles set before a diagram of the Tree of Life and concludes the ceremony by saying:

'From Thee comes all Grace'.

The inauguration is over. After a long pause the tutor then turns to the assembly, bows and begins to speak about the objectives of the group. The Work has begun. A new kabbalistic group in the long line of the Tradition is now in being. (See Figure 11 for the structure of the invocation.)

22. Objectives

The objectives of a group depend upon the circumstance. Conditions vary from place to place and from time to time. There is no one single aim, besides being of service to the Holy One. While all objectives relate to this ultimate, the way a group may be of use depends upon its historical context, the quality of its leader and the needs and talents of its members. Moreover, conditions change and, indeed, if they do not, then it is a sign that there is little or no movement in the group. So first of all the group must take into account the prevailing situation.

Beginning with the largest frame of reference, it should be pointed out that the background to all esoteric Work is Eternity. Without consciousness of this dimension, everything done is lost in the motion of the relative and particular. The Absolute must be the prime point, the unmoving firm base upon which everything is placed. This not only gives a sense of profound security but also an intimate perception of working in conjunction with the Divine. The phrase 'To aid God to behold God' can become a motto for a group. 'To help the Divine manifest upon the Earth' is another. 'To assist the Holy One to become known' is yet another that reminds each member what is the ultimate objective of the group. The use of such mottos for general and personal aims is a very good exercise, and each person should be asked to formulate her own at this point, so as to relate it to the main objective of the group.

The second level to be considered, after the World of the Divine, is that of Creation. This is where time and space begin and the first separation from the pure light of Emanation which allows for imperfection and the arising of Evil. Thus, this level is concerned with the creative processes of coming into being and the forces that seek to impede the impulse towards order and perfection. This requires an acute awareness of the impetus at work at the spiritual level where the oscillation between resolution, equilibrium and dissolution is manifest, not only in the galactic and stellar worlds but upon the Earth in all the corresponding processes of natural and human history. While the group can not be expected to grasp the significance of this level in detail at this point, it should be indicated as a reality that has a great bearing upon their future work. They should, therefore, be as aware as they can from this point on of the implications of celestial tides and rhythms in mundane affairs, for there may come a time when they may be asked to take part in some operation that could affect the balance of a global situation. The worldwide interest in meditation in the 1960s was one such operation. It has been said that if large numbers of people had not been meditating then the negative charge enwrapping the planet at that time would not have been neutralised and there might have been a World War.

This scale of view should never be lost in the group or its objectives will be split between a remote Divine connection and a human but petty preoccupation with personal development. The cosmic dimension brings the Absolute and the individual into a correct relationship in as much as the universe is the setting for the unfolding consciousness of the Divine reflecting upon Itself through mankind. This objective should be stated and repeated from time to time, not only to remind people of that field of activity but to place periodically whatever is going on in the group in its cosmic context. Too many people involved in so-called spiritual work either float up and away from life into an escapist ecstasy or sink into a deep abyss of over-analysis of the intricacies of their psyche. The continual consciousness of the universe's scale and the condition of mankind keeps the balance of levels.

The third World of Formation is concerned with the realm of the psyche and is the next area of objective. Here each member not only examines and works upon his own soul but contributes to the growing reserves of experience that will fill the emotional and conceptual triads of the group Tree. No one works for herself alone. The group is not to be a place where one comes just to take but also to give. This allows a reciprocal balanced flow to occur, in that the more that is given, the more is received. The study of the psyche's operations is a long and delicate business but it must not become just a therapeutic situation. This is not the purpose of a kabbalistic group. The psychological work during the meetings is not concerned so much with healing, though this happens, as development; this is not an idealised model of performance but the pursuit of what is right for that moment. In this way the personal matches and moves with the celestial and so the Divine can come directly through into the mundane. Here the tutor could ask all the people present to formulate a personal aim that relates to their particular life. It must be pointed out, however, that it should not be grandiose but should relate directly to an issue that already engages their attention, such as how can they add the spiritual dimension to their lives or in what way can they remember who and where they are for most of the time. These objectives will be quite hard enough to implement.

The last level is that of the practical. Here, the tutor periodically sets out the rules appropriate for that stage of the discipline. For example, the format of the meeting is explained in terms of theory and practice at the first session. Thus to begin with a time is given by which everyone should arrive. Latecomers will not be allowed to enter during the invocation. The rules and the reason for this are that 'The meeting shall be closed in order to hold the energy that will be generated'. And 'The meeting shall start with a silent meditation which will then be broken by the tutor invoking the sefirot of the Tree and the Names of God'. This is in order to raise the level of all present and make contact with the Worlds above. The invocation can then be followed by the lighting of the two candles, which represent the pillars of Mercy and Judgement, after a petition for the descent of the Holy Spirit has been spoken. The middle column is represented by the group at Yesod, the Foundation, with the tutor at the central sefirah of Tiferet. (Grace may or may not come down from Keter, the Crown, through the non-sefirah of Daat or Knowledge.) The group will then be ready for the session's work.

The work to be done might be pure theory or just practices, or a blend of the two in some cases. It could go on for precisely one hour; in others for as long as is appropriate when it will become apparent to the tutor, if not to the group, that they can go no further in their work. Then the meeting is closed. Each session should have a theme and an exercise to be carried out in the week before the next meeting. This might be to consider the deceptive power of the Yesodic ego or to remember the group at specific times of the day, like ten in the morning, noon, and three in the afternoon. To terminate the formal part of the meeting, the group can then be brought into a state of silent attention before the tutor speaks the invocation of return. In this, the Holy Names of the central column are said in their descending order and then the sefirot from Keter the Crown to Malkhut the Kingdom. The ritual is ended by the words:

"Holy, Holy, Holy
Art Thou, Lord of Hosts,
Thy Glory fills all the Worlds."

The tutor and the group then stamp their feet so as to earth and relax for the final part of the meeting. This is begun by asking for someone to act as scribe and write up a paragraph on the essence of what happened during that session. This is to be delivered, without fail, to the tutor at the following meeting. Next a volunteer will be requested to be the group treasurer. This person will collect a modest sum, to be decided, for the next week's wine, bread, coffee, milk and cheese, that the group will consume during the social part of the evening before they go home. Three or four volunteers will also be asked to make and serve the refreshments while the same number should offer to wash and clear up afterwards. There is also an official wine-pourer whose task is to retain the spirit of the session. This is a privileged rôle. While everyone is socialising the tutor can talk to people who have private questions or wish to express personal thoughts and feelings. When the energy of the meeting has reached an equilibrium all, it is hoped, will depart in good sprit until the next meeting.

As regards outsiders, talk about the group should be discreet. Only those who are likely to benefit, or be really interested, should be told about what goes on. Indeed, at first the rule is that nothing that occurs within the meeting itself should be discussed outside the group, except in general terms, and no names should be used. This is to preserve the sanctity and the energy that will accumulate over time. There are many other rules and regulations about group work but these will emerge over time at the right moment. The tutor's task at this point is to impress upon the group that it is responsible to itself, although the chair of Tiferet may guide it along the Path. Such a statement is sometimes misunderstood by some and their opinions on running the group may be offered. Much tact and firmness on the part of the tutor is required here, as this is usually evidence of someone who considers that he knows a lot and wishes to demonstrate it. Here begins the first of the many problems that come within the early stages of a group, for never is there a light lit without its corresponding shadow.

23. Early Meetings

The early meetings of any new group are a mixture of excitement, chaos and discipline. Outwardly they are held together by the tutor and the Teaching. In Kabbalah the focus is always upon the sefirotic Tree, although groups may come to it from different directions. Some, for example, will work from classical texts, such as the *Zohar* which is an encyclopaedic series of writings containing much information between long dissertations on the Bible. It was written originally in obscure Aramaic so that only the learnèd in this language have access to the original, although there are several incomplete translations. Many study alternative commentaries or lesser known writers on the kabbalistic view of existence. These can range from studies of the Hebrew alphabet and its symbolism to the contemplation of the Tree diagram. This last method is the one that has been the most consistent mode of transmission, because the geometric pattern of the sefirot and their paths is the least cluttered with the speculation of the ages and is the Teaching in its purest form.

In the group we are imagining, the basic Tree is drawn up on a scroll of canvas about three feet long and eighteen inches wide. It has been prepared by painting it with white emulsion paint to give it a priming ground and then drawn upon with waterproof Indian ink to mark out the circles of the sefirot and the paths. The surround is painted black or deep blue with the triads coloured in with waterproof inks. The traditional colours are red for the lower face of the Tree, purple for the soul and side triads, blue for the great triangle of the upper face and white for the supernal triad. The tones of each colour may be varied to differentiate sub-triads like the thinking, feeling and action functions. Some people make the awakening triad yellow. The lettering should be added after, to spell out the names of the sefirot and the operations of each triad. The same technique applies to the long Jacob's Ladder diagram with red for the lowest World, purple for Formation, blue for Creation and white for the top World of Emanation. The scrolls can be tacked at their upper and lower edges to wooden rods about an inch thick and

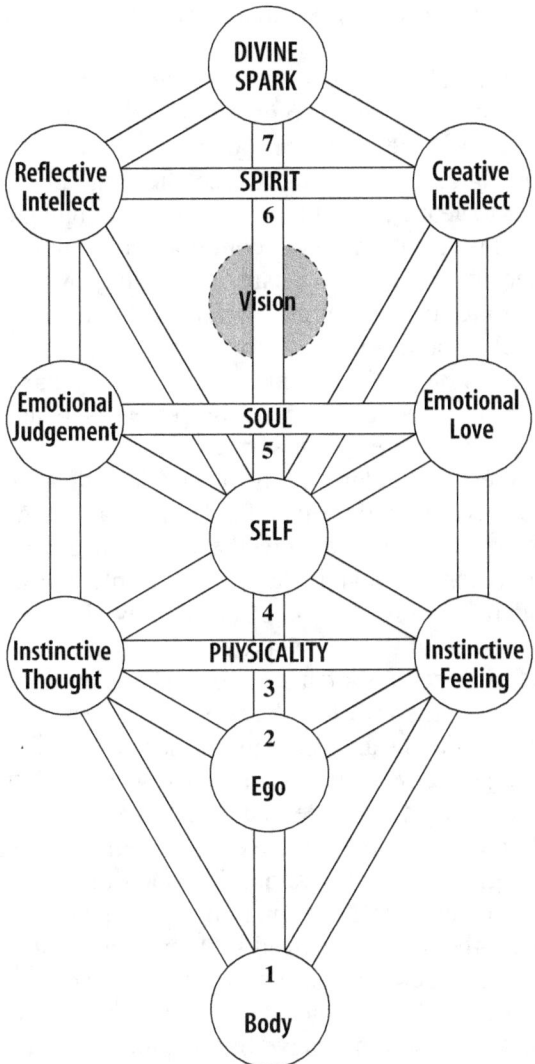

Figure 17—INTRODUCTION
One of the first things to be learned is how the Tree relates to the psyche, as it is the best way to see how the sefirot operate. Here only the general psychological functions are set out with the seven degrees of consciousness placed upon the central column. The bottom-most levels of 1 and 2 are physical awareness and the ordinary mind of the ego. Above these, at 3 is psychic sensibility and at 4 a state of sharp alertness. At the soul level of 5 is the ability to perceive a life span and beyond, at 6 cosmic vision. At the top is consciousness of the Divine. The psyche is in contact with all the other Worlds. (Halevi.)

have a tape fixed to the top so that they can be rolled up and tied when not in use.

The two scrolls should hang in a position where all the group can see them and the tutor can point out what is being discussed or practised in terms of the sefirot or the various Worlds. This is vital so that the group gradually comes to use the diagram as a frame of reference and to learn its terms as a kind of language that all will understand. This creation of a common communication is very important because it reduces misunderstanding. Most people have their own mode of expression about things, especially those concerned with esoteric matters, and many come into a kabbalistic group with terminology from other traditions they have practised or read about. This can be very confusing to the others and irritating to people who cannot understand why the rest of the group does not comprehend their particular jargon. It takes a little while, and some discipline, to leave the old terms outside and learn a completely new set of symbols. However, in time the reason becomes apparent as people begin to convey in an instant, for example, the state they were in by saying they were 'Yesodic' which, by then, has become a recognisable ego condition to everyone in the group.

The first few meetings of a new group are particularly exciting because everything is so fresh and, for people who have never directly encountered such depths and scale in ordinary life, every meeting is a mind-stretching experience that sometimes overstimulates the mental processes and feelings. Some people cannot sleep for hours after they have come home from their first meeting, others spend all their spare time on reading, then thinking about the topics discussed because for the first time they have real explanations for some of the mysteries of Existence. Yet others are so moved by what they hear and see at the meetings that they become emotionally elated and cannot come down to the mundane level. They go about their daily lives in a state of euphoric shock in which they have little contact with the earth. Older hands know better and will try to explain that there is a great deal of work to be done before these ideas and practices have any real meaning but this advice is rarely heard because no one can enter the door to the Path without that first flush of ecstasy. The social period at the end of each meeting is to release some of this excitement, for the power cannot be held as yet.

The chaos of the early meetings is not always outwardly apparent but it will manifest in side comments that are totally unrelated to what is going on because the person is either confused by what is being set out before her, wishes to demonstrate that she knows it all already or discovers that this is not the group for her now that she has come. Confusion will also arise because people are not used to the formal routine of the evening. They will forget when to be silent or get the sequence wrong. This fortunately cures itself by familiarity. Another reason for confusion is that some people expect the meetings to be in another form, and they cannot adjust the image that they had. This is common to those who know a little about Kabbalah and have a fixed idea of how it should be or have been in another group where they did it differently. Every group has its own way of operating and there is no ideal formula, except in kabbalistic folklore, and anyone who has been in the Tradition for long soon learns that even the most orthodox rabbis have quite different ways of doing things. For example, in the classical period of Second Temple Palestine the two great rabbinical schools of Hillel and Shamai were always differing in attitudes and methods. The only real criterion is if the group makes a contact with the upper Worlds. The perfect temple, meeting place, right costume and correct ritual and theory do not guarantee that anything will happen, whereas the motley group that meets in the upstairs room of a tavern may well be visited by the Holy Spirit because they are all truly present.

Discipline, at first, is applied externally by the tutor. To begin with, the rules of conduct in the group are very strict so as to communicate that, while a meeting is in progress, the personal has to take second place. The regulations of a group are designed not only to bring about a certain collective co-ordination but to instruct. Thus, the rule of waiting for someone to finish speaking is the implementation of ego or Yesodic discipline. Indeed, one kabbalistic aphorism is 'To make the speakers silent and the silent speak'. This indicates the bringing about of a certain equilibrium within the group as the dynamic learn to become passive and vice versa. Discipline also acts as a mode of working. Many people come to Kabbalah with an abundance of thoughts and feelings about the life of the Spirit. These are often unorganised and inarticulate in expression. Discipline creates a tool to hone down what is extraneous and ideas that are confused into the precise framework presented by the Tree. Thus, the elementary stage of theory and practice of Kabbalah is directly engaged the moment one enters group work.

Over the first few weeks, many changes will occur in the meetings.

Some people will go and new ones come. The former may leave because it is not what they expected or they disagree with the way the group is being run; others will leave on the basis that it will not give them what they want. For example, some individuals come because they think they are going to learn about magic. They soon find out, if it is a real kabbalistic group, that Kabbalah is concerned with the Way of the Spirit and not the acquisition of occult power. Very often at least half a group leave in these early days for a variety of reasons, both real and false. The more shrewd of the magician type, however, sometimes stay on to see what they can gain because they recognise that magic uses kabbalistic principles. Many who go at this early stage leave because they do not get fast results. They cannot stay any course and wander from group to group without learning anything but the most superficial grasp of a discipline. Very often they are the most verbose at the early meetings and leave after a brilliant flourish when their shallowness is exposed to people perhaps less informed but who penetrate more deeply in their experiential observations. Such people find it very difficult to face reality although they always protest that is what they seek.

During the first term 'X', the tutor, not only has to manage a boiling pot of personalities but cope with his own difficulties for to take a new group, especially for the first time, is an awesome task. Besides the heavy sense of responsibility that descends upon the tutor and the problems that occur before the meetings start to run smoothly, 'X' has to contend with his own inner world. The seasoned tutor is familiar with the upper and lower forces that focus upon whoever sits in the chair. He or she has the experience and the inner guidance to bring them into correct relationship. The first time tutor has not only these factors to contend with, but very personal issues, such as self-confidence, besides establishing a rapport with the group and its spiritual guide. In such a position he feels very much alone and, indeed, this must be so, so as to test and strengthen the integrity of the tutor. Thus, despite years of training, every little success or failure is snatched by the Yesodic ego until the Tiferet of the self establishes its ascendancy; and this may take a long time. Indeed, the excitement, chaos and discipline within the group is often a direct reflection of what is going on in the tutor. An experienced tutor has different problems because a group soon recognises and responds well to seasoned guidance. 'X', however, has yet to learn to command and no tutor of any calibre has avoided this ordeal. It is a trial of a primary order because it strains every fibre of the tutor's being to extend knowledge beyond its limits and tempts every weakness that Satan can exploit. Some call the next stage of the group the 'honeymoon' period but this is only for the student. For the tutor it is quite a different matter.

24. Honeymoon

After the sorting out of the first few months the group enters a relatively stable period. For the majority of its members the situation now becomes euphoric. Most people with any deep interest in spiritual matters spend much of their lives looking for others of like interest but never find them. Often they become disappointed because of this and compromise in their religion, profession and personal life. They perform the customs of their forebears without conviction because they know of no other way of the Spirit; they do their work without referring it to their inner world and make intimate relationships that only fulfil the lower parts of their capacity. Many become buried beneath the laws of mundane existence. Some hold on to their integrity but cannot act from the higher levels they know exist. Over time many begin to forget the spiritual ideal they had in earlier days. Occasionally, some become cynical and stop caring about such matters because no one around them understands. They may even give in and start to conform to worldly standards; they cease to look for and fail to recognise a contact when they meet one.

For those who continue to seek and eventually find their way into a working group where others are like themselves, it must inevitably be a most extraordinary experience. Suddenly they are no longer alone. They have found companions who are part of a living esoteric Tradition. This ignites and illuminates all the deepest thoughts and feelings about the spiritual life. They realise, in that first flush of enthusiasm, that they have come home; that they are with people of their own kind, as they perceive what lies behind the Work being done. Moreover, they have a teacher who will lead them through all the stages of development into a totally new world where many of the things they have read and wondered about are confirmed and become more real than the mundane. Now locked doors become ajar, revealing facets of other realities that they had not even suspected. Topics like the anatomy of the soul are examined in depth, various interior exercises give direct insights into how the Spirit operates and what its task is in relation to the psyche. The universe is looked at in a completely new way so that the scientific standpoint is seen to be the physical tip of a vast cosmic iceberg. Many other similar themes become areas of study and practice, so that it soon becomes apparent that there is a life-time's exploration and deep fulfilment ahead.

The effect on the newcomers to group work at this realisation is often profound. They become intoxicated with Kabbalah and greedily absorb everything discussed at the meetings, whether it be the spiritual metaphysics of the angelic levels or the physical fact that the central nervous system corresponds to the self of the body. Everything takes on great significance and they watch and listen to every conversation or remark that might reveal more of the Teaching. Sometimes, this attitude makes people lose complete sight of the tutor as a human being, as they credit him with an extraordinary beauty or power. While this 'transference', as psychologists call it, is partly projection, it also contains more reality as well because what is seen is a blend of their own elevated state and what the tutor may indeed inwardly be. The phenomenon of seeing the 'face behind the face' while in a heightened condition is not unknown. Many people under long discipline 'perceive' in this way by switching the level of perception from the physical to that of the soul. In the new student this phenomenon occurs spontaneously, because the novelty of being in a group is added to the power being generated which stimulates an ecstasy and a higher degree of consciousness. This is often greater than anything experienced before by the student.

The atmosphere of a newly formed group is highly charged not only because of the excitement of finding a gate onto the Path after being isolated for so long but also because, at this stage, the lower face of the Tree of the group is often filled by an influx from the higher Worlds. This means that the theory at Hod and the practices at Nezah are both operational in transmitting and receiving information and techniques. This causes all the sub-triads centred around the Yesodic ego level of the group to be highly active, giving rise to hyper mentation, feelings and actions, as well as creating the beginning of a group identity. The group Yesod or Foundation creates a growing sense of comradeship and not a little rivalry as people strive to excel in finding their place in the group hierarchy; because individuals as yet are still under the domination of the *Nefesh* or animal soul and perform just as they do in a natural social situation. Spirituality is not instant.

Very often such competition brings out the best and the worst in people. Those who think they know will feel that they are helping the tutor to explain something by giving their view while incidentally showing they are well along the Path. Others who know they know nothing will remain silent or will ask what they consider naïve questions which, in fact, are often more profound than the sophisticated enquiry which is often about books. A spirit of competition is usually motivated by goodwill and so many alliances and friendships begin to form between people who have certain things in common. For example, professional people like lawyers and doctors gravitate towards each other, as do artists and writers or people in business. This natural affinity is enhanced by the Work and many people suddenly find new and lifelong friends with whom they can socialise outside the meetings.

All this frequently generates the most tremendous feeling of love within the group. Much of what is felt is not just the relief at finding a circle of friends who share the same aims but a spiritual family in which one is secure and valued in a way that no blood clan or social crowd can fulfil. This love, however, is also the result of the Grace that descends upon such gatherings because with higher knowledge comes celestial care. Most people will not perceive the presence of this love, except during moments of silence in the meetings. It may happen while the group is pondering a question or during the pause after an interior exercise in which a clear sense of tranquillity pervades the room. This atmosphere comes and goes according to the receptivity of the group, although the tutor and one or two very sensitive or experienced members will know it is always there hovering over them.

One result of the added dimension is that a spiritualised projection sometimes places the tutor upon a pedestal. This occurs quite spontaneously because, for most of the people in the group, the tutor is indeed the spiritual connection as the Tiferet centre of the group's Tree. Thus, besides taking on the wondrous qualities of that position in the group's mind, the tutor has to live up to and hold this crucial position. Indeed, if he does not then nothing can flow down from the upper part of the group Tree, that is from Judgement and Mercy, Understanding and Wisdom, from Knowledge and the Crown and into the Yesod of the students. Seated in the Seat of Solomon, the tutor has to be the focus of the operation or the reality of the Tree will not manifest. Thus, the tutor holds the responsibility to act according to the principles being taught. This is not easy because, while no one may see the tutor's faults at this point, those who watch over the group from above will observe and test them in order to improve his performance.

The first trial the tutor is likely to be caught up in is the group euphoria. Many an individual who has been given the opportunity to be a tutor has fallen in love with the image that the group places upon the chair. This can cause a Yesodic-ego inflation in which the tutor adopts the modes and postures of what is thought or felt to be a master. This occurs because some degree of spiritual knowledge has been attained and, therefore, the temptation to believe that one is undergoing initiation. It has been known, for example, for some people who accept a group's projection, to dress up as a master with all the traditional garb like an actor which, indeed, is all they are. It has also been known for some individuals to adopt the rôle of knowing everything and hand out judgements to an ever-admiring circle of devotees who note everything and reproduce it in perfect imitation to show how they are walking in the master's footsteps.

When a group leader becomes so besotted by the group there is always the element of mutual seduction. This can occur with the psyche and body. Not a few have fallen for this temptation, for it is not at all difficult for a tutor with a gift for leadership or a weakness for praise to be seduced into playing the idol. Needy or adoring students will draw out everything they can by seeking advice and comment. Some even ask the tutor how to run their lives. Some tutors succumb to the rôle and lose touch with reality by forgetting their own limits. The classic temptation, for men, is the inevitable beautiful young woman in search of her spiritual prince who turns up at every esoteric group. Here the conditions for a love affair are easily created if the tutor opens it. This is because such archetypal rôles carry glamour and with it the possibility of sexual encounter that some tutors may not be able to resist. It should be recalled that even Merlin, the master magician, was beguiled by a beautiful maid and imprisoned by her. The power of enchantment is evoked very easily during this honeymoon period. It is a time when Lucifer, the bright and shimmering tempter, turns up to test the initiate at this crucial point in tutorship.

The honeymoon epoch usually lasts from a few months to a year or so. This depends upon whether the group retains the same members or has a constant turnover of people who have to go through this stage. When novelty has finally run its course and the tutor and the group come to a maturing equilibrium, then real Kabbalah can begin. This does not mean that the time has been wasted but that the gilt and dross have been discarded and that there is sufficient substance, experience and cohesion within the group for a new phase to come into operation. This does not occur suddenly but emerges slowly as the group works its way through a self-selective process out of a superstitious belief towards real knowledge.

25. Selection

The way a group begins to achieve stability is twofold. The first aspect is the gradual sifting out of people for whom the group is not appropriate and the second is the slow accumulation and synthesis of the material being studied and practised. The former process takes place spontaneously, the latter with deliberate consciousness. Here we begin to observe the alchemy of how a group starts to work. As one sage noted, 'Kabbalah either attracts or repels'. Thus, it draws together those who are in tune with it and expels those who are not.

An example of the rejection process is seen in those who come into the group in order to acquire psychic powers, for Kabbalah has the reputation of being concerned with such matters. This is so but they are assumed as part of the process of inner growth and not a specialised skill to be learned. This is magic. People who come looking for this kind of training are usually inadequate personalities seeking to compensate for their deficiency by having strange talents and they occasionally turn up at Kabbalah meetings hoping to gain some insight into how psychic powers may be acquired. Very soon they discover that they will learn nothing about the occult as they understand it, and leave to find a coven that is closer to their desire.

Another kind of person who quickly works his way out of a modern group is the scholar. He finds the meetings disappointing because they in no way conform to the traditional image of what Kabbalah is like. Most, if not all, of the members do not read Hebrew; no original texts are studied, therefore no authority is referred to. With no obvious connection to the Tradition it is an unacceptable situation although much of what is discussed and done is pure Kabbalah. Such people feel they have no option but to leave and seek a recognisable and approved teacher. They often finish up in an academic institution or in one of the orthodox *yeshivot* that teach the medieval form of Kabbalah. Yet another kind of early leaver is the wanderer who drifts from group to group. They are often very bright and do very well to begin with. Indeed, they often lead the students, drawing upon their previous experience which impresses those who do not know the

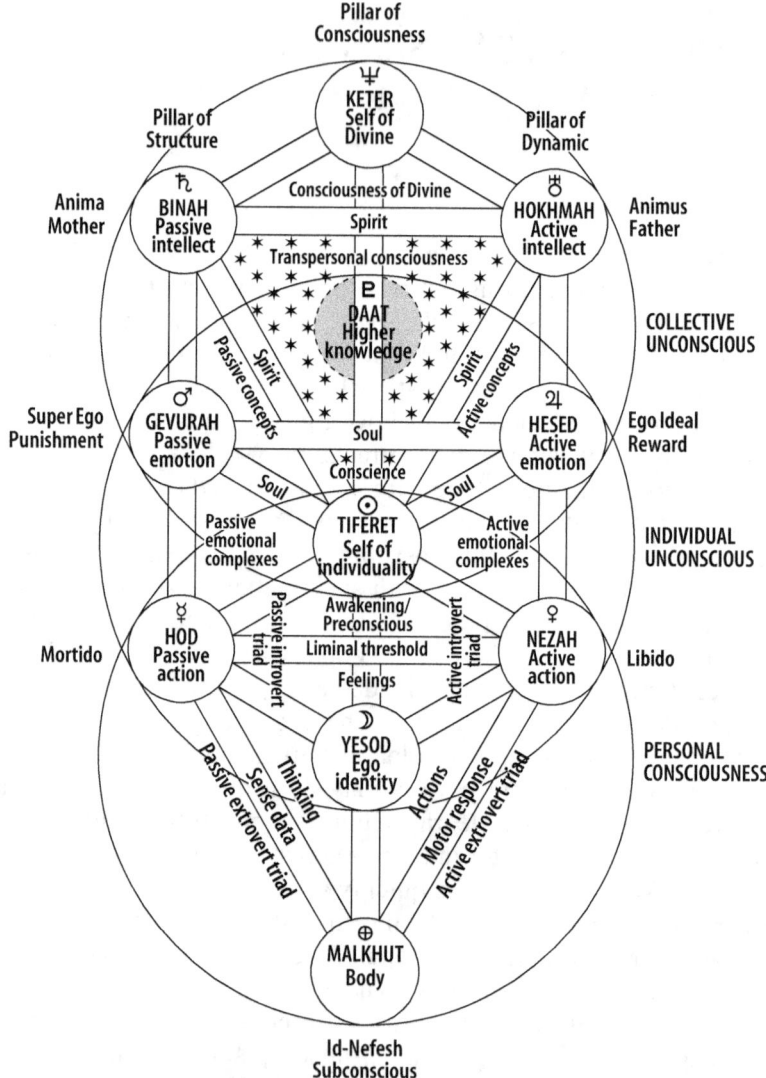

Figure 18—PSYCHE IN DETAIL

As a person develops, they need to know how their mind works. Here the triads and spheres of consciousness are filled in so that the student can pinpoint what their strengths and weaknesses are. This self-knowledge is vital if the shadow-side of one's psyche is to be identified, controlled and transformed. During group work, the interaction can stimulate latent problems that need to be resolved and gifts to be brought out. This aids not only one's self but others' as examples of what and what not to do. 'Know Thyself' was the maxim of one school of the soul. In Tree terms Tiferet is the individual Self and Keter the Self of the SELF. (Halevi.)

difference between information and knowledge. The separation begins to manifest when the person starts to run out of his material and begins to repeat what he has said. Slowly it dawns on everyone that there is little substance behind what is being given and the person picks this up as the integrity of the group heightens. The process demands absolute honesty from all, so that it soon becomes apparent if someone is embroidering an observation or distorting a statement. This phenomenon is the first sign that the group is moving out of the honeymoon stage and it is often at this point when those who should not be there start to become uncomfortable and drop out. Very often they justify their leaving by criticising the group for a variety of reasons and disapproving of the tutor. The clever ones then move on, as they have always done, just at the moment when they could break through their own inner barriers. One particular type is the eternal student who prefers always to be the brilliant prodigy, refusing to become an adult lest he lose the limelight to others who might surpass him. He leaves before this can happen. Kabbalah is not for those who have not the courage to change.

A quite different example of why people drop out is the psychologically sick. These are not always identifiable at first as, very often, they are highly sensitive people who are indeed looking for a solution to their problems. However, instead of going into analysis or coming to terms with the difficulties that generate their problems, they seek to avoid reality by reaching towards spirituality. Now while this is quite a legitimate approach, it is not valid if the person cannot face what they do not wish to know. Nothing can be done for anyone who is deliberately psychologically deaf and blind. Indeed, until they discover that they are not basically honest, everything they absorb will be distorted so that certain esoteric ideas are turned inside out to support their neurosis. The woman who chooses celibacy as a mode of spirituality is often avoiding her own sexuality or intimacy with men while the man who seeks only perfection is usually running away from his own psychological shadow. Both these and many other cases are repelled by their own and others' humanity. Spirituality without the human dimension can be as unbalanced as the demoniac who disregards others and seeks nothing but self-gratification. If there is any grain of honesty in such people then they will stay. If not, they soon take off because they cannot face the increasing isolation of their egocentricity as the rest of the group ceases to respond to the games they want everyone to play.

There are many other kinds of people who drop out of the group as the honeymoon phase passes its peak. These range from the lazy to the bored, as the novelty wears off; from the person who lacks sufficient inner experience to make use of the group, to those who have too much and need a higher level of instruction. This is rare but it does happen and, in this case, a tutor will recommend that the student goes on to another group or makes contact with his or her own teacher. Such a case might be when a person has come from another country, is seeking an esoteric connection and the group is the only lead that has presented itself. Here is where the tutor's discrimination and discretion is needed because he or she should not send an unsuitable candidate on to the elders of the Tradition. Here begins the positive side of selection.

Up to this point almost anyone who wishes can come to the group. This is because at this stage the group is at Malkhut, that is, at street level. As such it is designated, in some Traditions, as a 'preparatory school' which allows people in at every level without too much checking. This is necessary at the beginning, not only to attract members, because more than half will soon drop out, but to encourage those who are genuinely looking for a contact with an esoteric school but who as yet have no direct access. After the group has passed through its general enrolling phase, it can become more selective. This is done by closing the door of the group and confining newcomers to invitation only. Thus, while new people may still enter the group, they are either special visitors or prospective members. This screening increases the intensity of the work and raises the quality of the group.

The way people come to the meetings from this point on is through the recommendation of somebody already in the group or by direction from another group to the tutor. The chief criterion for entry is the degree of serious commitment to spiritual issues and self-development. Thus, while fewer people enter, the level of the group becomes higher. As the new phase proceeds, the meetings become more sober although they should never lose their sense of humour. The deepening which increases as the unsuitable elements diminish enhances the process of the group integration that now begins to emerge. Gradually, the individual and social relationships start to knit into a subtle fabric that forms the basis of a collective vehicle which can carry everyone and hold what descends from Heaven. This 'chalice', as it has been called, is also the 'Upper Chamber' which corresponds to the soul triad of the group Tree. At this stage it is no more than a fragile form but it has an existence. Sometimes uninvolved but perceptive visitors feel it although usually only the tutor and the more sensitive students are aware of its growing presence.

The formation of this inner vessel is more than a group identity, even though that level is there. Its quality is like a beautiful common room into which all members of the group can come at any time, either during a meeting, while alone or out in the world. This access is enhanced by the communal exercise of remembering everyone's face in the group at 10.00 am, 12.00 noon, and 3.00 pm. By this an ever-sharpening image is formed, not only in the psyche of each member but in the collective mind of the group as its structure and dynamic begin to be established in the archetypal Tree of all groups. This model pre-exists and simply needs to be consciously activated. The process is like a foetus; once conceived it gestates according to the laws of creation, formation and materiality, the lowest being the mundane level of the actual meeting.

This process of selection and synthesis in the group is absolutely vital for, while theory and practice may be diligently carried out each week, if there is no integration within the communal consciousness, then the substance gained will simply drain away, which is another reason that the group is closed to the public. This does not mean that it becomes exclusive—that would be a cutting off—but that a discriminating relationship is formed between the above and below; for as the potentiality of the group builds up, so those who oppose the Work will appear from either direction to test, destroy or even steal from what is becoming an access point between the Worlds. At this stage we enter into the realm of the supernatural in which factors other than human become interested in what is going on. However, before we examine this dimension, let us summarise what has happened so far to make the study and scheme clear.

At first an individual who has reached a certain level in Kabbalah is commissioned to take on a group. This is composed of people who are directed towards the tutor or have been guided by Providence into the preliminary meeting. Then comes the phase of excitement and confusion with the gradual loss of those who do not wish to or cannot tread that Path. Now we have an embryonic group of people seriously committed to the Work who, by dint of effort and considerable Grace, have come to a stage when there emerges a distinct communal entity. This delicate vessel, held by solid labour and the Teaching, becomes a focus not only of knowledge and love but also of power which may be used for good or bad objectives. Here is the moment when people come into direct contact with Evil for the first time.

26. Evil

According to ancient Jewish legend Lucifer, the Bearer of Light, was once the highest of all angelic beings. In kabbalistic terms he stood at the level of the seventh heaven which is just beneath the place of the Creator at the centre of the Tree of Emanation. This gave him an exceptionally favoured position until the coming of Adam. When man, the complete image of God, was brought out of the realm of the Divine and created on the sixth day, all the angelic hosts were aware that there was now a being in existence who was more perfect than they for, although they might excel Adam at that time, he would ultimately outgrow them in experience and knowledge of all the Worlds.

Most of the angels from Great Michael downwards acknowledged Adam as the Son of God; but Lucifer would not for he could not see how this as yet innocent creature could ever be his master. A contest was therefore arranged by the Divine to demonstrate that, while Lucifer had wide powers, he did not possess the complete likeness to the Holy One nor the special favour that was bestowed upon Adam. When Lucifer lost the contest he felt his pride had been humiliated. He therefore left the Heavens in disgust, taking with him all the dissident angelic beings who then became part of the demonic hordes that were to serve Lucifer in his rôle as Satan.

Satan, in Hebrew, means 'the Tester', and as such he is employed by the Holy One, as nothing in the universe is wasted, even though it may be degraded in rank by misconduct or choice. Therefore Lucifer, possessing the subtlest form of intelligence in Creation, was drafted into tempting mankind, beginning with Adam and Eve in the World of Formation, better known as Eden, the realm of the soul. The place left vacant by Lucifer's fall was eventually filled by Enoch who was the first human fully to realise all the levels within his being. Thus Enoch rose up through the Worlds, superseding the angels who initially objected to this creature who still smelled of Earth, to take up the position vacated by Lucifer. From here Enoch, who then became transfigured into the great Archangel Metatron, began his work. This was to teach mankind how to evolve and to realise that, in the mirrored relationship between the microcosm and the macrocosm, God beholds God. Lucifer is understandably opposed to any human being who might reach Enoch's level. Therefore, it became a matter of personal honour for him to test, try and trap anyone who was entering on the path to Self-realisation. This is quite a different operation from general evil which seeks to make chaos and promote hate at the collective levels of nations and petty differences between people. Lucifer is especially interested in those individuals who possess some spiritual capability because this is the area that is of greatest pique, as he still yearns for his lost glory.

As you might expect, the person who is the most vulnerable to the attention of Satan is the tutor. Now, while a tutor may have had previous encounters with Evil in the form of other people or external events, this particular assault is mounted from within. To possess knowledge is to have access to power. However, this can only be manifest in relation to something else, be it a situation or a person that can be manipulated by knowing what to do and what will happen. When such skill is applied in service of something good, like a doctor seeking to heal a bodily malfunction or a judge finding a fair solution to a conflict of interests, all is well. But in any esoteric situation where the issues are far more subtle, there is a very fine line between directing and manipulation. In the early stages of a new group the situation is simple because the rules are obvious, like turning up on time and only speaking when one has something to say. Later, as the group starts to integrate and the more psychological levels become active, there is a less clear definition to rules as each situation becomes more complex and peculiar to itself.

Take, for example, an individual coming to the tutor for marital advice. The case might seem obvious and the tutor may be tempted to issue a comment that could be taken as an express instruction by the student who would then carry it out without further question, because he believed the tutor always to be right. Clearly such a situation is suspect because no one can always be right and certainly not about another's marriage which always has factors known only to the partners. Nevertheless, there are some tutors who have run groups, and even schools of groups, who issue edicts that deeply affect many students' lives and not always to their benefit. This comes about because the leader has come to believe, with the weighted attention given to his words, that he is an esoteric oracle. When this occurs it may be taken that Lucifer has succeeded in blocking the Path for the tutor, and for many in the group.

That Lucifer is seen by some Kabbalists as an entity in his own right and as a cosmic principle by others does not matter. What does matter is that, at a certain point, anyone in the position of tutor is taken to a pinnacle of temptation and there offered dominion over their world, in this case the group. Such a moment occurs when the dependence and adoration of the group, enhanced by the increased flow of power gained by sitting in the chair, opens the Tiferet of the tutor to self-pride which inflates the Yesodic ego. Most people in the group would not be directly aware of this crisis in the tutor but it usually comes just as the meetings are really getting underway. It creeps up on the tutor and will manifest unconsciously until it comes into notice in such ways as the nonchalant gesture or holy tone of voice that suggests a hint of arrogance. In some people this phenomenon will be quite affected and even theatrical, in others it will only be discernable to the perceptive who will see the group slowly shifting its course from the Tree and focusing upon the personality of the tutor. This crisis is the first major one of many to come for the group, as well as the tutor.

In some circumstances, and here we draw on many Traditions, the tutor becomes so identified with his rôle that the people cease to see who he really is. Indeed, some lose all sense of individual identity as they gradually take on the outer trappings of the Tradition. Such situations are to be witnessed in Hindu India and Islamic Persia, among the Hassidic Jews and in the Orthodox Church. Many leaders' charisma derives from collusion between themselves and their followers. Inflation based upon an original inner connection and subsequent possession is not uncommon. In this a person is taken over by their own Lucific aspect and acts out the rôle of spiritual leader without consciousness or conscience. The result is that a lot of people are led astray by identifying the Tradition with that person and cannot go beyond the child stage until they have outgrown their teacher or leave the organisation over which the leader presides.

This issue is a very grave situation for not only do some have their inner growth arrested but many very talented people are lost for a while, to themselves and their destiny, by being tempted from the Path by what appears to be a spiritual way of life. This is where the Lucific principle is extremely skilful. It can convince a person that he is right when this is obviously incorrect to anyone outside the field-force of

Lucifer fascination. While it is often a case of the Emperor's new clothes it is not always obvious, for sometimes it is not a question of right conduct but of motivation. Fortunately, if an instruction does not come from goodness then no matter how correct it may seem at first, it will eventually become perverse in manifestation. Thus people are made to fast for the wrong reason or carry out severe exercises that cripple rather than strengthen. Illness or a breakdown is the ultimate check. Misused or rather distorted knowledge takes people out of reality and into the eccentric realm that the Lucific tutor allows through the chair of the group. This naturally cuts off the source of flow from the upper Worlds so that the quality and integrity of the group gradually drops until there is a distinct sense of fantasy or, worse, deadness at meetings. At this point a group begins to disintegrate, if not corrected, as the most perceptive members leave those who cannot see to worship at the shrine of the possessed teacher. Such groups can linger on for many years. Some people are infatuated by the strange charisma and fall under its spell until what substance there was has been burnt up and only a wick is left. Sometimes something dramatic removes the tutor, like an accident. In other cases, the group gradually runs down, the tutor takes to drink or plays some self-destructive game which perplexes many of the group. Fortunately, such situations are not common and many skidding tutors, after several warnings from their elders or from Providence in the form of significant incidents, turn back in time and continue the Work much wiser than before.

Most of this is unnoticed by the majority of a group. The more sensitive or intelligent might detect that the tutor is having a difficult time or that they are occasionally a little too severe, clever or even casual. Such a crisis manifests in different ways according to the temperament and state of the tutor. Some students might suspect that something is amiss, because the tutor is acting out of character, but put it down to some private problem and so not realise it has directly to do with them. If the tutor has recognised the situation, then he or she usually has to work extremely hard to remove the encrusting rôle that has been built up around them. Some might maintain a very humble attitude until Lucifer withdraws, knowing he has lost this round. An encounter with Evil is not quite like most people imagine because it involves a conflict within the soul between what is called, in Kabbalah, the two impulses of good and evil. This situation makes mankind unique, in that we have choice. However, the gift of free will is not fully tested until we move up from the routine ego processes into the awakening triad that leads into the place of the soul. As all tutors have to be in the Seat of Solomon between these two triads at Tiferet, so they are open to a maximum of temptation and any weakness must be corrected before the group is allowed to go further under their guidance. Reliability and integrity are paramount and Satan is there to check them.

27. Theory

So far we have dealt mainly with the psychological and social aspects of the group, showing how it is brought about by a set of circumstances originating in the general needs of a time and the particular requirements of those individuals who are drawn by Providence or fate into contact with the tutor. While all the various levels and subtle activities are being sorted through, as experience begins to fill out the inherent structure latent in the group, the more obvious aspect of Kabbalah goes on. This consists of the theory, devotions and rituals that are studied and carried out each week under the direction of the tutor. The first stage of any group, after its initial organisation has been established, is to learn the rudiments of the kabbalistic scheme. This is usually done by the systematic study of the Tree of Life diagram and the doctrine of the Four Worlds.

To begin with, the tutor will give a general outline of the workings of the Tree. In this the unity of the whole structure and its dynamic are demonstrated and restated constantly as the detail is examined. It must never be forgotten that the whole of Existence emanates from one point as it unfolds into a multiplicity of facets that together express the unity of everything, extending to their maximum and then returning to that point of singularity at the Crown of Crowns from whence they came. This notion of Unity will be stressed again and again because those who see only the apparent will discern dualities, triplicities and many other seemingly opposing or disparate contradictions that can be resolved by an encompassing Unity. The importance of holding to the idea of Unity keeps the concept of God as being quite separate from the Mirror of Existence, even though it may faithfully image the Attributes of the Divine. This reality will be experienced at some point and one will know that, indeed, while the world may be God's place, God's place is not the world. This makes the universe and the Holy One utterly different in their orders of reality. The reflection in the mirror, no matter how perfect, is never the One Who gazes upon it.

Having established the difference between the Absolute, its manifestation and how all the aspects relate to and emanate from the

One, the tutor will then show how the various great laws that govern Existence operate. After the principle of unity, symbolised by Keter, the Crown, comes polarity, represented by the two outer pillars of the Tree. Here the group will be asked to observe examples of expansion and contraction, tolerance and severity and the many polar phenomena that are met with in life that express duality within a totality. The observations should be real and concise, such as the polarity seen in the relationship between energy and matter or in the interaction between people when, during conversation, one is usually speaking or active while the other listening or passive, until the rôles reverse. Indeed, if they do not then the relationship becomes one of conflict, if both are simultaneously active or if both are passive. The examples brought into the group by students should be based upon events of the week and not something from the remote past or from a book, so that fresh and uncluttered observations are given.

Next the processes of the trinity should be examined. Here the interaction of the three pillars and the lesser triads are explored both metaphysically and practically. The principles should be set out by the tutor, like the notion that all triangular situations have an active, passive and a neutral element, and then illustrated with an example such as the lever with its active and passive arms on a fulcrum. After the group has discussed one idea in detail it should then go out and seek its own observations of the law. Some will see it at work in the home and others in their profession. This project should be the week's task with each person bringing in an example from their own life. Twenty or so such observations about a principle seen in operation clarifies the law of action, passivity and neutrality with more lucidity than the best metaphysical discussion, for a group sees the law at work at many levels and ways through so many different eyes. This kaleidoscope view of principles in action is one of the chief gifts of a meeting.

After the processes of unity, duality and trinity comes the principle of quaternity. Here the group is asked to perceive how the four elements of Fire, Air, Water and Earth express the notion of consciousness, intellect, heart and body; or, seen another way, to find examples of will, spirit, psyche and flesh. These levels have to be clearly differentiated because not only do they reflect the four aspects of a human being but also the composition of Existence in the four Worlds of Emanation, Creation, Formation and Action. Many examples of this four foldness can be brought into the group. One might be how a person wishes to build a boat. Having decided to do so (will) he then thinks about what kind of boat (Creation—intellect). When he has clarified his specification he then begins to design it (Formation—emotion), so that it is not only efficient but a work of art. After modifying and completing his drawings he then builds it (Materials—action). Here we have the process descending from a single impulse of will, through the realm of ideas to a design which is then constructed. Having set out the main laws of Existence, a detailed study of the Tree and the four Worlds of Jacob's Ladder can begin.

First it will be seen how each World is a complete Tree, echoing at a lower level the original Divine Tree of Emanation. Besides the purely metaphysical angle, the ten sefirot, plus one non-sefirah, are also studied in their human manifestation so as to catch some notion of how they might operate at other levels. Here Kabbalah follows the ancient esoteric maxim of 'As above, so below'. Thus, each week the sefirot are examined in terms of ordinary life. Starting at the bottom, people may be asked to bring in observations about Malkhut, the Kingdom, which traditionally is associated with the four elements. Students might see, for example, how all earthly processes are an interplay between solids, liquids, gases and radiation or how the body is an elemental machine, like an old-fashioned steam locomotive. So too is the internal combustion engine with its petrol (liquid), vapour (air) and spark plug (fire), set in a solid cylinder (earth) that moves its piston when the firing process begins the cycle. Yesod, the ego, might then be examined in the following session. Students could be told to observe their own ego image as well as others and pictures of themselves. People might bring some revealing examples of false faces, well controlled personalities, charming façades or cunning masks. From this exercise the ego will be seen to be a complex set of interacting functions that resolve into an image within the lower psyche. Ego may be considered as a villain by some and a good servant by others. Both these views can be equally true. It depends on motivation and objectivity. Here we have the beginning of discrimination between levels of consciousness.

After the two lowest sefirot have been examined, the group could then go on to identify the functions of Hod and Nezah, the two sefirot of thinking and action. Here it will be discovered that Hod or Reverberation is reflective and responsive in its duties, such as listening and collecting data, while Nezah or Eternity, on the active pillar, is found to be an impulsive and spontaneous initiator, as well as the

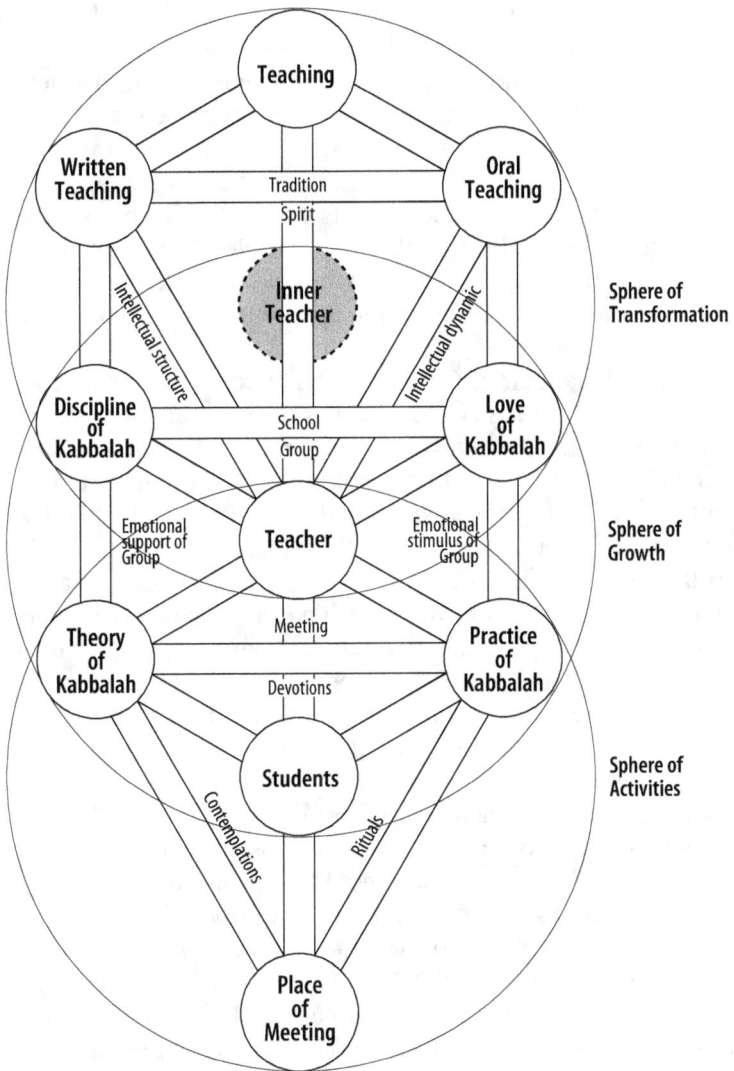

Figure 19—WORK

Here the various functions of the group Tree can be seen in operation. While each student must perform their individual exercises, the meetings are equally important as the collective mind is more open than most individuals can manage. Because of this a school, or even a group, can operate and be effective in the outside world. It is said that first one must work for oneself, then the school and then for the Work for its own sake. Out of such esoteric efforts civilisations have been born. Islam, Buddhism and Christendom all began with a small circle that became a school. Their founder holds the place of the Inner Teacher. (Halevi.)

principle that stimulates the cyclic heartbeat and lung rhythm. These two sefirot will also emerge as the gateposts of the threshold that hovers between the body and the psyche. Two weeks should be devoted to just these two sefirot so that students can recognise such things as the difference between the love of rhythm in Nezah and the fascination with tone of Hod. One person might observe, for example, that Hod is related to picking up subtle hints from the air, that something is imminent, while another might note that Nezah has gut reactions to events when they happen; or that while Nezah is the basic instinctive desire in courtship, Hod writes the love letters and makes the delicate and subtle response.

The emotional pair of Gevurah and Hesed are worth several weeks of study. These are easily identified as the stern and loving aspects of the psyche. Later the reasoning and prophetic sefirot of Binah and Hokhmah can be related to the polarities of the intellect. The group should work its way through these thoroughly so that it can see how they and all the other sefirot and their paths focus down and up and into the central sefirah of Tiferet or Self. By the end of a term, the group should begin to have some idea of how the Tree works as a whole. It will be noted, both in theory and observation, that everything that happens on the Tree, be it in one of the sefirot, on a path or in a triad, has some connection with this place of the Self. The Seat of Solomon is that which observes from somewhere deep within. It is that which watches and knows all that goes on, even if it is unknown to the ego. Here is where the group begins to define the difference between the conscious and the unconscious, as marked off by the path between Hod and Nezah. They should also start to observe, especially during the meetings, that this Self-consciousness is enhanced as they become aware of being present with others in the same state of development. This reveals the difference between the mechanical triads of thought, feeling and action that surround the ego and the triad of Awakening, just above the threshold line and between the ego and the Self. All this is aided by group effort.

When such phenomena begin to occur then there is usually a shift in the level of the meetings. People become more alert, watch and listen in quite a different way. It is no longer a gathering of interested people receiving and sharing information but a body of souls which is beginning to become receptive to something more than what is being said. Indeed, it will be noted by some that many things are revealed during the occasional silences that occur while looking at the Tree which is always referred to for explanation. Some of the more sensitive people present may even detect the presence of the Spirit of the group that begins to manifest openly at such moments. This is because the gradual raising of the level of the group's consciousness increases each time everyone at the meeting crosses the threshold of the group Tree to enter into contact with the Awakening triad, headed by the tutor. This level, however, is a vulnerable area for it is here, in what is called ecstasy, that Lucific intrusion can occur. The balance between vision and illusion at this stage is very delicate. Thus, the group must plod steadily on through the stolid routine of learning and practising the kabbalistic principles. Such groundwork weeds out those who seek only excitement, or are just curious, and keeps the group well-earthed as it begins to become familiar with experiencing the lower levels of the upper Worlds. Running simultaneously with the theory being studied are some of the practices now given.

28. Devotion

In the early stages of the group any devotions that might be practised should be simple. This is because until the group begins to coalesce into an operational unit nothing can be held or focused that is of any use at the collective level. Therefore the process of building up to the formation of a sustainable communal vessel to contain the 'Dew of Heaven', as it is traditionally called, requires a series of definite stages, beginning with the simplest mode of devotion for the individual.

No doubt several of the people who come to the group already have devotional practices. These have to be set aside for the moment unless there are exceptional reasons, perhaps being part of that person's religious day such as the saying of the *Shema* for a Jew or the Lord's Prayer for a devout Christian. This is because it is wise that everyone in the group starts at the same place so as to get a sense of unity of purpose, as well as learn a particular technique because, contrary to popular belief, one has to learn to pray. Most people learn by imitation of the outer form and so we have the empty words of the service in the synagogue and church that drives the seeker after God to look elsewhere to find a real way of communicating with the Holy One. This is why so many deeply religious westerners are found in Sufi and Buddhist groups and not within their own Jewish and Christian communities.

Whatever other methods an individual may practise should either be discontinued or kept for strictly private practice. While in the group the students should scrupulously follow the practice specified by the tutor, so that they can develop without distraction. The first thing to be learned about the art of devotion is exactly what it says, that one is devoted. This means that a connection through the feeling triad of Nezah, Hod and Yesod is to be developed, alongside the thinking triad of Hod, Yesod and Malkhut. These triads are worked upon to increase their capacity to analyse and become more sensitive to the moods of ordinary ego consciousness. Normally, the feeling triad influences the ego with ups and downs but, under discipline and guided direction, it can become the agent by which the ego contacts the inner Worlds in quite a different way from responding unconsciously to what is going on beyond the threshold of the psyche; for under direction awareness can be reversed so that the will commands the ego, instead of being dominated by rhythmic or remote states of mind such as Monday morning blues or a sense of deep depression about something going on in the unconscious.

Training the feeling triad takes time, because it is the most unstable of the three triads set round the ego. First it must taught to stand still, like an unbroken horse before a bridle can be put on. This is achieved by working from the other triads which support and contain this volatile function. The active triad is given the task either of remaining in the same physical position, like some traditions use certain bodily positions, or by patterned movement such as the Dervish turners who spin upon the axis of the big toe. Both solutions take up any excess energy and focus it upon a still centre to be occupied by consciousness in the feeling triad. Likewise, the thinking triad is given something to contemplate. It may be the words of a prayer or a mantra in Hebrew, English, or whatever language is appropriate. It might be, in this case, simply to repeat the phrase 'Be still'. The combination will create the right structure and dynamic for a devotional experience.

Initially, such a practice should be carried out in the group under the direction of the tutor. The first session might be for a whole evening, so as to make it clear to everyone just what and how it is done. People can ask questions, both on practical matters like speed or whether the phrase should be said aloud, or on theoretical matters such as a more detailed account of how the triads work during a meditation. The exercise should then be practised at home during the day, so that people can find out what they can and cannot do. Some might, for example, discover that they cannot concentrate or hold the suggested physical position. These problems can be solved privately, but preferably at the weekly meetings so that everybody can see and share the successes and failures of the exercise. This is most important because in this way not only do people realise they are not alone, either in their difficulties or in surging ahead, but it also builds up the communal reservoir of group memory that is so vital to it as a living organism.

When the first devotional practice has been established, it may be used to balance the theoretical and ritualistic side of the meetings either on a regular basis, in which every third evening might be given over to devotion, or irregularly when the going is too heavy on the intellect or body. To introduce ten minutes of meditation during an intense period of intellectual or physical work can bring in a fresh dimension and alleviate whatever negativity is gathering in the atmosphere. Some groups have a special devotional meeting once a month while others might spend a part of each meeting in meditation. It depends upon the need of the moment and the inclination of the members. Some groups, for example, more interested in contemplation will have only a short devotional period before getting into discussion. It is, however, recommended in such cases not to minimise devotional practice lest the balance be upset and the group turn into just another debating society that does some practical work. Feeling must also be present.

As the group matures, so the devotional practice can be elaborated. By this is meant that the depth of the meditation techniques is increased—but not just in their outward form which so often happens. People might, for example, shift their attention during the practice from the feeling triad into that of the awakening triangle, just above the liminal line that stretches between Hod and Nezah. This will make them aware, as they meditate, of their psychological processes as well as being physically conscious. Clearly this is not so easy as the simple exercise of just holding a mantra in focus. But with determined and diligent execution it will precipitate quite a different type of prayer. For example, the person will become aware not only of himself but of the states of other people in the room. This may not be advantageous to begin with because it will cause distraction but, in time, the presence of the others will enhance the personal and communal meditation and give greater power to any group prayer. This is why churches, mosques and synagogues exist. Unfortunately, most congregations have all but forgotten the real reason for their gathering together. Such meetings have, more often than not, become social or tribal occasions. While remarkable individuals can reach a great depth or height on their own, the vast majority of us have to work with others in order to gain any elevation in our prayer. Thus, the collective effort enables even the least spiritually developed to be lifted up by the power generated by a congregation. This was their original purpose.

Later on, a group can develop specific devotional practices. These may be designed to serve a single occasion or build up, over several months, to a climax perhaps based upon a religious festival. Such celebrations were specifically designed and timed to correspond with certain moments of the year when some particular balances of cosmic and spiritual energy were present. All these devotions, of course, would be related to kabbalistic principles so that there would be an ordered resonance with the laws of the universe. Thus, for example, a dawn meditation might start with consciousness of Malkhut, the physical World, beginning with the four elements. This might be done by experiencing each state of matter as it stood, flowed, blew or radiated through the body. The next stage might be on awareness of the ego and its surrounding triads and their work, passing on to the awakening state in which the lower psyche and the body were held lightly in view before going on to the place of the Self where one saw one's whole life and the moment now, in which one sat or stood observing the Sun touch the horizon with a number of companions on the Path. This would lead to a change in dimension and, while one might still be resonating a specific prayer of petition or praise, the consciousness could then shift from the physical and psychological Worlds into that of the Spirit. Here altitude would be maintained by holding on to the core of the prayer, phrase or word which would then begin to take one up into the higher regions of the World of Creation where one might be allowed through to experience the Light of Divinity; or be held until those who had gone on returned and began to descend in an ordered sequence to the Earth.

The gradual deepening of each meditation session should move in unison with the work of contemplation, so that people perceive the theory of Kabbalah come alive during their devotions. In time they will come to see how many prayers are carefully constructed upon spiritual principles, as are many festivals. The early temples, for example, are revealed as great prayers in stone with every level set out in the form of circles, chambers or altars. Even the fragments of prayer that have come down to us will be recognised as vehicles for devotion based upon the same principles, although the mode may be through this god or that myth. Esoteric knowledge has always been with mankind ever since Enoch, the first human being to become fully realised, brought back from the upper Worlds the body of higher knowledge that has been transmitted down to us. Prayers, perhaps long familiar since childhood, often take on quite a different meaning in the light of what is studied and practised in the group. The Lord's Prayer of Joshua ben Miriam of Nazareth, for instance, has the whole kabbalistic scheme within it and the Jewish prayer of the same magnitude, the *Shema*, has the most profound implication in the words when translated fully into 'Hear!' (or 'Awake!') 'O Israel', (or

'He who struggles with God'.) 'YAHVEH is our God. YAHVEH is One' (that is the unique Unity). If the words of these prayers were fully experienced as they were said, then the devotee would be illuminated with Divine Light. However, most of us are so well attached to the earth that we have to use the mode of the physical to raise our level by ritual which is the Way of Action used in conjunction with the ways of Devotion and Contemplation.

29. Ritual

The essence of ritual is that something done in the physical realm is related to the higher Worlds. This may be a simple gesture of the hand or an elaborate ceremony. It can be working consciously in everyday life, so that quite mundane actions become full of meaning, or a carefully designed ritual acted out for a specific occasion. The principle is that, because all the Worlds are based upon the same sefirotic model, so intentions executed in one World will affect all the others. This is why, in the traditional Jewish approach, so much attention was given to quite ordinary things like leaving and entering a house and the act of love. Ritual is the mode of formalising action and giving it not only meaning but creating a contact with other Worlds.

In the early stages of the group nothing too complex should be attempted. This would only confuse because to act and be conscious simultaneously takes some time. However, people should not believe the notion that to perform a ritual is enough. It is not so. Indeed, when a group does nothing else but this then it is either time to discard that particular ritual or even disband the group. Rituals have to be built up in the same way that a music piece is composed. First one must learn the language of notes, then the structure of chords and bars and so on until the composition has a series of movements that express a progression leading up to a climax and a resolution that returns the performers to a place of equilibrium after the peak of consciousness.

The chief instrument of ritual is the body. This is the tool of action and expression. It is also the perfect reflection of all of Existence and therefore can be used in many ways to evoke different levels and principles. The initial step in learning the vocabulary of the body is to see it as the Tree of Life moving about and operating within physical space. So the first exercise is to make room in the meeting place where people can manoeuvre, as individuals or in concert. To begin the process of ritual, the group should clear and clean the working area so that it is regarded as something special. Chairs can be taken out or arranged to define the space to be dedicated and used. This seemingly ordinary procedure must be viewed as a ritual in itself, so that people begin to regard whatever they do as a sacred action which, in turn, starts to affect their attitude towards quite mundane tasks.

Having created a rudimentary working area, people should dress specially for the occasion. This is not only a practical consideration so that the body can move freely and take up any position, but serves to indicate to the animal soul that it is involved with the operation. Moreover, the men of the group should dress like men and the women like women. Traditionally this is to make people move about according to their natural inclinations before they begin to develop the male and female aspects within their individual Tree. Many people are unbalanced as regards their sexual identity in that some women are excessively assertive and some men overly passive. Dressing according to sex re-orients the pillars by containing or allowing certain types of movement which are the root of physical and psychological attitudes. One must start from Malkhut and Yesod which are sexually emphasised one way or the other. During this first stage of ritual one must begin at the beginning in order not to distort the gradual development of the pillars with current ideas about masculinity and femininity. One truly has to understand what one's sex is before tampering with its balance. Therefore, skirts and trousers are not to be regarded as social or conventional but symbols of physical differentiation and their respective gifts and qualities in action.

Initially, people work as individuals even though they will be operating in a group. It is like musicians who have to learn to master their own instruments first before working fully in an orchestra. All early lessons will be concerned with and based upon the general scheme of the Tree and the body. This is done by the group standing in lines of ten and carrying out the following instructions. To begin with the body is seen as a whole organism. That is, it is a unity despite its many facets. This is done by standing quite still but moving the consciousness from the Crown of the head down the Lightning Flash of the Tree through the hemispheres of the brain (Hokhmah and Binah) to the face and throat (Daat), to the lungs and heart (Hesed and Gevurah), to the solar plexus (Tiferet) to the hips (Nezah and Hod) to the genitals (Yesod), and down to the feet (Malkhut). This is done slowly so that each level is noted and fixed in consciousness as a particular place and function. Thus, for instance Daat, the area of knowledge, is related to speaking and the cognitive senses of tasting, smelling, hearing and seeing. Here is where the Tree perceives the inner and outer Worlds, as against the solar plexus which relates all the events of the body to the psyche. After familiarising the sefirotic positions in the body, the simple exercise of leaning to either side will soon demonstrate the balance of the pillars and reveal how, in most of us, the right side is indeed the more active, as we work with the right hand while the left side holds the object steady. This exercise will also show how, beyond a certain point, we can lose our working equilibrium if it is not corrected. One must operate within the optimum range of the three pillars or become subject to the destructive influences of the demons of extremes. Next the group divides itself into two, one half standing and the other kneeling. If this is done in sequence, or with alternate people, then the upper and lower faces of the Tree will be experienced as individuals look up and down at each other. This may seem like a child's game but it is extraordinary how deep these apparently simple exercises go as the body's intelligence registers what the psyche does not notice and holds it for years, like never forgetting how to swim. The Tree body-image is then deepened and enhanced by the exercise of raising the arms so that the hands are above the head with the right palm up and the left palm down, like the Dervishes. This symbolises the receiving and imparting of what is flowing down from the Crown above the head. The descent of Grace is consciously assisted by the student who brings both hands down to cover the face, then to touch the heart, solar plexus, hips, genitals and finally grounds the flow by touching the floor. The reverse is to begin by touching the earth at the feet and then ascending, by way of the same sequence of levels, to stretch out and hold the position of the raised arms. This ritual is often used to begin and end ceremonies or even just to prepare for or terminate personal meditations.

This is the basic model for most rituals. Without the physical relationship between the Tree and the body, no action can be performed in a kabbalistic way. Other traditions use the chakras or especially designed robes and ornaments. Kabbalah uses the Tree in the body, so that there is a direct link between all the Worlds and what is being done by physical analogue. The body is the ritual garment.

After the group has become familiar with the Tree in the body, communal exercises can be started. These may be simple arrangements of people taking up sefirotic positions. Some groups actually mark out the eleven positions of the Tree on the floor of the room and practise standing on each station in meditation or contemplation to gain some insight into the nature of the sefirah it represents. Later, the paths between the sefirot could be laid out and people walk backwards and forwards between various sefirot in order physically to shift from one station to another and perceive what the quality of the joining path might mean. This exercise could be a weekly ritual so that students slowly build up a physical image of the Tree from bottom to top by simply acting it out.

A method of synthesising this stage of the training is to hold a ceremony at the end of the term, in which chairs are set out in the various sefirotic positions. The tutor then leads a progression up the Tree from Malkhut to the top, ceremonially describing the qualities of each chair that he sits upon. He might say about Tiferet, for example, 'This is the Seat of Solomon. The place of the Watcher. The wise one's position;' or 'Gevurah: this is the place of discrimination, discipline, control and judgement;' or 'Hesed: this is the place of loving kindness, tolerance and forgiveness', and so on. After the tutor has spoken the short descriptive invocation for each seat, there should be a short silence and pause before the tutor stands up and moves on to the next position. As soon as the tutor has vacated the position, the chair is filled by a student whose seat is then taken by the one that follows him or her. After the tutor has reached the top chair of Keter and spoken the evocative description, he or she should get up and stand to one side as the group moves up the Tree and passes through the Crown position of the top chair. During this group progression the tutor should sustain the beat and flow of the chair-changing movement by saying, for example, 'This is the route by which you will enter Heaven–(move)–This is the way so trod by the mystics–(move)–This is the path of the initiates–(move)'; and so forth. When the ascent is complete and all have left the Tree of chairs, the process is reversed and the tutor leads the descent of the Tree in the same manner, using all the experience, imagination and inspiration possessed to deepen the experience as the group is brought back to earth by the time they each sit on the chair of Malkhut. When everyone has got up from Malkhut then the ceremony can be terminated with the words:

'Holy, Holy, Holy,
Art Thou Lord of Hosts,
Thy Glory fills all the Worlds.'

This could be the culmination of a term's physical work, and the beginning of a cycle of rituals which are performed at periodic intervals in order to earth, strengthen and unify the group and the practical work it will do. Initially such ceremonies should not be too complex nor performed too frequently. However, over time many subtleties can be added and aspects deepened. Many people, for example, find that the same outer form takes on a new meaning each time they participate. Nor is it unknown to experience a direct and transcendent glimpse of the upper Worlds while carrying out what appears to be a simple physical operation. But then this is exactly what ritual is meant to do; symbolic action, filled with consciousness, to resonate with and attract a response from the higher levels. Running parallel to the exercise of the group's working methods is the slowly developing interaction of people at the meetings, so let us return to the very human realm of a group's dynamics and politics, for these also are areas of learning for the Kabbalist.

30. Relationships

As a group becomes more solid and deepens its study and practice, so its complexity increases. After the honeymoon period is over and the first shedding of people who do not wish to work in that particular way has happened, there occurs a consolidation within the group built upon a commonly forged language and shared experience. The language is a crucial factor, because it develops and becomes more and more precise, subtle and sophisticated as the group progresses. In its extreme this is witnessed in certain kabbalistic manuscripts, to comprehend which one has to be a scholar's scholar. While this might be quite acceptable within a learned circle, it is not so applicable to men and women operating in the world at large. Thus, whilst the *lingua franca* of the group works towards an exact mode of expression about kabbalistic matters, it must not lose its clear relationship to ordinary life. Here the balance is held correctly between the Worlds. This does not mean to say that anyone can easily understand what is being discussed in the group but that it should not become pure jargon and unintelligible.

The slow accumulation of shared experience, based upon what is brought into the group from outside and what is experienced whilst there during the meetings, will begin, over time, to fill out the various triads of the group Tree. Thus, people bringing in observations about different principles seen in life, like the thinking, feeling and action processes, are integrated into a communal memory, as are those events which are gone through at the meetings such as in the chair ritual. The filling out of the triads and deepening comprehension of the sefirot, however, not only unifies the group but starts a subtle differentiation within it that becomes more pronounced as the group grows in calibre and capability.

The first stage of differentiation is the sub-groups of people who have social, professional and temperamental affinities. Here, like is drawn to like and with it all the dynamics of human relationships. Some people will get on well for a period, as their yesodic egos relate in that personal area. Later they will discover that there is another layer in which they have little in common at a deeper level, although they may still be committed to Kabbalah. Another set of people might find that circumstance brings them close, in that they live in the same district and therefore share transport to the group. This may be a connection of convenience but little else, for it does not follow that because one is a member of the same group, intimacy must necessarily occur. Quite a number of people prefer for various reasons to be strangers outside the meeting and this they must be allowed, for one must not presume on the goodwill generated during the meetings. Friendship must still be a natural affinity and not forced. Indeed, some groups make it a rule that no one who is not already a social or professional acquaintance should cultivate a special relationship on the basis of the Kabbalah, although the connection may be silently acknowledged in people meeting by way of circumstance. The rationale for this is twofold. The first reason is because in some cases it is exceedingly dangerous, in certain countries, to acknowledge openly a connection that could be seen as heretical, subversive or revolutionary and the second is that it is a discipline designed to hold consciousness above the ordinary level of social intercourse. The Masons keep this rule although it can eventually become a corrupt form of exclusivity.

The most intimate form of relationship, the love affair, is likely to occur in a group as it develops. This is a perfectly normal phenomenon but it can cause great problems. Nothing is more rare and exciting than to find someone of the opposite sex who is both desirable and committed to inner development. This dream come true is fine, provided the people involved are mature enough in outlook. Then the relationship can run its theoretical course towards marriage and life commitment. But, as everyone knows, this situation only occasionally occurs. However, while the ups and downs of a love affair should be conducted outside the meeting, its alchemy often affects not only its protagonists but those close by—which usually means other members of the group. Generally speaking, the tutor should not be drawn into the situation but sometimes it cannot be avoided, if it affects the group by the creation of a negative atmosphere after a lover's quarrel or during the breakup of an affair. The tutor's responsibility here is to respond only if asked by the two concerned or intervene if there is a threat of disruption in the meeting. Then it may be necessary to ask one of the two to stay away for a while until the atmosphere settles down or alternate their coming to the group until they have come to terms with each other. No one should be put out of the group if he wishes to continue Kabbalah, unless he means to hurt the ex-lover by destroying the group's harmony, as sometimes happens.

Another problem likely to occur is when a married member of the group with a spouse who is not interested in Kabbalah falls in love with someone who is. The situation in which such a person finds him- or herself is not easy, and by no means uncommon, when at home nothing is shared but the chores and children. With the passion of the early marriage years gone and only a pleasant or unpleasant routine, many people begin to yearn for something else, to search for a deeper meaning to life. At a group devoted to inner development there are many friends who become closer than one's own family. They are real companions and, in among them, there may be a man or a woman who corresponds exactly to an ideal partner in body, soul and spirit. This is a most powerful attraction and one cannot presume to judge people in this position because when an individual reaches this stage of development the ordinary criteria of social convention do not have the same meaning. A person, for example, immersed in a marriage that breeds nothing but bickering or, worse, a dulling lethargy of the soul, might be shaken by meeting another individual who brings out the best in them. It is a difficult problem of morality, fate and decision which the people concerned have to work out in relation to spiritual principles. In one case it might be quite correct to terminate a decaying marriage and begin a new relationship. In another, it might be right to carry on because of some unfinished karma or task to support and even help the original partner. Here, the tutor has to be most careful not to interfere and, when asked for advice, always to reflect back the wider and deeper implications of the situation. In such considerations the criteria should be what is real, what is to be learned and what will the consequences be for each person involved.

Besides the social and intimate relationships that should begin to emerge in the post-honeymoon period, there will also appear the first stratification of the group. As noted, there are already those who either know something about Kabbalah or have been under some spiritual discipline before. Initially, these will form the inner core of the group as they usually contribute much more than others. Some of these people would have gone in the first release of those who did not wish to work that way and some of those who remain may, by this time, be surpassed by more advanced people who now know as much, if not more, having mastered theory and practices. This can, in some cases, cause competition and friction at the ego level, leading to difficulties for the individuals and the group at large. Here the tutor has to act as a cross between a diplomat and a regimental sergeant major, that is Hesed and Gevurah, in order to placate and encourage peoples' Yesods to give up an image of knowing a lot when in fact they know a little, which too often becomes apparent as the rest of the group develops. Tact and truth are vital in this delicate operation or a potentially good student can be lost by being exposed too abruptly to his own ignorance.

Out of the original core of the group, those who come into the place where a certain degree of awakening has been achieved will become the students closest to the tutor. These people may not necessarily be friends or even get on well together. What brings them close is the conscious commitment to the group. This is quite different from an unconscious collective attachment which other members might experience. This inner core is the growing point of the company which, about this period, begins to stratify into three distinct spheres. The first is the core close to the pivot of the tutor, the second composed of those who recognise the value of the Teachings but are not wholly committed and the third, those who see the group as a semi-social meeting place where one talks and does interesting things. It must be added that many highly intelligent and somewhat advanced people come into the last category because they never really commit themselves to anything, fearing that they might lose what individuality they have acquired by 'submitting', as they see it, to the tutor, the group or the Teaching. Undoubtedly 'consent' is a better term. No one is required to be a slave. According to kabbalistic Tradition the Holy One wants co-operation, not subjection. The degree of commitment differentiates the various levels within the group, although any individual may vary his or her status within it because most of the time one is never in the same state of consciousness and therefore consistent in integrity. For example, even those of the inner group can undergo lapses as they realise their potential capability, and consider themselves, with a little Lucific help, the brightest after the tutor. Here we have the first of the serious tests that all committed students must pass as they encounter the Opposition's resistance to the group's development, as it generates the phenomenon of the star student.

31. Star Students

As a group begins to develop its infrastructure there emerges a hierarchy within the three levels of uncommitted, half-committed and totally committed. This ladder of involvement will range from the merely curious, through those seeking solutions to personal problems to those to whom Kabbalah is a way of life. Of the last there is again a subdivision into those who seek the Work as service to God, those to whom the Work has become a reason for living and those who see it as a mode of the highest expression of themselves. The last of these has the potential for great good or evil.

Of the first kind, these are people who already have a deep religious conviction. Usually they have had some mystical experience and a certain amount of training. This means that they have not only encountered an esoteric teaching and its disciplines but have practised what they have been taught in life. Very often they are people of mature years who have seen much and experienced a great deal of interior change. Such a person might be a professional army officer, born into a military family who, finding that this was not his way decided to resign his commission at the only time it was possible, in a small gap between two wars. It was as if Heaven had taken care to remove him while comrades went on to fight what turned out to be an unjust and disastrous conflict. People on the Path are often preserved from the whirlpool of mass events by what appears to be providential intervention because there are so few seriously committed people in the Work of the Spirit. Another example of the deeply committed person is the woman who endured great suffering from a physical disability and immense loneliness. Out of this came a profound courage that developed her faith so that she could withstand the sense of uselessness that would crush most unemployable people. This gave her the maturity and insight to see that conscious spiritual work was the way to give and serve others in difficulty by intercession on their behalf. This was her work.

People like the above are vital to a group. They form the kernel to the core and act, in conjunction with the tutor, as the link in the soul triad that is beginning to emerge out of the triad of awakening. They form the first inner group of whom only those who are at the same level can be aware. These people come each week without fail, in bad weather or from great distance. Nothing deters them for they recognise that it is crucial for them and the group that the Work goes on, if only for the Holy One's sake. They are not always those who speak or are conspicuous in any way. Very often they say nothing and yet contribute more at the soul and spirit level than the most brilliant and voluble speakers. If one of these individuals, because of extreme circumstances like illness, cannot come to the meeting then it soon becomes apparent, to the more sensitive, that something is amiss in the group. There is a lack of light, less grace is present and people are aware of something absent until that person returns and the group regains its equilibrium.

The second section, of those to whom the Kabbalah has great meaning, are the majority of the inner core. They see the Tradition as helping to integrate themselves and everything they think, feel and do is related to its Teaching. This gives them a structure and dynamic that only a spiritual teaching can supply. It makes both the great and small events in their lives take on a deeper significance so that they can see what their place is in the scheme of the universe. These committed members are usually extremely diligent and carry out every exercise and instruction of the tutor. They go out of their way to be of use and will often do things at great cost to themselves, in order to be useful and repay the debt they feel they owe the Tradition. This is often worked out in relation to the tutor who, to them, represents the embodiment of the Teaching. Here, unfortunately, lies a danger in as much that the quality of devotion is sometimes excessive and the tutor, if he or she has not been seduced by such adulation, has to temper these devotees constantly by demonstrating that he is also human. The issue of loving admiration is encouraged in some schools as a way of teaching by imitation but, for those who live in a modern context and wish to work through individuation, it is necessary to realise that the tutor is merely a connection, not an embodiment, or all the energy generated by the meetings will be accumulated and crystallised at the Tiferet of the group which is not the point. Some tutors, recognising the danger signs of adulation, have been known to be deliberately vulgar in order to disillusion potential worshippers. The traditional way of avoiding this problem is for the tutor to practise constant modesty.

The phenomenon of the star student is related to the problem of identification and projection. Such people very often come into a group with a considerable amount of previous knowledge and experience which gives them a tremendous advantage because they know more than almost everyone else except the tutor. This not only makes them stand out as an elder but gives them a special relationship with the tutor who needs someone experienced enough to take over the chair when he or she is absent for some reason, like illness or a kabbalistic commitment of greater priority elsewhere. This Number Two rôle is usually accepted by most of the other members of the group except those who feel or think they are equal or superior to the star pupil. Such a situation can cause some friction which reveals to everyone, especially those not involved, the power of the animal soul and its desire to excel and be top dog. When the people involved realise their motivation has been exposed they either leave, because they cannot gain what they see as a commanding position, or they acquiesce to the fact that the star student is indeed the most suitable candidate to be assistant to the tutor. This stage is a very informative experience for everyone, as it demonstrates the subtle and shadow elements at work in the lower psyche that have to be identified and controlled.

There are, however, always those who do not accept the situation but are prepared to wait, perhaps for years, for the star student either to discredit themselves, because this does happen, or bide their time until the star student is given a group of their own, thus leaving the job of being close to the chair and its power vacant. Strange as this may seem in a group devoted to esoterica, such things do occur because it is under just these very conditions that Lucifer works best. Here lies the lesson, 'the highest treason is to do the right thing for the wrong reason'. This brings us to the particular temptation of the star student. Very often such people appear to exceed in effort even the best of the most committed students. They spend much time with the tutor and nothing is too much trouble in assisting the Work. They ask questions of increasing depth and learn everything they can from their mentor, observing his way of life carefully, reproducing every aspect, down to having the same books and objects as well as modes of expression and conduct. Usually the tutor is aware of the beginning of this identification and indicates, by tactful comment or action, that while to emulate one's teacher is useful, one must not be just a copy. However, sometimes the star student, in the grip of the rôle, does not see that the comments are directed towards her for the situation is not critical enough to be recognised. This indicates trouble ahead.

However, the tutor may not take action for he must give the student the benefit of time in order to correct the aberration herself. Such acts of diplomacy have to be tried so as to exercise the student's self-consciousness before any exposure is applied. Trust is a delicate business when dealing with the level of soul and spirit.

Most star students pass through the stage of faithful imitation and go on to express their knowledge and being in terms of their individual lives. However some, consciously or unconsciously, do allow themselves to be used by that subtle demon shadow in all of us that seeks to destroy those we most love and oppose all authority. This rebellion against teachers, parent figures and God can cause a very deep crisis for the tutor, the star student and the group, in as much as the Lucific element takes possession of the student at the critical point when the student's inflation is eventually checked by a confrontation with other students or the tutor. This precipitates the issue of pride, as their special status is threatened. Such an initiation requires great psychological honesty and spiritual integrity and some star students cannot manage this Tiferet test. They feel shocked, humiliated and angry for their real motivation now emerges for them and others to see. Very often they suddenly decide to leave the group rather than lose face, because they have fallen from Tiferet to the level of the Yesodic ego. If they stay on it can become a crisis of the first order for the group until it has been worked through. This is one of the ordeals that a star student may have to endure if he does not heed the hints of the tutor and circumstances early enough to offset the temptation. Occasionally, some who fail the test badly actually turn against the group and tutor and even speak maliciously of the meetings in public. This can cause much damage but it usually brings misfortune to the person, as he cuts himself off from development. To become a tutor in his own right is not uncommon for star students but it cannot happen if the prerequisites of integrity are not met.

The dramas described above usually occur amid the normal routine of the group work. Indeed, many members will not even be aware they are going on because the main attention of meetings is always devoted to developing the individual and strengthening and deepening the group's capability and techniques.

32. Sacred Space

The first of the techniques to be worked upon and refined is the method of practical action. Generally this is applied to ordinary life in as much as the main part of practical work is in fact carried out not in the group context but in the home, at work and in day-to-day circumstances. This is an important factor in Kabbalah for although the development of ritual is a vital part of the Tradition, the reality is that most of ordinary living is the area where the way of Action is practised. By this is meant that every activity from dawn to dawn is part of this method; making breakfast, walking to work, applying a professional skill; in leisure; dancing, sport or making love. Here the application of conscious action transforms a mundane incident or operation into a kabbalistic exercise so that all the Worlds are present in that activity, shifting the level of the person and situation into a different frame of reference and influence. This is the Work of the Kabbalist.

An example of this is when a person makes others aware of the larger implication of what they are doing during, perhaps, a committee meeting or bringing a higher level of attention into the using of a tool which then produces finer work. Another situation might be in a game when a deeper understanding of what is psychologically involved gives greater insight into the interior activity and what goes on between the players. Many quite physical situations can be converted in this way to take on a deeper significance and, indeed, it is the Kabbalist's job to transform their daily task in order not only to help personal development but also to aid the universe, if only in a small way, to realise its own reality. The principle here is that every conscious activity directly affects all the Worlds at that time and place so that, while the conscious actions of individuals may be very limited, the work done by groups has a greater impact.

When several people come together to do something, the power that is generated is more than the sum of all their efforts. This is because an additional factor emerges that unifies what is being carried out and focuses its dynamic and structure into a potent and new

177

Figure 20—PLACE
This space in a private home became sacred once a week when an invocation was spoken before a group meeting began. Such a conclave could be held out in the open, in a room, in a tavern or a formal chamber dedicated to just such a purpose. Such meetings were held in synagogues, mosques, churches, in Masonic lodges, royal chambers and even in the ruins of ancient temples. In Kabbalah, they usually took place discreetly in the study of the rabbi, so that women could attend. Later, when the tradition became too popular, such gatherings were only publicly permitted for married men over forty. (Photograph, Halevi.)

manifestation. Thus, when all the elements of an aircraft are assembled and it is fuelled it has the potential of flight when conscious direction is added. It is the same with group work. Individual members can carry out various personal operations but they cannot accomplish what a group does because they do not have the scope and power created by the collective variety or the development and capacities to which the group has access. This does not mean that a group is superior to an individual. Such a notion has led to the distortion of the idea that a group always takes precedence over its members who must be subservient to it. While this may be true, it only applies in certain areas of operation where a group can accomplish what is impossible for the individual, like the combined effort of a crew running a spaceship. Indeed, the parallel is useful in as much as a group is the physical manifestation of a subtle vessel that is being built up to enter higher space and collect the Dew of Heaven.

In order to develop a group vessel there are various collective exercises. Here, we begin to deepen and widen the personal techniques which are the alphabet and grammar of the co-operative ventures that are to follow. Let us take an example and show how the base plate of a kabbalistic space ark is laid and built up.

Let us assume that the group has a largish room in which it holds its meetings. Periodically, say once a week or month, the chairs are arranged around the walls or a long rope is stretched out to form a circle. This is to segregate a specific inner area from the outside world and form the basis of a Holy Space. Let the spatial seal be perfect, except for some kind of gate for people to enter and depart. This might be a symbolic door, such as a screen especially designed for such occasions. The axis of the circle should be towards the East with a Tree diagram or candlesticks on an altar as the focus. In some spatial settings the entrance is in the West, to form the pole opposite the altar. The North and South may be marked out by other symbolic devices to give the group a directional orientation, as it was done with the Tabernacle and camp of the Israelites.

At the centre of the circle some groups set a single great candlestick or cube. These act as the vertical axis to the circle as the East-West axis does the horizontal. Certain groups drape the cube with an elaborate or simple cloth and mount the candle on its top. There is no hard formula. It is a question of illustrating principles. Many groups, for instance, have devoted a whole room permanently to this purpose and, over the years, built up a space whose walls, floor and ceiling form a chamber not of this world. Traditionally, signs of the zodiac or quotations from the Bible may be set at crucial angles while the floor could be made into a great chequered grid to calibrate all positions. Some groups have put four great thrones at the quarters to signify the elements and Worlds while others have marked out the Tree along the West-East line across the room. There are many variations of how to create a sacred chamber. A few Kabbalists go to the other extreme, merely by lighting a candle on the mantlepiece. This, one must add, can only be done by individuals who are advanced in Kabbalah and can charge the level of a space by altering their state of consciousness so that other people present notice there is a distinct difference in the room. However, before the above example of practical skill can be reached, most people have actually to act out the process many times before it becomes part of their being.

Having now created a separated space (and that is the meaning of the word 'sacred') no one can enter it without having undergone a ritual of cleansing or covering of the body. This may be accomplished by actually having a bath, donning special clothes or by symbolically bathing and robing in an act of imagination. One could, for example, stand outside the circle and, one by one, enter the arena to wash in a laver marked out by tape or ring of cord. This action very often has the most profound effect on people who have been busy in the world, as they find their cares are indeed washed away before they take their place inside the circle. The robing area can, again, be elaborate or plain, according to taste and temperament. Some groups find that a simple object, like a chain around the neck or a hat or carrying an emblem, is enough to remind the wearer where, why and what he or she is.

When the whole group is assembled within the circle the invocation can be said to invite the Holy Spirit to be present. This action, carried out by the tutor or leader of the operation, brings together not only the group but whoever else is interested from the Worlds above, as the level rises during the ceremony to fuse all the levels into a unity. The power of such ritual acts should not be underestimated for to perform and speak according to kabbalistic principles will always evoke a response, both below and above, by virtue of resonance and so such ceremonies should only be carried out if the intention is to serve the Holy One. Indeed, nothing should be begun and ended without referring to the Sacred Name. This not only evinces deep respect for holiness but protects the operation from any intrusion by the opposition. The form of the invocation at the beginning and end of each operation can be built around the now repeated formula of ascent up the sefirotic Tree and the Sacred Names of: ADONAI or Lord, EL HAI SHADDAI or Living Almighty, YAHVEH-ELOHIM or the The Holy One, EHEYEH ASHER EHEYEH or I AM THAT I AM; followed by the words, 'If it be Thy Will, Let Thy Holy Spirit descend upon this company, so that we may know Thy Presence'. The termination of the session is the reverse procedure, starting with the highest of the Holy Names and sefirot and finishing with the by-now familiar phrase, 'Holy, Holy, Holy art Thou Lord of Hosts, Thy Glory fills all the Worlds'. The group should then stamp its feet to earth the energy and consciousness, as it does at the end of all meetings.

As the sacred space is set up and used over the months, so its form will condense into the World of Yezirah. Thus, each time the room is re-arranged or entered and charged, so the subtle vessel will increase in structure, power and capacity. This means that some residue of the higher Worlds is left after each session that can be detected in the room when the ritual has finished. As time goes by this presence of the higher Worlds will develop to such an extent that anyone entering the space will become conscious of their psychological and spiritual state quite spontaneously. People have found the same phenomenon in the *tekke* of the great Sufi, Rumi, in Konya and in the Ari Synagogue of the Spanish Kabbalists in Safed. While such places should be protected from sacrilegious actions that might spoil the atmosphere, they must not be an excluded area to reverent visitors. Some groups spend much time and effort bringing these spaces into balanced and pure perfection by work on the practical level in keeping it spotlessly clean or repainting any elemental decay. However, a few people become so obsessed with the physical aspect that they forget that it is only the spot where Heaven and Paradise touch the Earth. It is not the fabric of the building that is important but what happens inside. If the group has to move then the sacred space should be deconsecrated so that its energy cannot be misused by an improper takeover. This is done by opening all the doors and windows and asking for whatever has been gathered to be dispersed to its respective Worlds. This should leave it in a depotential state that the Opposition cannot pervert. With the space dissolved, it becomes just another room with an atmosphere of something very special having happened here. The ark moves on with the group to the next venue.

33. Action Tree

The body is an organic symbol of the sefirotic Tree. The point above the head is the Crown; the two hemispheres of the brain, Wisdom and Understanding; the face and throat, Knowledge; the two chambers of the heart, Judgment and Mercy; the solar plexus, Beauty; the hips, Reverberation and Eternity; the genitals, the Foundation; and the feet, the Kingdom. Much can be done to use this set of correspondences as a method of working the Tree. We have already explored the individual exercises of applying the different levels within the body in order to get to know the four elements and we have also seen how the arms, placed in certain positions, can bring a consciousness of different sefirot so that a series of movements and configurations move the body in a series of dance-like postures based on the pillars, pairs, triads and the Lightning Flash.

When a sufficient number of individuals have passed beyond the learning stage of these basic body sefirot movements and come to be familiar with the structure and dynamic in each position, then the group can begin working in concert so as to create a communal ritual for studying and acting within the Tree. Now the Way of Action operates through awareness, even as the methods of the heart and head facilitate emotional and intellectual consciousness. This means that whatever is studied or practised is not being 'thought' or 'felt' about but 'sensed' in consciousness. Many people mistake thinking and feeling for consciousness which they are not. They are functions through which consciousness perceives. Thus, to move through the motions of a ritual is to be acutely aware of what is happening in a deeply physical way in that the body has its own intelligence and is, in some areas, wiser and more intelligent than the head or heart. That is why it is sometimes a good thing to get the intellectuals and sensitives in a group to perform a ritual, in that it reveals the state of their action triad which is usually stiff or rusty. It also gives the person who likes to perform a chance to develop her talents in the direction of consciousness, providing that the ego does not grab the show.

Let us suppose that the tutor wishes to instruct the group in a nonintellectual and non-emotional way of comprehending the Tree in order to balance too many theories and an overdose of poetic sentiment. First the room is cleared and set up with its energy contained within a circle of chairs or tape. Then the floor is laid out in the form of a Tree with tapes representing the paths between the sefirot, made up of cards. The colours of the cards can be as follows. Malkhut is brown for Earth. Yesod can be silver with Hod and Nezah as yellow and green respectively. Tiferet can be gold. Gevurah and Hesed should be red and blue with Binah and Hokhmah as black and white. Daat might be a black transparent disc with Keter as an iridescent luminous circle. The colours are a mixture of traditional with some adaptation to modern materials. The paths can be made of a light colour.

Having set out the scheme, ten members of the group then enter the area and stand at the base of the Tree while the leader makes the invocation for the Holy Spirit, adding the petition that it be granted that they might learn much from performing the ritual. The tutor then proceeds to Malkhut and, after making a brief statement about the nature of each sefirah, moves on up the Lightning Flash with each next person in line stepping into the vacated positions behind as all move. This process is carried out until all the places, except Daat, are occupied. Having completed the operation, everyone faces up the Tree towards the tutor who raises the hands above the head in a mode symbolising being ready to receive. After a pause, in which the full significance of this gesture is perceived, the person at Hokhmah does the same followed, after another pause, by the individual standing at Binah. There is then an extra-long silence as the flow is held at the empty position of Daat. At the right moment, and this will be known if the person at Hesed is alert, he or she will be inwardly instructed to raise their hands. The progression of raising hands on each sefirah should continue on down the Lightning Flash until it reaches Malkhut where arms in the upward position are held for a long moment before the tutor, at Keter, lowers his arms; which is the signal for the rest of the people standing on the Tree to lower theirs in sequence. Such an operation fuses the human Tree into a unity as they await the next stage of the ritual.

At first the timing of the ritual will not be good but, over a period, it will improve as people begin to use their sensual perception to become aware of what is being acted out around them. As for interior instructions, these will come as people increase their level of consciousness of the Spirit that will come down during such rituals. The repetition of this operation is not just to become proficient performers, like soldiers trooping the colours, but to raise the level of the group to co-ordinate with the Tree of which they are part. During their time on each station people will experience the power and quality of each sefirah and this is developed further by performing a mime in character with that position. A mode that can be used are the images of the planets which correspond to the sefirot at the level of the World of Formation.

Thus, the person at Malkhut can roll themselves into a ball representing the Earth and inch their way round in a circle to represent the four seasons while the person at the Yesod alternates between being the slender Moon goddess, Diana, with her crescent bow and the many-bosomed Artemis at the full. The qualities of Hod could be demonstrated by the quick and restless motions of Mercury and that of Nezah by the sensual and rhythmic dance movements of Venus. The place of Tiferet might be represented, for example, by a posture of proud Apollo with a solar face and lyre. Gevurah is evoked by the martial positions of defence and attack and Hesed by the jovial demeanour of Jupiter. Binah has been described in the sombre countenance of Saturn in deep thought and Hokhmah by a mime that suggested prophetic vision. The place of Keter might be represented by a Buddha-like position or the outer and inner attitude taken up by a high priest.

All these ideas are merely suggestions and much work might be needed by the group to catch the quality of each rôle. These could be developed a sefirah at a time as individuals build up their versions of the parts and then later in a concerted effort with everyone in different positions at each session. One could then work up the ritual into being a symbolic journey where people moved from place to place and acted out each station and its lessons in personal terms as they ascended the Tree of Initiation. There are many ways in which this particular format could be exploited both for individual and group comprehension of the Teaching through the mode of action. All this, of course, is the basis of miracle plays and sacred dramas.

Taking this exercise yet further, people who are stationed on the Tree could, after the drama of the sefirot had been enacted, begin to exchange places by walking along the paths noting, as they moved, the differences in the field force that will collect around each position. Here the pattern of the Lightning Flash is disregarded as students begin to study the relationship between different sefirot. As they trace the paths again and again, moving around the Tree in circulation, many things that the ordinary intellect of Hod and the feelings of Nezah cannot grasp will become apparent. It will be noted, for example, that the path between Yesod and Tiferet is a special one that arouses consciousness, as against the one between Gevurah and Hod which seems to evoke pedantic constriction or that between Hesed and Hokhmah which stimulates one into a strange state of illuminated emotionality. This exercise has many possibilities in which the paths can be explored by direct sensual experience that leads to a deeper comprehension of their nature.

Another practical exercise which can be applied to this method of action is to get people to relate in triads. For example, the three people at Gevurah, Hesed and Tiferet can form the soul triad and see how their respective positions and characters give their unit a particular quality. Likewise, Yesod can be the centre of Malkhut, Hod and Nezah so that three triads and their demands on the ego consciousness at their focus can be experienced and demonstrated. The great spiritual triad of Hokhmah, Binah and Tiferet, when acted out, could be highly informative to both participants and lookers-on, in the Tree and outside the ritual circle, if they can evoke in their rôles the potencies of these sefirot. Out of this exercise might emerge a profound appreciation of how each sefirah, like the person occupying that position, has a complete Tree within itself, thus being able to be in resonance with another sefirah. This could be an evening's exercise in itself. So too could be the position of Tiferet with its three connections with the Worlds of Action, Psyche and Spirit. Much might be learned by anyone trying to hold these three levels of the Self simultaneously while attempting to deal with a difficult Yesodic ego in a psychodrama designed to show an imaginary crisis being demonstrated in the realm of action.

All the foregoing and more can be extracted from just this one ritual set-up. By it we see how kabbalistic principles can be applied and explored at the physical level as one develops a sensitivity towards the upper Worlds by acting out symbolic gestures that generate a definite response. Here we have the direct application of the ancient maxim of 'As above, so below', for by this method we gain access to the higher levels that are normally invisible. This is done by conscious action that brings the dynamic and form of those Worlds to the material level. Thus a group begins to carry out the brief of Kabbalah which is to bring about a unity between the Worlds so that God may behold God in the reflection of the sefirot through our experience. Having seen how the body may be used to develop an access into the greater universe, let us now look at a deeper application of the Way of the Heart that uses another kind of imagery for its working method.

34. Inner Temple

The development of the Way of the Heart within the group may take many forms but its essence is to awaken and refine an emotional sensitivity to the upper Worlds. By nature the heart is related to the World of Yezirah or Formation as the Way of Action has a natural affinity with the physical realm. The Yeziratic World is what it says, in that it contains in form what has once been a dynamic idea but is not yet a physical reality. Here is the realm of imagery that is ever changing in its cosmic element of water. It is also the level in which the psyche moves and has its being. Thus this approach is concerned with symbolism in its purest sense for beyond this level there is no form at all and, indeed, all perceptions of the Creative and Divine Worlds are only perceived and transmitted via the forms of Yezirah. Having understood the essence of this principle, the group now starts to explore the language of symbols and use it to begin to penetrate beyond the physical.

All things in Kabbalah must be done in a proper sequential order. Therefore the group should use a familiar device as a base for launching an excursion into the upper Worlds. Thus, in this particular exercise the chairs in the room may be arranged into the shape of a heart with the axis of the configuration along the line that is oriented to the altar or Tree design at the eastern end of the room. The upper part of the heart shape should open to the east to allow whatever will come from that direction. The point at the bottom of the heart should be occupied by the leader of the meditation. If the group is fortunate to have an even number of men and women, the men should be seated on the right of the heart with the women opposite. If the number is uneven then whichever sex is over-subscribed should lend its excess to the other with the understanding that they are honouring masculine and feminine principles.

Having set up this arrangement and performed the invocation to the Holy One, several things will become apparent. Here is a good moment for the group to reflect, through the leader, upon their reactions to the clearly sexist situation. This pausing at crucial points to make observations while learning to build up a kabbalistic operation is vital, so that people share each other's experience and make a communal memory of what they are going through. It should be done throughout the construction stage of every enterprise because it not only enriches the group but helps those who are inarticulate or feel out of the creative process at that moment. Many people, for example, do not have a talent for visualising symbols or seeing with the inner eye and they are very much aided by their more imaginative colleagues in that slowly the skill is drawn out of them by example because it is inherent in everyone.

However, to return to our exercise. The division of the sexes in Kabbalah is not just biological but a question of pillars in emphasis; and here we continue the notion that people should find out to which pillar they naturally relate. The body and psyche of each sex is the first way of identifying this tendency. Let any sexist reaction be put aside as part of the Yesodic image of social rôles because here we are concerned with Divine principles which unite both the masculine and feminine. From this configuration of the male and female sides of the heart much can be learned about the true function of sex. This will only become apparent if the group considers the situation objectively. Another observation that might be made during the first pause for reflection is that the heart-shape of the chairs evokes a certain emotionalism. This is because the arrangement stimulates an archetypal form that carries a high charge. This will be perceived in the tension created by polarising the sexes which provokes many unsuspected feelings about men and women in opposing and complementary relationships. Further, the men will sense their togetherness in their way and women in theirs and quite strong attractions and antipathies will arise quite spontaneously that should be noted both by individuals and the group.

Having recognised that the situation has a wide potential, the next stage is to set the structure and dynamic of the group heart in motion. This is done by the leader asking the men to build up a pressure in their heart and solar plexus areas while the women take up a receptive status in the same triad of Tiferet, Gevurah and Hesed. After about twenty seconds the men are then instructed to direct their energy towards the women who not only receive the power but note its effect, as do the men. In the pause after the exercise, observations are then made on what happened. The process is then repeated but this time in reverse with the women performing as the active force and the men in the receptive position. This is commented upon by the group in the following pause. By this time the group should begin to see the operation as a heart-pumping action. This idea should be executed in the next sequence when the group alternates the active and passive rôles between sides, over several minutes, with the tutor calling out 'change over' every time the psychic pressure reaches its maximum. This 'beating heart' ritual should not only bring everyone together emotionally but prepare them for the next stage of the exercise.

Here an altar is created by the communal imagination of the group under the direction of the tutor and is placed at the centre of the heart. Its form should be reinforced by people describing, during the reflective pause, how they see it. Experience shows that, except for minor details, it is often essentially the same for everyone. Thus those who cannot visualise anything can join in, in as much as they have a composite image to go on, even if it is not their own. After the altar has been established, the walls of a temple are imaged. These extend round and behind the chairs of the Heart in the slowly emerging dimension of the World of Formation. After the combined comments about the nature and design of the walls, the group should begin to experience the sense that the temple is as real as the physical room in which they are sitting. This illusion or vision, according to one's orientation in the Worlds, is enhanced by the group placing, under the tutor's direction, a domed roof with a hole in its centre over their heads to rest upon the walls. Such a ceiling not only encloses the force field building up but protects the group from any intrusion of the Opposition who are often attracted by the power generated by such operations in the Yeziratic World.

Having created and formed a Temple, the group now proceeds with the object of the exercise. They begin, again under direction, to say aloud, but softly, 'Lord, Thou Art God'. This is repeated in unison four times and from then in silence. This does not mean that the group dissolves into private meditation but continues to operate closely as a unit. This stage can last for ten minutes until there slowly emerges the beginning of a most extraordinary feeling in the atmosphere of the now fully emergent Temple. This is held until the tutor is instructed to bring the group back down into the room, not only to make observations upon what happened but to hold the tendency in some people to float off when experiencing ecstasy for the first time. After the observations have been shared with minimal comment from the tutor, the group is then taken back into the Temple where the prayer state is entered into

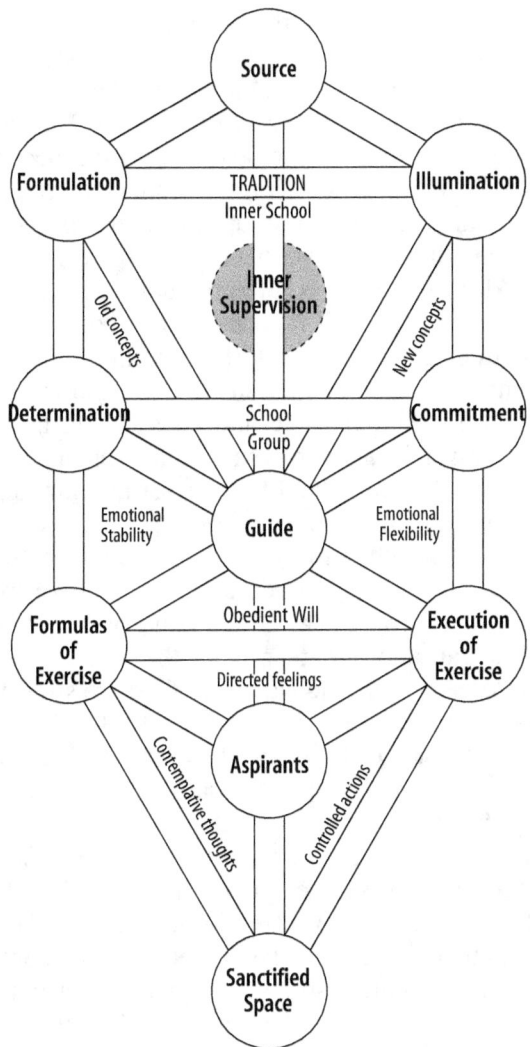

Figure 21 — DISCIPLINE
As in any school there is a curriculum. It may be very strict or quite informal. However, all require those under discipline to carry out its precepts or a school can become just a talking shop or mindless gym. Moreover, everything must be done with attention and have a recognisable aim. The discussion of ideas has to be thoughtful, rituals mindful and devotions practised with a willingness that generates a personal will power that can be consciously applied. This gives the school a practical, emotional and intellectual balance and capacity to discard what is no longer useful and develop what is. All this gives rise to the higher functions of the organisation and its further development. (Halevi.)

again until the atmosphere is at the level it was. When this has been reached, the tutor will call for total silence. This is also held for about ten minutes before the group is brought slowly back to earth again. In the following pause, observations are made once more. These will probably be quite different in character, as people become aware of their body and lower psyche trying to distract their concentration. Many quite trivial things will rise up into consciousness and small aches will become large in the ego's attempt to resist the procession of ascension. All this should be noted by individuals and worked on.

When the group has said all it needs to say about the experience at this point, the tutor should then ask them to think of a problem they have and formulate a question about it. Having done so, the group should then return to the Temple and enter, using the sequence of outer and inner prayer for about fifteen minutes, into a period of interior silence. This state should be held for at least ten minutes in order to tune the body, psyche and spirit. At some point the tutor will know that all the questions to be inwardly addressed to the Holy Presence will have emerged out of the deep stillness attained by the group. Some people will receive answers and some will not, according to their need. After an appropriate period, the tutor should speak the invocation of descent. Here the Names of God are spoken and thanks given for what has been received. Then the sefirotic Tree is descended, after which the phrase, 'Holy, Holy, Holy art Thou O Lord of Hosts. Thy Glory fills all the Worlds' is said. The operation is again terminated by the stamping of feet, after which the group should sit for a little while in silence before making their final reflections on the experience. When these have been made, the group should then silently leave, in pairs, via the space vacated by the tutor at the point of the heart. After the chairs have been dismantled, wine and bread and good conversation with a hot drink should complete the earthing process. If the exercise has been effective the Temple will still be there in the same space but in the World of Yezirah.

Over time this inner Temple will become more and more real as its structure and dynamic are strengthened by the accumulated work of the group. Some groups like to make a physical symbol for the Temple, like a door, so that they can have access to it even during routine meetings. Others prefer not to as they are able to go there easily although they may be miles away from the group's meeting place. The maintenance of the Temple, like the efficacy of prayer, is based upon devotion which is the essence of the Way of the Heart. The purity of such an interior building is held by love, truth and discipline, by all the qualities of the soul; only here it is a shared sacred space within the group's consciousness. Those with eyes to see will know of many such temples around the world although they are not always set in great religious complexes. Many such 'upper chambers', as they are called, are to be found in the most unlikely places, such as back rooms in city centres or stone circles in the middle of the countryside. During the destruction of the synagogues in the Old City of Jerusalem, vandals did not desecrate the kabbalistic meditation room of Bet El school because they did not recognise the house as a holy place. Its reality was in Yezirah.

35. Seminar

The development of the contemplative aspect of the group's work arises out of the theoretical sessions at the meetings. These, over the months, change from the simple relaying of information by the tutor to a seminar in which the group, having been given a theme to consider during the week, come back and relate their observations.

This develops into a tutor-led discussion within a kabbalistic context. After several terms, perhaps a year, a new and highly disciplined form of contemplation should emerge in which the group grows, both in shared experience and reflection. People will, for example, not seek to interrupt each other but wait for a suitable moment when they catch the tutor's eye. Nor will they compete to make the most brilliant comment or interesting observation because, by this stage, it becomes clear, in the presence of the Spirit which comes after the invocation and the lighting of candles, that cleverness or fantasy is only too apparent. The lucid atmosphere of honesty exposes the ego.

By the time the group reaches this level of integrity in discussion, most of the people should have moved in the quality of their inner and outer lives. Many things would have happened to their values and frame of reference and, for some, the group might be the only place where they can speak of the things they most care about. So, besides the gradual improvement of communication, there will be a deep emotional commitment to the exploration of esoteric ideas. Let us take a recurring topic as an example and see how it would be dealt with by a group at this stage.

Suppose, one week, that the concept being studied is the notion of free will. This was probably introduced as the result of a question arising out of the previous week's discussions. It might have come up during a session on the function of the soul or while someone was describing a turning point in her fate. It could have arisen as a totally new direction in contrast to a theme on, say, the nature of angels which had been worked to the limit of the group's knowledge and experience and the tutor may have decided to earth the company at that point, because some members had begun to fly too high. The idea of free will may have been introduced at the end of the previous meeting with some direction as to how to consider it. For instance, the tutor might ask people to note how much free will they believe they have and test it in life; and to reflect on those moments when they exercised this remarkable gift. With these instructions the group holds and observes the theme of free will throughout all the week, that is, as often as they can remember it consciously. This in itself is an exercise.

The group, having performed the invocation to inaugurate the current meeting, now sits silently, after the candles have been lit, and ponders the topic. The tutor then restates the question, 'What is free will?' and delivers a few introductory remarks to remind the group what they are about because some wil surely have forgotten. To set the scene for the discussion, the tutor might say that free will operates in the soul triad, according to the Teaching. 'Why?' the tutor may ask, giving the group the starting point to work from. The tutor then might say it was interesting to note that Tradition said only human beings had free will. To be provocative, the tutor could ask, 'Is everyone in the form of a man or a woman, human? There are many people with the outlook of stones, plants and animals in the world. Do they have free will? Is it possible for a person in the animal state driven by impulse to exercise this right? Could a vegetable or mineral type of person who is totally preoccupied with materiality or survival have the same option?' After a moment's reflection a member of the group might say that it seemed impossible to exert free will while in those two lower states of being. Another could add that perhaps that is why crises occurred, in that they shook people out of these imprisoning states. Here the tutor might point at Yesod, the ego, on the Tree diagram for those not yet familiar with kabbalistic psychology, adding that indeed such upsets did force individuals to wake up out of their habits and perceive the world from another level.

The group could then deepen the discussion, each person adding an observation. One member might see that she had only a limited choice while another could begin to differentiate between routine decisions and real free will. Somebody might give an example of this in the difference between choosing this or that professional method and altering the course of one's life by changing his job. This could bring out examples of people at a crossroads in their marriage and professions where they clearly could stay, move forward or go back from a particular situation. The discussion might then go on to fate and how much is preordained, bringing in the question as to what exactly is free will, if things are already set out by Providence. Here the tutor could intervene with the notion that it is not the external events that are perhaps so significant but one's relation to them. This alters the scale of reaction to occurrences transforming them, for the Kabbalist, into quite a different game. Someone might then ask, 'Can you change the pattern of fate?' The reply would be that general events cannot be altered, because they are part of a grand design into which the components fit. However, because most people did not exercise free will by choice, the flow of events goes the way of a general trend. This mass tendency did not apply to those who were, to some degree, awake in the soul triad. They could modify their personal fate by choice, as observed by many present in the group, although this may disrupt the routine of the world about them. While this was not a bad thing in itself, one had to be reasonably responsible not only in regard to others but to one's own karma. Therefore, quite often free will was more concerned with interior choice which changed the quality of life for that person and those around them without tampering too much with the external situation. This often precipitated a greater change in the long run, as the inner influenced the outer. A deep transformation of the energies involved usually breaks patterns which hold habits and repeating relationships.

The discussion might then turn to the theme of fated moments and how everyone had them at some point in their lives, so that no one was deprived of the privilege although they may not appreciate it at the time. People might speak about their moments of choice before going on fated journeys, being married or deciding to come to the group. One person said, at one such meeting, that it was only a split second between his taking off for India or staying where he was. He might have wasted years looking for what they had near his own home. Another one reflected on how it took a very long time to make up her mind about coming to spiritual work but that, when she had, things began to change. Someone else had come to this decision by the observation that he had been ready but circumstances were not right. This took the discussion into the notion that free will cannot be exercised just at any time, but only in moments when certain things were possible because, as one person remarked at this particular meeting, 'one can only choose if there are choices'. This had led the tutor to bring in the idea that free will was related to incidents of development or regression within the soul, in that all else below this level was concerned with mechanics. Such an idea could cause some consternation among some ego-oriented people and the discussion might become a debate; the issue being that the soul is the only part of the psyche that can operate freely. Using the Tree as the guide, the tutor would explain how the lower part of the psyche was under the unconscious Assiyatic laws of the Earth while the upper part was under the Beriatic will of Heaven. Here the seminar might open out some deeper implications.

All the way through this session people could not only be taking in what the tutor says and placing it in the context of the Tree but what all the others have to contribute. These observations are absorbed into the communal mind and placed in the respective triads of the group's emotional complexes and intellectual concepts. Those ideas which are stimulating, like free will existing only when one's soul is awake, will be filed in the active triads and those which build structure, such as 'one must wait for the right time', go into the passive triads. All this material slowly adds up over the weeks, months and years to give the group vessel a tremendous depth to draw upon that is felt even by newcomers who are given access to the collective psyche that the group has grown over time.

Another factor to emerge in these seminar-type discussions is the fact that, while the theme being examined may be simple in essence, each person brings a different facet to it. The very different types and temperaments add a greater richness to the group's understanding. For example, the housewife might well see more clearly what the professional man cannot, and the artist may describe in his work the same law that the scientist discovered in her laboratory. The psychoanalyst and the gardener could well share a similar view of growth from different angles and the lawyer and yoga teacher have a quite contrasting view of, say, the principle of manipulation. The sheer variance of the contributions enlarges the group's vision and is vital to perceiving the Worlds from every tangent. Yet, it will be seen over time that behind all practical actions, psychological forms and even the spiritual dimension, all reflect the essence of the Divine Tree which is the pattern, dynamic and will beneath everything called forth, created, formed and made.

The seminar is drawn to a close so that the tutor might ask for some conclusions that have emerged during the session. By now certain ideas will have begun to be related and clearly seen in terms of Jacob's Ladder. Other themes could well still be obscure but at least they have been considered, whereas before they may have appeared to have had no relation to the issue of free will, such as the fact that one may choose to be under-privileged. One or two ideas may have dominated the session and these might have aroused certain comment or have been of particular interest. They might be on the theme of accidents; or what is the hallmark of the 'right moment' which, the tutor might point out, is the time when the three lower Worlds are in alignment and things can happen. This particular notion could evince a number of questions and so the tutor, judging this to be the theme of the coming week, might propose the following exercise. This is that everyone observes his or her own life very closely that week, to see how near they are to a critical point of change when all the factors of their inner and outer Worlds are present and ready to move. The giving out of the week's theme usually gives a clue on the next step. After one or two people have asked for some details or clarification, the meeting is then closed with a silence before the descending invocation is said and the candles blown out. After the formal meeting has been dissolved volunteers are, as usual, invited to make coffee, clear up and pour out the wine, as well as one to act as treasurer to collect money for the next week's supplies. A scribe is also co-opted to write the notes up for the group's book on weekly meetings that is periodically photocopied and distributed.

During the social period in the latter part of the meeting some topics will be enlarged upon in smaller groups with some people talking to the tutor about more personal matters relating to the group's discussion. Despite the clatter of cups and plates, the work of the group should go on as the process of psychological digestion is begun before everyone goes home. After all have gone, anyone standing silently in the empty meeting place might perceive the residue of the meeting that is still present. This is quite an experience. This leads us on to the most directly mystical approach in the method of guided cognition.

36. Gateway

Having developed a stage further the three approaches of action, devotion and contemplation, let us look at the fourth approach of direct cognition. We are dealing now with quite a different order of things. In the other approaches the three small triads centred at the ego of Yesod are worked upon to develop their particular faculties which are principally functions of the lower psyche. Here the effort is directly conscious so as to penetrate the threshold of everyday awareness and enter the inner and upper Worlds. This means that there is a distinct shift from the ego's appreciation of the familiar world about one to the level of the self at Tiferet which has access to the higher Worlds. It must also be added that the path between Yesod and Tiferet not only takes one out of the realm of sensual consciousness but up the stairway, as some call it, to the beginning of the spiritual way. Joshua ben Miriam of Nazareth called it the *Malkhut HaShamaim* or the Kingdom of Heaven which, to the Kabbalist, is the first of the seven great halls.

The transition from mundane reality into another World is not a common experience although everyone, at some point in his life, has had a moment of extraordinary lucidity as he has been spontaneously lifted out of the ego state and into the triad of awakening formed by Hod, Tiferet and Nezah. This is known as the place of the first ecstasy. In most cases the state of lucidity quickly fades. However, it does leave an indelible mark on people who often recall it as a high point of experience or memory. In Kabbalah one seeks to attain this condition at will and hold it consciously for as long as possible, so as not only to explore that level of reality but unite it with everyday living. This cannot be done without a technique and much skilfully directed practice given by someone who has the experience first-hand and knows the pitfalls which are many. The most common of these traps is not to be able to tell the difference between inner reality and pure fantasy. In many people the two are mixed, resulting in either confusion and cynicism or superstition about anything pertaining to the other Worlds. This is why one needs instruction and companions to validate one's experience.

In group work the situation is set up so that people can receive informed direction and compare experience in order to see what might be an objective reality in its own right; in the same way two scientists might relate constants that occur in different experiments in the same field of investigation. One method of doing this is to assemble the group in a circle with a gap for a gate in front of the Tree diagram. In the space between the Tree and the 'gate', just outside the circle, a chair should be set quite apart that faces the Tree. This is to be the 'Seat of the Disciple'. After the session has begun by the ritual of invocation and lighting the candles, the meeting should fall into a deep silence in which all draw together as an intimate assembly, by recalling every face present and those of the group who are absent. This will begin to build up the sense of the vessel that should, by this stage in the group's life, slowly emerge from the Yeziratic World and hover over the company. In ancient times this was called the Merkabah, the Chariot or Vehicle for ascending into the upper Worlds. However, Tradition states that one has to go down in the chariot in order to go up. By this is meant that the Kabbalist must first penetrate deep within the inner parts of his being, that is the body, psyche and spirit, in order to contact the corresponding universal levels of the physical, psychological and cosmic. When sufficient energy and structure has been manifested and the group is ready for lift off, the tutor will begin the preliminary stages of a limited ascent because it is unwise to go beyond a certain point until one knows how to get back.

In the following exercise the journey will be confined to making contact with what is called the 'Inner Teacher'. There are several views of what this means for each case is different for every person. Thus, for one individual it might mean recognising those aspects of his psyche that are interested in personal development while in another the 'Inner Teacher' could be the essential self that is at the centre of her being. Likewise, for someone else it could be a quite objective contact with the discarnate entity who is instructing them. This might range from a personal mentor concerned with details of one's life to some illustrious saint or sage. Here it should be said that such *maggidim*, aside from Elijah, generally only communicate with those with a vital task to carry out, like the Vilna Gaon who was the rabbi responsible for holding the integrity of the Tradition in his time and place. Such people are rare and we will address ourselves to less exalted expectations and objectives. This is important, as some people can easily come to believe they are chosen to perform some prophetic task like being the mouthpiece of a long-dead sage. One must always be watchful in this work and await confirmation from other sources before accepting what might be a Lucific diversion, for this is the zone where many fall into self-delusion. This happened to Shabbetai Zvi, the 17th century pseudo-Messiah who did Kabbalah a great disservice.

The tutor begins the process of interior penetration by centring everyone in the body. People are asked to be aware of the four elements at work and the appetites and sensibilities of the vegetable and animal souls. Then the ego is observed with all its functions that form an ever-changing image of sense, mood and thought within the mind. This situation is then perceived from the place of the Self and held in view as the tutor begins to lead the exercise on to the next stage. First the group is asked to lift their consciousness up out of the meeting place and into the 'upper chamber'. By now this inner Temple should be a familiar sight to the eye of the imagination. Here the group is asked to pause so as to establish a stable relationship with these Yeziratic surroundings. The floor, walls and ceilings are examined and people make comments on anything unusual or what they had not noticed before. After a time the Temple should not only become more solid in its own terms but become modified according to the collective mind of the group. In some cases it might become increasingly beautiful, like the Palace of the Alhambra in Granada, with gardens and fountains outside. In other situations it might be a very simple room with plain benches and a desk. A different group could conceive of it as a Greek temple or the interior of a monastery while others might visualise an alchemical chamber full of instruments or books. Whatever the scheme, one factor in this situation must be present and this is a door.

At the earthly level, the door is represented by the ' gate' in the circle in front of the Tree and the empty chair. This outer reality is related directly by the tutor to the inner reality, so that there is a synthesis and cohesion between the upper and lower Worlds. When the orientation has been well established, the tutor then asks each member of the group to formulate a question, giving each two or three minutes to do so before going on. The tutor then instructs the company to wait and listen until they inwardly hear their name called. When this happens they are to rise and go through physical gate-door of the circle and sit down on the 'Seat of the Disciple' facing the Tree which represents their inner teacher. They are to wait until they are told, by an interior prompting, to address their question. If they do not receive an instant reply, which is often the case, they should wait until they do. If no reply is forthcoming they should then listen for an instruction from the tutor to return to the circle. This requires enormous sensitivity on the part of the tutor. When the next person is called, she should arise and repeat the same operation and so on. After all those who are called have completed this process, the group should reflect in silence, so as to establish what has happened, before the tutor begins to disengage the group-vehicle and bring it down from the upper chamber back into the meeting place and the more mundane levels of the psyche and body.

After a moment's pause in which to regain a natural orientation, the debriefing can begin. This should be as concise as possible at first to allow all who wish to speak to do so. Afterwards general comments and conclusions can be made.

Some people's experience may have been quite spectacular and others seemingly dull. Each account should be assessed according to its own criteria so that the maximum information may be gleaned. For example, one person might find himself in a palatial salon occupied by a fairytale king while another could discover themselves in a monk's cell. Some teachers look like magicians, others like sages or even an admired friend. Occasionally, people encounter non-human mentors. In one instance a person saw nothing but a spot of light and heard a voice. It has been known for people to see Jesus and even the Devil. None of these experiences should be dismissed because they reveal something of the influences at work in that person. They can be very useful intelligence in becoming familiar with the nature of the Self and its counterfeits, as well as who might be one's mentor.

If the question posed to the 'Inner Teacher' is crucial then the answer, if any, should be taken seriously but tested against common sense and spiritual experience. Sometimes what comes back is not always what is expected. For example, the answer to a personal problem may be long and detailed—or curt—while an apparently more profound question about the laws of creation can be totally ignored. The experience of an encounter with the Inner Teacher, if contact is made (and not everyone does each time), is deeply affecting because it makes the group realise that they are being supervised. To know that one is being watched over but not interfered with, because free will must never be impeded is, for many, a deeply reassuring feeling when they are periodically perplexed by the trials Providence seems to send to those on the Path. The communal experience of entering the 'upper chamber' and going through the same door, to be received and to receive, reinforces the group's identity and capacity, for very few individuals have direct access to their Inner Teacher, who or whatever that might be.

For many, the group operation may be their first conscious excursion into the higher Worlds. Initially it is an awesome experience but, after a time, the ascent becomes less perturbing so that one can observe the scenery quite calmly and even explore the field. With practice some people become so skilled in the process of ascension that they contact this level on their own by inwardly willing a shift in their consciousness. However, as traditional literature often warns, there are certain dangers at this point which we shall deal with in the next chapter.

37. Dangers

As one begins to penetrate from the level of the Yesodic ego, where everything is relatively intelligible, into the zones beyond the frontier of ordinary consciousness, so the individual and the group start to encounter factors which are unfamiliar. Subjects like sorcery, possession, ghosts, angels and demons might be fascinating to read about or see on television, where there is the option to turn the page or switch off, but this is not the case in a direct encounter with the real thing. To experience the supernatural can disturb the unstable elements in some psyches or give access to the entities that exist in the invisible Worlds. Here it must be said, in accordance with Tradition, that one should not proceed with these interior imaging exercises if one's psyche is in a state of disequilibrium. A tutor should always be watchful for the unbalanced student and dissuade him from taking part until he is ready and stable which, in some cases, may not be in this lifetime. Such people must be helped but not in such a way that will disrupt the work of the group for they can attract hostile and mischievous intruders who seek entrance.

In order to place what we are considering in context, let us look at the theoretical topography of the danger area. The lower part of the Yeziratic Tree relates to the World of Formation. This is the habitat not only of the ego level of the psyche but also of those entities who inhabit the lower psychic realm, in the same way that plants and animals exist in the natural World. As below, so there are creatures above of every species, some friendly and some otherwise, some highly intelligent and others stupid. Moreover, as this lower level of Yezirah roughly corresponds to the subtlest levels of nature, so it constitutes the zone where the newly-dead spend a brief time before going on. It is also the place where those who refuse to believe they are dead, or are still obsessively attached to the senses, reside and wander about seeking a contact with the living. Generally speaking, little connection is made because normally there is no means of communication except under special circumstances, such as in dreams, at the approach of death, during a major psychological crisis or at a seance. Sometimes a contact can be made in the kind of exercise that has just been described if the normal procedure of protection by invocation or prayer is not correctly executed prior to ascension.

Usually the passage from the earthly level to the higher realms is quite safe provided the operation is placed consciously under the guidance of Heaven and the Holy Spirit. However, some people do not always follow the tutor and go off on their own without a guide during the ascent or are lured away from the group by voices originating either in their own psyche or from entities that are attracted by the field force that is generated by the circumstance. The method of dealing with such a situation is for the tutor and student to centre in the Self of Tiferet and place themselves directly under the Holy One's protection by prayer or the repetition of a Divine Name. A dramatic alternative, when the individual cannot cope, is for the group rapidly to return to earth, stamp their feet and enter into normal sensual consciousness. This, of course, will terminate the ascent. Generally speaking, a group should pass unmolested through the critical zone of lower Yezirah, as one does every night when going to sleep.

An awareness that there are potential intruders should not frighten people with knowledge and goodwill. Like any earthly adventure there is always the factor of danger and this is intended to put off the faint-hearted or those who are not yet ready. They should stay on the Earth and go about their natural business. However, for those who do want to take the risk, there is no need to be foolhardy. This is where a group is invaluable because, like mountain climbers, they are roped together for mutual support and have an experienced guide. The fact that creatures of these zones may come close to examine one need not put the climber off. Neither should the occasional storms of Yeziratic weather nor the difficult psychological corners and cliffs on the way up. All these can be dealt with by calm persistence, skill and increasing experience. Indeed, each ascent should make this psychic foothill section easier until one is no longer unduly bothered by the hazards of the lower Yeziratic slopes because one knows what to expect and do.

In practical terms, one should keep one foot in Malkhut so that one never completely loses contact with the Earth; that is, a dim sense of the physical World should never be lost. For those people who have a weak link with ordinary reality, this should be strengthened by developing their sensual perception. The tutor could help here by giving exercises in touching, tasting, smelling, hearing and seeing what is taken for granted. These faculties should instantly be put into operation if, during an ascending session, a person begins to panic or lose touch with the reality the others are entering. The same technique can be applied to the occasional hysteric episode that occurs with someone who may be temporarily disturbed by some personal breakthrough or breakdown. It is a good thing, if possible, to take the individual outside the building and into the open so that she may make direct contact with the physical elements to calm her down. Cold rain or warm sun will earth most people. Another rare phenomenon is the occasional epileptic fit. If this does happen, and it may take even the tutor by surprise, the group should remain calm and allow a qualified member to deal with the situation. If there is no one, then the epileptic should be lowered gently to the floor to avoid self-injury and the airway of the mouth made clear while the tongue should be protected from being bitten by using a handkerchief wad until the fit has passed. One must be prepared for anything.

As will perhaps be realised, this zone is the one used by those who practise low magic which harnesses the more subtle powers of nature, corresponding to the upper face of the Natural Tree, to dominate and direct the creatures of the lower face of the World of Formation. Traditional literature insists that this is a very dangerous game as once control has been lost over these entities they can turn on their erstwhile masters and hurt them. This is why magic is forbidden in the Bible. Kabbalah is concerned with serving God, not with the manipulation of occult power, however well-meant, because no person, no matter how skilled, can know the full ramifications of what they are doing to others, themselves and the universe. It is said that the art of magic is to adjust the structure and dynamics of the World of Formation in order to effect the configuration of causes that will bring about changes below in the natural World. While this is technically possible, it is not always ethical or correct to interfere with the way a situation is developing, especially if the magician wants it to go in a particular direction. As with all magical operations there is a price; and while the sorcerer may gain a limited success, the universe will inevitably assert its need for equilibrium so that the situation will revert to its original flow. This is why black magic always fails in the end.

What is known as white magic is often an applied correction to a disturbed or blocked sequence but within its laws. For example, certain groups use kabbalistic principles to set up healing situations and while this is not improper in itself it is often done by people who do not

205

Figure 22 — DANGERS
With Higher Knowledge comes psychic power. This can be misused by irresponsible, ambitious or evil people. The Arts of Magic carry great temptation. Some clever individuals who believe they are Magi consider themselves above the Law and apply what they know to manipulate the Universal Order. However, if one opens the door into the Astral realm, as here shown, who knows what may be let in that cannot be controlled? Only a spiritual Master can contain such psychic forces by being in obedience to the Divine. (Rembrandt engraving.)

understand the full implications of what they are doing. It may be likened to the early use of penicillin which was seen, like many other wonder drugs, as a cure for every ill by destroying the evil bacteria until it was discovered that it also debilitated the good bacteria, thereby weakening the whole system if used indiscriminately. Many good people who practise this kind of psychic healing operate from a naïve base of a little knowledge and much sacred superstition. Belief, alas, is not enough! Faith and knowledge are needed. However, in this context it is not the studied manipulation of subtle forces that is required but taking the problem up to the Most High and asking for intercession. Then, if it is willed from above, the miraculous that arises out of the Beriatic World of Creation will work on the World of Formation which, in turn, will bring about a change in the physical World. In this case, the entire universe is taken into account by the Absolute who knows exactly what is needed to allow a healing to occur without creating tension or disruption elsewhere.

The temptation to be diverted from the Path is one of the tests that confronts both the individual and the group when encountering the entities and powers of the upper Worlds. Indeed, many people are drawn to the study of Kabbalah because of the magical mythology that surrounds it. While it is true that there is a magical aspect, even within the Judaic line, its operations were always related to Divine Will. Some people, for example, soon forget what Kabbalah is about as they become absorbed in the theory and practice of contacting angels; and those who are intrigued by the devils quickly cease to remember who they are because such interests open the door to possession. Now while this may sound medieval, the reality of this supernatural phenomenon is recognised in every culture. We may, in modern times, know it by clinical names such as schizophrenia, or use such terms as archetypes and sub-personalities, but these are merely other ways of describing the points of contact and entry between the psyche of the individual and the hosts of the Yeziratic World. According to traditional Kabbalah, an angel and demon watch over the soul triad aiding and abetting the action of free will. In the psychotic and insane this privilege is forestalled by the inflation of one of the psychological functions, such as Nezah which can be taken over by the archetypal entity of Venus which produces the nymphomaniac; or the Hodian possession of the Trickster that underlies the criminal, conman and kleptomaniac. Lesser possessions can occur within the emotional or conceptual complexes where certain entities live off obsessions or fears, as parasites do off blood or sap. *Beelzebub*, or Master of the Flies, was not just a quaint old name but a poetic and precise description of Lucifer in action.

Lucifer will enter the field of the group when a sufficient number of its members have begun to generate a cohesive power structure because as the group acquires a collective potential it becomes vulnerable to tests. Thus, while the less sensitive members may not initially suspect what is going on beneath the weekly routine, there will appear the shadow side of the group identity. This demonic element can emerge from any direction out of a smoothly-run situation, because sinister factors are present in everyone including the tutor. It may manifest privately in personal difficulties or in friction between certain cliques in the group. It can creep into an obsession with regulation or arise out of the petty politics of a growing organisation. It can also come through a key factor, like one of the star students who dramatically precipitates the group's first major crisis which could destroy all that has been made.

38. Crisis

As a group moves through the stage of consolidation, so it begins to establish a firm Yesod, or Foundation, which is quite separate from its members. People may come and go and the group can lose most of its founder members and yet retain and develop a distinct identity. This is usually related to the tutor's way of working for there is no classical form to a kabbalistic group except in essentials. The human element must always leave its stamp and this is determined by the tutor's character and calibre and those who are drawn to that mode of operation. As a group reaches its first plateau of maturity, so a certain stability sets in. By then certain ways of doing things are performed as routine and people align and relate according to their level and personal inclination. The situation resembles that of a large family with the tutor at its head. This is inevitable because all collective human activities reflect this pattern whether it be home, club or occupation. Thus, there are those close to the leader, those in the middle stratum and those below and remote from intimate contact with what goes on at the top of what is becoming an organisation. This does not mean that the leading elements cut them off but that the less committed and advanced levels are usually unaware of the subtler events that take place in the group except through hearsay and then often much later in a distorted form.

What has been described now begins to show the characteristics of a greater family situation with all its positive and negative sides; intrigues, loyalties, opinions and ambitions. For most of the outer circle of the group the way things are done is probably quite satisfactory because they have never experienced being in esoteric work before. Everything is new and to doubt is seen to be disobedient, even though the tutor may have said test everything before accepting it. For these people the wonder and privilege of being in such a group over-rides any criticism they may have of its organisation, the behaviour of senior students or the tutor. This is a lifeline for many newcomers and to question would be to deny what help was being given.

The middle level of the company, which usually constitutes the majority of the group, is usually content to carry out all the duties and operations of the group with little disagreement. To them the regular meetings and cyclic exercises give them a deep stability and a sense of belonging to something worthwhile. They might query a detail here and there but this is in order to understand why this or that is done. They would never dream of disrupting the group over any issue, because it is their support, and to undermine it would be to destroy what they valued, in many cases more than anything else in their lives. They might hear people gossip about each other, even though the rule is never to speak about someone negatively unless to their face, and they might even gather snippets of comments or criticism of the tutor but they would never be disloyal. Indeed, they would defend the tutor's honour as their own. However, such loyalty can breed both a sense of security and the seeds of destruction because it can encase a group in a citadel psychology which eventually generates resistance and rebellion against its authority for a variety of reasons.

As well as the family structure, the group will also start to exhibit the dynamics of an institution with its little customs, routines, and rôles. This is inevitable but it must not be allowed to become excessive. Certain people, for example, will always volunteer to write up the notes on the meetings and thus become the scribes while others will claim what they think are certain privileges that go with preparing the meeting room or even just being in charge of the cleaning party. Some individuals become identified with their official tasks, like being group treasurer, while others of more subtle nature cultivate the friendship of senior members of the group for reasons other than being esoteric. These motivations might be to gain access to what they think is the inner circle of the group or just professional or social considerations. All these and many other problems have to be watched out for, checked and eliminated, preferably by the people themselves. However, within this very human situation with its complex relationships and drives, there are always individuals who are never at peace. Such people are often knowledgeable because they tend to drift from group to group looking for a solution to their problem which is that they know more than most but can never gather any people into a group which will come under their rule.

People of this kind are to be found in every organisation whether at work, leisure or in a spiritual pursuit. They are ambitious for power although they speak always of the common good. In esoteric groups the approach may be disguised but the motivation is quite discernable to the experienced eye. Such individuals are often highly intelligent and will plan and wait until they see an opportunity to take the group over. Sometimes this is done quite legitimately by being an excellent deputy, in which case they earn much respect and often mature in psyche and spirit by dealing honestly with their preoccupation with power. If they do not then it is not unknown for them to start a quiet rebellion by questioning, in private conversation with other members, the way in which the group is run. At first they will not attack the tutor directly but seek to discredit those close to the chair by implication, using what errors all people make to bring their credibility into doubt. Sometimes such accusations are just and need correction, but they are not relayed to the tutor who should be told of any important misdemeanours. This happened when, for example, a senior member was over-zealous with a class practising a ritual and became a bullying regimental sergeant-major. Incidents and others like this, if not curtailed, can destroy the collective confidence. Potential usurpers edge any situation towards this as they hope, like all revolutionaries, that it will lead to a chaos in which they create their own kind of order. This is their fantasy, conscious or unconscious.

Such an extraordinary notion is not without precedent. More than one group has been destroyed from within by internally stirred dissension. The most classic case was the Karaites in the eighth century who, on the face of it, were a breakaway sect which rejected Talmudic law and refused to accept the authority of the rabbis. The real reason, however, was an internal power struggle in which their leader, having lost the position he thought his by right, created a separate rejectionist sect over which he ruled. A more recent example was the issue that split an esoteric school between those who wished to walk in the footsteps of the dead master and those who wanted to change the system and go another way. Such crises do not erupt overnight but are the result of many months or even years of quiet dissension in which someone wishes to take over an already existing organisation.

Perhaps the most difficult situation is when the star student, closest to the tutor, is the one who is at the root of the rebellion. This can occur when the person sees he is never going to be more than a deputy and will not be allowed to direct the group according to his understanding. It is very hard being an understudy especially when he hears of problems that never get to the tutor's ears, or so he thinks, ignoring the fact that he does not pass the information on in order to isolate the tutor and increase his power. While such a practice may seem horrific, when the Lucific element in all of us tests our integrity it is amazing what a person can lead himself to believe if he considers that he is behaving for the good of all. Quite a number of star students fall for this temptation and, contrary to their belief, their game is often closely watched by their tutor who has been through this same test. Strange as it may seem, the process of deception and self-deception is not tampered with because the tutor must not interfere, beyond hints in the early stages, with the issue of free will, but allows the student the maximum opportunity in which to see and stop what he is doing, preferably by his own effort.

If, however, the situation becomes critical, that is it begins to affect the group adversely as a whole, then the tutor must act. This might be through a number of private conversations with other senior members, who could tactfully warn the student of the collision course so avoiding loss of face, or it could be a personal confrontation in which the tutor presents the situation and the way the star student is undermining the group and discrediting the Work. In most cases the person, realising what has happened, seeks to correct the situation but occasionally the culprit might be unrepentant and speak his mind about how they see the group. The tutor in this situation might reply that it would have been better for the student to have spoken of their disagreement earlier. If the student still maintains this position and adds, as is often the case, that there are others who agree with the criticism, then the tutor has no option but to recommend that the student forms his own group and works independently. This solution is, in fact, a formal invitation to all those who do not wish to continue in the present group to leave without any ill feeling. Some may jump at the chance to set up a separate group which may or may not succeed according to the reality of their cause. If it is only opinion, fantasy or a pursuit of novelty that makes them break away then the seed of their enterprise will not fructify. If it is a genuine concern, then they must flourish.

The ideal solution is for the star student to realise that it is time to work on his or her own. This should be acknowledged by the tutor who, if genuine, will encourage and bless the prospective tutor by sending on suitable candidates to help form the base of a group. If it takes root, then this may be the beginning of a school of Kabbalah as the process starts again with a newly initiated tutor instructed to propagate that Line.

Here is another level of Work as the Teaching and training extend in the form of related groups which generate a particular style of operation. This will be recognised by other schools and the world at large by its reputation.

39. Reputation

As the embryo school begins to grow so it will start to develop in a different dimension. A kabbalistic school is more than just two or three groups, its members and their activities. It is an organism with a character that is quite independent of any individual although it can be guided by a Teacher. While it may be said that a group moves in a tutor's particular way and attracts a certain type of student, there does come a time when something transpersonal emerges from the collective effort of several groups to manifest a distinctive entity. This moment occurs when a sufficient amount of energy, structure and consciousness have been generated to unify all the groups into a recognisable configuration. A parallel phenomenon is when a collection of individual actors, in rehearsal, suddenly become a company at a certain point when they start to relate to their parts. It is a definite change of state in which the spirit of the play takes over. In the case of a kabbalistic school it is the spirit of the Line manifesting the Tradition in that particular situation with those particular people.

While this order of reality may be present, it will be perceived by most only at the group level, although perceptive visitors might, perhaps, be more aware of it than those immersed in the school. Such strangers might, moreover, note the flavour which distinguishes that particular school from others they may have visited. Less sensitive people could pick it up as a distinct atmosphere that made them feel at home or definitely outside a meeting, as if there were a higher space into which only members could enter. This field force is quite real and exists in the psychological World of Formation as a hedge against subtle intrusion, although sinister elements can still enter under the cover of people who do not know they carry a shadow within their psyche. This is inevitable and should not preclude such individuals from joining a group. It may be the only place from which they can get help.

This brings us to the issue of new members to the group. In the early days, large numbers were needed to make up for the natural wastage of people leaving because it was not their way of working.

Now that an organisation is well established and has a growing core of committed members, the rate of entry and loss is considerably less. Therefore, the selection process must be more rigorous. Gone are the days of zealous honeymooners seeking to convert any likely client at work or social gathering. Members are still on the lookout for suitable candidates but they have to be more prudent. There are several reasons for this. Besides it being a sign of maturity to act with restraint, it is better if seekers come looking of their own accord. This eliminates the merely curious. Also by this stage the school will have begun to generate a reputation and will certainly attract those interested in occult power politics. Thus increased discretion is required of all members.

Reputation is acquired in two ways. The first is that which emanates from the groups at the subtlest levels and is picked up by those also in the Work, be they good or evil. This means that they are beginning to take their place in the esoteric network that exists in that country. If the emergent school has any capacity, then it will certainly be closely observed from above and below. The other way is by word of mouth. This can happen through recommendation or gossip. It is a general rule that little or nothing is said about what goes on at meetings or between members outside the context of the school. This is not only to stop outsiders getting a fragmentary and distorted version of what happens but to preserve and build up the vitality of the organism. However, people are people and talk does occur. Among the more disciplined such conversations will be confined to discussion about general esoteric matters amongst themselves or with others who are perhaps in another branch of spiritual work. These discreet exchanges can be very useful and help communication between different disciplines. There are of course the dialogues between people in relationship with others not involved in the group, from husbands and wives to interested acquaintances who seriously want to discover something.

With non-member partners the issue can become very difficult as sometimes the school is seen as a rival in attention. This must be handled very tactfully or a deep hostility will develop which can not only affect the relationship but lead to many malicious things being said about the school. A similar problem occurs when a relationship breaks up and one party leaves a group. Very often the one who leaves slanders the tutor as well as the people with whom he was intimate. It is a real test of integrity for all, especially when several members depart *en masse* as sometimes happens during an ideological crisis of personalities. This can precipitate a tremendous burst of back-biting as the departing shake themselves loose from the loyalty and discipline of the school. This is why there is the strict rule that while courteous relations with ex-members are maintained, no active attempt is made to contact them for it could feed their ego-justified anger. This rage, it must be added, is often a negative projection of their own inadequacy unless, of course, their grievance is genuine, as with a corrupt situation. The neutral position of remaining members allows people to run the course of rejection and reflection without interference but leaves the door open for them to return should they wish. No one should ever be cut off from the Tradition although they might be advised to join a group with no connection to that particular school.

Undoubtedly such incidents feed the negative side of a school's reputation and they are likely to reach the ears of those interested. Such stories and distorted facts can be used as ammunition by people who feel their little empires threatened and by those who seek to discredit any kind of spiritual work. Such individuals often appear to be involved with self-development when they are, in fact, working against it. These dark teachers usually run groups that take the inexperienced up to a point and hold them there for many years in suspended spiritual animation. They are sometimes persons who have had higher knowledge but will not let anyone pass beyond their level because they must be, in their ego-oriented world, the master. Here is where reputation is useful because, to the discerning, much can be gained from the grapevine about certain groups and teachers. An example of this is the man who says all the right things, infatuates all those who come under his spell and yet leaves a trail of broken minds, hearts and bodies behind him. This is why reputation has to be taken into account. It reveals something about the quality of the Teaching being propagated.

The emergence of a new school into the esoteric community can be a simple addition to the numbers and quality of those operating in an area or it can be the beginning of a new epoch. At the time of Joshua ben Miriam of Nazareth, there were many spiritual schools besides those in Jerusalem and at the Essene community by the Dead Sea. Only a few people would have suspected that the group of twelve from the Galilee, with their north-country accents and ways, would have generated a New Testament out of the Old. While such cosmic events only occur every few millennia, the possibility is there, if in nothing else but in the matter of degree. Thus, when the time for innovation occurs, there usually arises a new formulation of the Teaching that brings a freshness to the Tradition for that generation. This pattern usually manifests in groups that do not follow the format of the more conservative schools. Naturally, as these innovatory groups begin to take place and inevitably draw those who would have otherwise gone to the older schools, there will be some tension with those who do not understand that the Tradition must move on. Orthodox Lines, well-established and conservative schools will be highly suspicious at their best and openly hostile at their worst to any newcomers in their field. This will clearly define those truly on the Path from those merely preserving an old, worn-out formula. This does not mean to say that the ancient ways are invalid but that those who practise them, even as those who take up the new for the wrong reasons, are not always in line with the living flow of Kabbalah.

If people cannot see an esoteric school at work and how it transmits the Teaching, then all they have to go on is hearsay and what is picked up out of the ether. This is why what is projected by each member of a school is their responsibility. The reputation of a school is the result of everything that emanates through thought, feeling and action and is filtered through the member's conduct and strained by any recipient's limited comprehension.

The image a school may have among peer organisations will be built up as it becomes increasingly cohesive and creates a focus of reception and transmission between the upper and lower Worlds. Thus, as a school develops, those at a similar level will become inwardly aware of its presence. Such a capability takes some time to generate and, like people, a school can fail at crucial points in its career. There are many surviving remnants of withered or dead schools operating long after the spirit has left them; certain occult and masonic lodges are an example. Finally, the emergence of a school is such a rare occurrence that its effects must be felt unconsciously by the general community. This contact might be in the subtle presence of spirituality or through the personal connection with members and their values which modify the way of life of those around them. This is the function of reputation.

The mundane dimension is not only a very practical one but the chief mode by which a school transmits its contribution into the world for, while the higher influences do exist, they are not apparent until there is contact between a kabbalistic school and ordinary life. At this stage of development, it might be the only way its members can pass on what they have learned about unifying the Worlds in order that God might behold God. This greatest of undertakings is not as remote as it might seem, for every act, emotion and idea should express this objective in the life of the Kabbalist. A school's task is to train and support individuals so that they may carry out this operation and be an agent for what comes through from above. When members of the school find themselves in situations that need a lift in level, they can call on resources far beyond the capacity of one person. Initially they are the Malkhut point of the Tradition until each individual operates within the larger range of an organisation that must inevitably grow as the school develops.

40. Organisation

As time passes our imaginary school will expand, proliferate and consolidate into a confederation of independent groups working within an annual cycle of three ten-week-long terms, like an academic institution. Indeed, the natural breaks between terms occur in the same way, in order to move with the natural rhythm of the seasons. Thus, the groups begin their year around mid-September, after everyone has been away on holiday and the body has been rested or exercised, the psyche has had time to reflect on the previous year's work and when the spirit is just beginning to miss the subtle food that can only be obtained in the school. This last factor is quite crucial because the three summer months away from the meetings usually reveal that the inner life of many people, which is fed and held by the Work, begins to be run down after a time if it is not replenished both in the individual and in the school as a whole. So when the first meetings are convened there is usually a deep hunger as well as the pleasure of seeing well-loved and familiar faces again.

For the tutors the summer has a special meaning. Taking a group is extremely demanding and by June the tutor will be exhausted and will look forward to a private holiday and to the research that can be carried out over this long recess. Some tutors will simply take time off in some far away place while others may indeed take on more work, like a summer course in the country or abroad. Others might stay at home to reflect on the larger scheme while someone else may want to finish a book or devote the time to a project such as relating scientific data to the Tree. Yet another might go to Israel to follow up the trail of certain traditional schools or go to see a particular rabbi with whom a contact has been made. Some summers might be spent in places where Kabbalah was once prominent, like walking the streets of old Gerona and Lunel or going to the Jewish quarter in Amsterdam and looking and listening with the inner senses. Sitting and meditating in the ancient synagogues of Toledo and Posquières or the study house of Rabbi Karo in Safed reveals more about what went on there than a book can tell.

As the evenings of Autumn draw in and the attention becomes more introverted so the Work of the school begins again. By now a group procedure will be well established. People arrive just before the meeting and prepare the room for whatever is to happen there. They will then take up their places and await the tutor coming. On his arrival the group will fall silent and go into private meditation. The tutor will then begin to raise the group level with a series of formal instructions, such as, 'Let us come together. Let us rise up. Let us enter the Holy Chamber'. The group, under these directions, will rapidly knit together and ascend into a different time and space, carrying even those who are not too familiar with the operation. The tutor will then speak the invocation of the Tree, light the candles and call upon the Holy Spirit. After a short pause in which the group adjusts to the shift in dimension, the meeting begins with the tutor restating the exercise of the summer. This was the theme to be considered over the holiday. It might be 'How does free will relate to fate?' The tutor will then ask for observations. By this time most of the group will have entered into the 'upper room' and in a few moments it will be as if they had never been away.

This phenomenon is due to the fact that a group now has momentum because the structure is sound and the dynamic constant. Such a state takes at least three years to reach. Its basis is a reliable tutor and a stable core of members who carry out all the things needed to keep such an organisation running. This means not only putting effort into the purely theoretical and practical side of Kabbalah but all those small housekeeping jobs that keep a place operational for meetings, meditations and rituals. Very often only a fraction of the group bears this responsibility and a tutor should periodically remind the group that it is their concern, not the tutor's, to maintain its machinery; that is their contribution and vital reciprocation to what is given from above. While knowledge is freely imparted they have to provide their own facilities. As one Kabbalist said, 'The Lord will supply the food but you must lay your own table'. The responsibility is sometimes left entirely to the tutor, who has more than enough to do, or a minority who value the Work; but this is not correct. People who just take and return nothing to the Work remain spiritually immature. Each person's offering is according to the gifts Heaven has provided him. The artists have their skills, the scientists theirs, the housewife her knowledge and the businessman his. The poor give what they can when money is needed and the rich repay their fortune by providing what no one else could afford.

Out of all this effort will emerge some kind of organisation. In some schools the functional base is kept to the minimum, so that groups might meet in private houses, while another decides to formalise its position and go as far as drawing up a constitution of a friendly society. Some schools elect a central committee and hire people to manage the practical affairs of the organisation because it has become too large to be run on a voluntary basis. This means that certain people will be responsible for finance, planning, looking after buildings and their maintenance. Perhaps there has to be permanent secretary to answer the telephone and deal with paperwork as well as co-ordinate activities in order to alleviate the load on the head of the school. Such a person would need to have an inner council of advisers who would be responsible for general policy decisions. With this scale of organisation many things become possible. Special premises can be rented or bought in which ambitious projects can be realised. More people could be accommodated, as inevitably greater numbers must be expected as the school's influence and magnetic field draws them in, for it is not unknown for schools to grow, at this point, with great rapidity to many times their original size, so that what was once a small meeting of ten or twelve has become an organisation of two or three thousand members. The early Church began this way.

Clearly such an expansion brings its dangers. With all organisations comes temptation and corruption. However, in a kabbalistic situation more is at stake because people's souls are involved in the running and purpose of the system. There must always be a careful watch for any person who becomes identified with a position, no matter how petty, who seeks to misuse the situation. Normally, the tutor will deal with this kind of problem but it is better that those around the individual contain it before it gets out of hand. For example, the chairman of the central committee of a school has been known to imagine that he is the charismatic reflection of his teacher and issue edicts accordingly; and some secretaries have been observed to decide who can or cannot see the master. Another problem that arises is when a person always takes on a particular job because no one else will do it. This sometimes inflates their sense of importance. Thus, it is as well to have all such positions filled by a series of people. These are samples of the many hazards of esoteric management that do not occur in ordinary work where the objectives are quite different.

In addition to the weekly group meetings, another possibility might be the introduction of weekend meetings of thirty or so people from

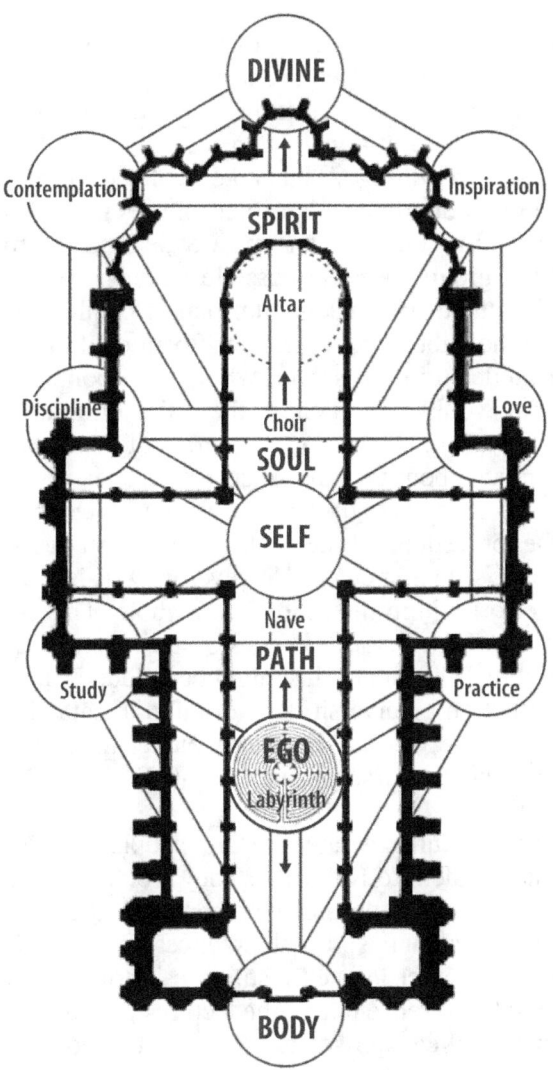

Figure 23 – INTERACTION
Schools of the soul often co-operate. The medieval Cathedral of Chartres was built by the Masons, a school of the soul. They no doubt consulted the enlightened priesthood, then present, and the rabbinic school just across the street. As can be seen, the Tree is part of the design with the Choir and High Altar representing the soul and Spirit. The famous Labyrinth is the ego that wanders in circles until the seeker finds there is a way out and up to the Self at the Tiferet point at the centre of the building. The famous twin Sun and Moon Towers are the side pillars of the Tree with the middle door as entrance to the central column of Ascension. (Prof. Keith Critchlow.)

different groups. These could occur during the national or religious holidays and extend from a Friday evening to a Sunday afternoon. These would allow concentrated and sustained work which can bring people to a level the normal meetings cannot. Such an inter-group operation could be held at a well-sited residential conference centre that took care of everything. A bus could collect those without cars and a weekend without domestic responsibilities might release much energy to enhance a course taken by an experienced tutor. Cheaper trips abroad for groups become possible with charter flights and a hired coach in attendance makes pilgrimages painless. In this way, places such as the kabbalistic centres of Spain could be visited with an informed guide from the school who would point out things no ordinary tourist would see, such as the pillar of Isaac the Blind's synagogue embedded in a wall or the garden of Rabbi Nachmanides which tell so much about the Kabbalists of Gerona.

As each group expands to the limit of manageable numbers of forty people so the procedure of delegating senior students to take a beginners group is implemented. However, now it is a question of a co-ordinated effort within the school as a whole. This is an entirely new operation, perhaps holding a series of introductory lectures in an academic building. The aim of this might be to launch an impulse that has a direct effect on a university city or cultural capital with a view to influencing people who might not encounter the esoteric in daily life. This could be the first project mounted by the school in the mainstream of life.

Initially, such lectures would prepare people in a general way before introducing them to Kabbalah. They would hear about a wide variety of traditional mystic and philosophical ideas and be given simple psychological and spiritual practices to do in a form that resembled those of other learned institutions. However, there would be a fundamental difference in that the lectures would have a back-up that no ordinary college possesses. The organisation of such talks would be no problem because of the skill and discipline available throughout the school. The lecturers, for example, could be drawn from a pool of advanced tutors and the running of the practical arrangements would easily be managed by those learning how to do such things under experienced supervision. Out of such an enterprise could emerge a totally different order of work. It would not only unite all the school in a common aim but create a greater vessel to act as a medium of transmission between the Worlds. Although this widening of scope might enlarge the dimension of the school, it should not detract from individual and group activities. The human scale must not be lost in either the exciting or dull times that must, inevitably, come and go.

41. Dull Times

While the birth of a school is inspiring to be part of, it is dependent upon many hours spent on routine work over terms and years. Because of this there are inevitable periods when nothing new seems to occur and there develops a dreariness in both the individual and the school as it pauses between the ebb and flow of inner growth. One task of a school is to create the best environment for its students to evolve and so its programme should be designed to meet this need. However, this objective is not always recognised as the ego always seeks the easy option. The cyclic round of ritual, meditation, contemplation and mystical sessions, as well as holidays and informal meetings can, at some stages, become stale despite the fact that everything is related to Kabbalah. These dull periods are sometimes more gruelling as tests than any traumatic crisis for they call upon the deepest levels of discipline and commitment. For relative newcomers this lethargy in a group is not encouraging and those who cannot see the point of trudging on drop out and not a few old-timers fall off at these times. For the tutors and the central core of each group the situation is both difficult and more urgent. They must take the Teaching to an even deeper level of theory and practice so as to draw upon their innermost resources. During such moments the depths plumbed reveal the Teaching in a new light, so that apparently well-worn themes and exercises in metaphysics, devotion and right action become yet more profound, as people realise that they know so little about Kabbalah and even less about the art of practising it. This precipitates a well-known phenomenon in esoteric work.

Joshua of Nazareth gave a parable of seeds being sown on different kinds of ground. Some sprang up quickly but withered just as fast. Others fell on stony ground and could not grow beyond a certain point and yet others, being in good ground, took their time, fulfilled their full term of growth and bore rich fruit. The fast but shallow growers usually leave a group quite early. Of those that remain, there are some who bide their time to see what will happen and some who stay because they know what is going on. The former usually leave when the going gets rough, but the latter carry on for a variety of reasons; for example, some are interested in the Work but relate it only to themselves and personal development. Such people will stay as long as it benefits them which, in itself, is not an evil motivation but it has limits which are reached when the school enters a barren period.

Now a school, like any living organism, has times of work and rest, excitement and depression. In the early days such cycles moved quickly but in the epoch of maturity, when most of the outwardly creative work has been completed and the adolescent episodes of inflation and projection of both students and tutors is over, there ensues a slower and more powerful cycle of progression. Generally, this gentler but more potent oscillation carries the school into a more profound penetration of the Teaching and over the times when nothing seems to happen. To those with experience or discernment, these dull epochs are when something is either being digested or prepared for a transformation. Alas, not everyone in a school can perceive this subtler level of activity, even though they may have studied Kabbalah for many years, for they either miss the inner situation altogether or interpret it as stagnation. Those who still hanker for some excitement or outward manifestation find these slow passages frustrating and begin to criticise the system. People who understand what is happening usually realise that this is where they must give back to the school what they have taken, return the energy and hold its structure with conscious endeavour.

This type of crisis reveals the various levels of comprehension within the school. Those who only wish to take become agitated in the meetings because they are not getting what they want while those who value and recognise what is needed put their effort into support. This is called by one esoteric tradition 'super effort'. In this the intent is doubled and trebled so that a breakthrough can occur both for the individual and the school. Each tutor knows this principle but will not go beyond indicating what is required because the chair must not do the work of the group; that is their responsibility. Those who do not understand the need will blame the tutor for the added tension and project fault on all those students who seem to want to force the pace beyond the usual limit of labour or interest. If they do not voice their dissent in public they will certainly speak of it in private, either amongst themselves or to their tutor who will listen and then try to explain the deeper implication of what is happening. Some dissidents will hear and rejoin the others to aid the school and some will not because they cannot perceive the real problem and only see a technical knot to be untied by a superficial alteration which is quite different from transformation.

Such moments in a school's life can precipitate the most extraordinary events. People who have been under its discipline for perhaps years can suddenly become belligerent, seek radical changes and even threaten to split the school into factions. Sometimes they threaten to leave when they see that the school is not going to alter its form of the Work and introduce some new and more exciting ideas. The right to comment is there and if the suggestions are honest, real, sensitive or creative, then the school should adopt them, if they are considered to be helpful. This situation, however, is rare because more often than not it is the registering of a complaint based upon a personal difficulty which is projected onto the school, so as to avoid facing it. A tutor can usually spot this. Such criticism might arise from an innate laziness or wilfulness, a sense of not being accepted or a desire to be noticed. They do not see that the real problem is transpersonal; that what they propose is just cosmetic. A solution can only come by the conscious transcending of form; that is, for example, by performing a routine ritual with fuller attention to its meaning. It is usually just before a breakthrough that people turn aside to do something new. Only those who work through the critical moment, when resistance is at its greatest, pierce the veil and enter into the mysteries. Thus, even the daily exercise of putting the body into a Tree configuration can, in a super effort, suddenly give a profound insight into the levels of correspondence so that touch is seen to relate to lower Action, taste to upper Action and lower Formation, smell to upper Formation and lower Creation, hearing to upper Creation and lower Emanation and sight to the pure light of the upper Divine. Such a breakthrough is indeed a transformation.

The response to support a school during a low period and not tear it apart also comes from a sense of debt in those who remember their former state of being. Without such a contact they would still be lost and on their own. A school is the product of thousands of Kabbalists down the ages who have kept the light burning. An awareness of this dimension is most important because it opens up the school's consciousness to the wider implications. Many people in spiritual work fail to realise that schools do not just happen but are the result of hard and sustained effort on the part of many people because the forces of ordinary life are naturally opposed to consciously accelerated development. Only those who can be masters of their instinctive and lower psychological patterns can make real use of the Teaching. Dull times bring out a craving for novelty and a contrariness that is sometimes hidden in the most unlikely students. Indeed, quite often the most reliable members of a school are those who are doubtful, who check everything to see if it is so and whether it works or not. Many such individuals are frequently puzzled after many years as to why they are still there; and yet these are usually the most loyal and conscientious students during the dark times because they have really processed their experience.

To keep a balance in our account of a school going through a bad patch, there are times when the situation is indeed stale or some form of stagnation has appeared. This can occur when certain operations are badly managed or people have become exhausted. Generally this situation is pointed up by some acts of Providence, like petty quarrels, inefficiency, accidents or a key person falling ill. Such signs should not be ignored for they may reveal that indeed something fundamental needs to change. If the symptoms of disorder are not seen in their early stages, then odd things begin to happen. For instance, tutors start to become remote or the school's secretariat begins to dominate decisions on policy while the repair unit that maintains the meeting house allows it to become dingy. These are the signs that something is wrong. The rot has really set in when observations made at meetings are repeated every term and there is a lassitude or unpleasant tension at the end of each session. This can mark the death knell of the school if it is not dealt with.

The possibility of a declining impulse or even the demise of a school is ever present in this Work. There is no guarantee that the Spirit will come down each term and stay for ever. The path up Jacob's Ladder is very narrow and the Lucific principle will always seek to make members slip and a school fall from Grace. It is not hard to bring about. The end of a school may be instant, in the sudden decease of a leader who leaves no one of sufficient calibre to carry on, or it can be a genteel decline of an ageing company which spends its last thirty years in what becomes a pleasant esoteric social club. Dead schools can become coffins of rigid institutionalism in which the rules are everything and the individuals nothing. Inmates of these esoteric cemeteries sometimes consider their loyalty to a dead organisation as the point, not realising they worship an atrophied idol. Many such people are willing slaves of a mummified form, usually administered by a usurper who took the place of the teacher once all rivals had gone. This is the tail end of a takeover story that occasionally occurs. The state of the game is usually recognised by the extraordinary demands of such leaders. For example, one such character insisted on being addressed by a fantastic title. This stage is the last phase of decadence and can be discerned in many organised religions.

The likelihood of such an advanced rot occurring at this point in the story of our school is remote but the roots of it can be sown at this time. Nothing should be taken for granted. A careful watch must always be maintained by all who care for the Tradition. A good leader will carefully consider all constructive criticism emanating from groups, private persons or through comments of visitors. Indeed, it is vital for every member of a school to be aware if something is amiss or it will be placed in jeopardy. One way to avoid decay and keep the Spirit present is to repay one's debt by serving the school when it needs most help during its dull times.

42. Service

The principle of paying one's debt is important in esoteric work. Initially, like a child, one is brought up and educated to a certain point. Because of this people assume that knowledge and assistance are free on the spiritual path. This is not so. As those who have gone beyond the nursery stage will inform you, the rest is the result of individual effort with occasional assistance of Grace at crucial moments. The Work, or *Avodah* in Hebrew, is exactly what it states. Consciousness does not rise spontaneously but through experience which everyone should know is not always just letting things happen. If this were the case, then mankind would still be at the animal and vegetable level of its evolution. Seen on a larger scale the Work is to continue the process begun by Enoch, the first individual to achieve full realisation. As Divine Scribe it is his task, as Metatron, to transmit the art and science of self-evolution by means of a Line of Teaching that has been maintained over the millennia by immense effort on the part of a few in each generation. Many people come to the Work assuming it to be free; and so it is to begin with until they realise it is their task to take on the responsibility to help those who follow. It is only then that they are truly on the Path, for there can be no movement until one's place has been filled and one can move on. This is the paying of the debt.

In the early stages of a school, the tutors bear most of the burden of organisation and raising the level of the students. Later, the elders aid in lifting the meetings by their conscious efforts and co-operation. As the groups become more than just a collection of people, others begin to contribute in their way by practical help that frees the tutors from concern about matters such as chairs and coffee cups. This means more energy is available to take the group higher because every tutor has only a certain amount of power on the human level. Yet more energy is released when senior students begin to take a sub-group in order to key newcomers into the language of Kabbalah and its principles. This allows a tutor to take the more advanced people yet deeper without being distracted by elementary questions or loss of force caused by people who do not as yet know how to work in concert. These subsidiary tasks not only pay back the debt a student owes to the Tradition but increase the amount of knowledge available to any student who gives extra time and effort. Take the case of the student running a sub-group. Here is a most fruitful exchange for it is a well-known fact that one learns more from teaching than from being taught. The same is true of any service rendered in the right spirit.

Service for what has been received is also observed in the form of students taking on various obligations. In one case it might be the maintenance team that keeps the school building in order and clean. Another example might be where a student is designated to be in charge of particular rituals, such as a morning meditation, or certain routine operations like being responsible for running the group's bookstall or making sure the kitchen is efficient. Some students might take on the task of researching a particular background subject that is of special interest to the group at this point, such as ancient theatres, time, biology or King Solomon. An example of this was the architect who presented a paper on the construction of early temples from a viewpoint of Kabbalah while another student gave a talk on mythology and its archetypal relationship to the sefirotic Tree. In one case, an assorted number of musicians gave a concert of esoterically-oriented music while another group presented a play in which the actors and the audience sought to maintain a conscious participation. Much was given and received on both sides.

Once a school has passed beyond the Malkhut, Yesod, Hod and Nezah stages and reached the Tiferet level, so much more can be done. If the hazards of over-organisation can be avoided, by periodically changing people's rôles so that they do not become too identified with their tasks, then many things are possible that were not available in the early days. For example, special study units can be set up to examine specific topics. One such group might be concerned with mathematics and the Tree or kabbalistic cosmology and modern astrophysics. These units would be for those especially qualified or interested in a subject that would be beyond the scope of many in the general group. Another project might be the detailed study of the human body in terms of the Tree while a different unit relates contemporary psychology to Kabbalistic principles. Yet another research unit could be concerned with tracing the historic connections between Kabbalah and other esoteric traditions. Sometimes, a school has students who know other languages, such as the man who could read Turkish and Aramaic as well as Hebrew. These skills could be put to good use.

Some units could specialise in the development of physical practices, like creating a repertoire of kabbalistic movements of the body or the exploration of new meditation techniques that require concentrated attention. Selection for specialist activities requires much discrimination and time, for to build up such units in a balanced way is no easy task. Many unready people, excited by a subject, would apply but if anything is to be accomplished only those judged likely to stay the course should be accepted.

Other less formal activities carried out by students paying their debts to the Tradition are those services which few see or even know about. These would be the individuals who help people in distress. It might be a one-off situation, like a student who is incapacitated by a passing illness, or a chronic situation in which someone needed constant support or special treatment. For example, sometimes there is a doctor in the school who deals with maladies as a kabbalistic physician which is exceedingly rare in the profession. Occasionally, there are psychotherapists in the school who give their service to people going through major crises during a transition period in their lives. There are many examples of people offering skilled assistance within a kabbalistic frame of reference. This is a real service because most professions are confined to a non-spiritual dimension in their outlook. Very few lawyers consider a case from the viewpoint of karma as one Kabbalist barrister does. The courts see only the immediate, never the long term effect on a fate.

Yet other people, perhaps less specialised but just as important in their service, might perform dozens of tasks that only someone under kabbalistic discipline could do. Just being around when needed could be crucial in someone's life. Knowing how to listen with conscious attention is another. These might not seem exceptional qualities to any decent person but here is the added dimension that the awareness generated includes the influence of the higher Worlds, so that a flow can pass through the listener or watcher and into the needy person or situation. One meets many people in various difficulties who require help, sometimes without realising it. The discerning Kabbalist will recognise such situations and, if it is appropriate, will take action ranging from direct practical intervention to a silent consciousness which draws the attention of the person out of the ego into the self by the Kabbalist merely being present at the level of Tiferet. This is often enough to induce improvement. Some people will remember perhaps a crucial conversation on a train with a stranger, not knowing they were being consciously advised in relation to their problem, and others in distress might not ever know that they were helped through prayer by a passerby who had interceded on their behalf. Service or *Avodah*, which is another meaning of the word for Work and worship, is not just confined to those in the specialist groups.

A special unit devoted to spiritual healing is a fine example of kabbalistic giving and receiving. Here the unit, under direction, rises up in consciousness from the elemental level, through the body and vegetable and animal intelligence into the awakening state. It then proceeds by degrees into the consciousness of the soul and the connection between everyone in the room. This is the Place of the Vessel that has been forged out of the Work done by the school. Here the unit might form a ring around the rim of the chalice and carry it up into the realm of the Spirit. This is done by ascending through the levels of Devotion, Purity, Sincerity, and into the fourth Heaven of 'Being with God' at the sefirah where the three upper Worlds meet at the Keter of Yezirah, that is the simultaneous Tiferet of Beriah and the Malkhut of Azilut. This is the focus of the Worlds of the psyche, spirit and Divine. Here a petition is voiced by the unit leader that the vessel be filled with Heavenly Dew. After a long pause of silent devotion, permission is then asked to transmit what has been accumulated down into the lower Worlds. Then, after taking leave of the Divine, the company slowly descends, carefully carrying the brimming chalice back to the place where the three lower Worlds meet at the Tiferet of the psyche which corresponds to the self of the unit. Here the Dew of Grace is dispensed either to a particular situation, if it is right, or allowed to flow wherever the Holy One wills to some place or people who particularly need it on Earth. The unit then makes the final descent back into the psyche and the body before stamping their feet and giving thanks to terminate the healing operation.

We now see that 'X"s original seed group has turned into a forest. From the tentative collection of unrelated people it has become an integrated organisation which has now not only matured but multiplied and developed its own methods, language, and way of operating between the Worlds. By now a distinct hierarchy will have emerged within the school and this leads to the issue of ordination in which individuals cross from the outer to the inner court of the Temple.

43. Ordination

A school is a co-ordinated association of groups, sub-units and individuals dedicated to propagating the Teaching. Such an organisation does not come into being without much preparation on the part of some very deeply committed people and without not a little help from above. Let us now look behind the scenes to observe what happens as the school reaches a crucial point when it takes a quantum jump. So far only the tutors are under any formal view of obligation and, as such, they form a conclave. Now there comes the time when the most advanced students have reached a level when they too can enter the inner council. This is done through the procedure of ordination which brings them into the circle of conscious responsibility.

Ordination in the priestly Line of Judaism died with the destruction of the Second Temple in Roman times. While the family name Cohen, or priest, still carries a courtesy rank, it no longer has any spiritual authority. This went to the Essenes and the rabbinical schools who possessed the *Barakah*, or Blessing, which was passed from master to disciple. The word 'Kabbalah' may also be translated as 'Tradition', or that which is handed down. In the rabbinical Line there has been periodic discussion about reinstating the ancient institution of ordination and whether it is permissible again without the Temple. While the debate about the outer form has gone on over the centuries Kabbalah has continued to practise a discreet mode of ordination in which individuals who 'knew of themselves', as the Tradition puts it, were invited into the circle of those who had dedicated their lives to the Work. Recognition was the primary reason for this acknowledgement but it also gave an authority to someone who, for example, was to start a new school or carry out a special project.

The saying 'many are called but few are chosen' has particular significance here because although certain people might appear to be ideal candidates they are never selected to be ordained for various reasons. There is no element of certainty in who should, for instance, succeed their tutor because many things can happen to block the potential individual. Such a person can be shown, under particular circumstances, to be subject to egoistic inflation or panic in a crucial moment of spiritual tension, thus destabilising a group. Indeed, it is observed that the most talented often have some fatal flaw that emerges when the person is given responsibility, like the man who could not resist misusing his gifts in order fascinate and seduce women who came for instruction.

This brings us to the qualifications for ordination. Reliability in itself is not sufficient because it could indicate a lack of imagination. A candidate has not only to know the theory and practice of Kabbalah from experience but be able to teach it in a living way. It is not enough to imitate a good teacher faithfully. One must make it one's own without getting in the way of the Teaching. The ability to deal with a group is a major consideration, as is the skill in handling a crisis, both in public and private situations. This means the person must have an advanced degree of personal maturity and several years experience of spiritual work, so that most of the problems likely to be encountered have been worked through and resolved into a true 'self'-confidence; that is, he has his own Tiferet connection. Here we have the traditional criterion of Kabbalah that a person should be an adult in worldly matters and steeped in the Teaching. The qualifications of marriage and sex should be interpreted according to the values of local conditions in which attitudes to partnership and spiritual commitment are taken into account.

Throughout the training of students a tutor will be on the look out for suitable candidates. Over time it becomes apparent who is likely to qualify for ordination. To check their calibre, these particular students are given tests in order to reveal their limits, both to themselves and the tutor. Increasing responsibility and temptation are put in their way and if they come through what sometimes appear to be arbitrary or even unjustified exercises then they are seriously considered as possibilities for what will be the inner conclave of the school.

If there is an element of doubt, because tutors are aware of their bias, then a second opinion is requested. For this tutors often turn to their own original tutor for consultation. This will result in a procedure in which, unbeknown to the prospective candidate, two already ordained people will be delegated to turn up at a meeting, perhaps at the beginner's group which the student is taking, to assess the ability and suitability of the person in relation to bearing witness to the Tradition. Very often the observers are total strangers to the student who sees them as casual visitors. Alternatively, they might meet over

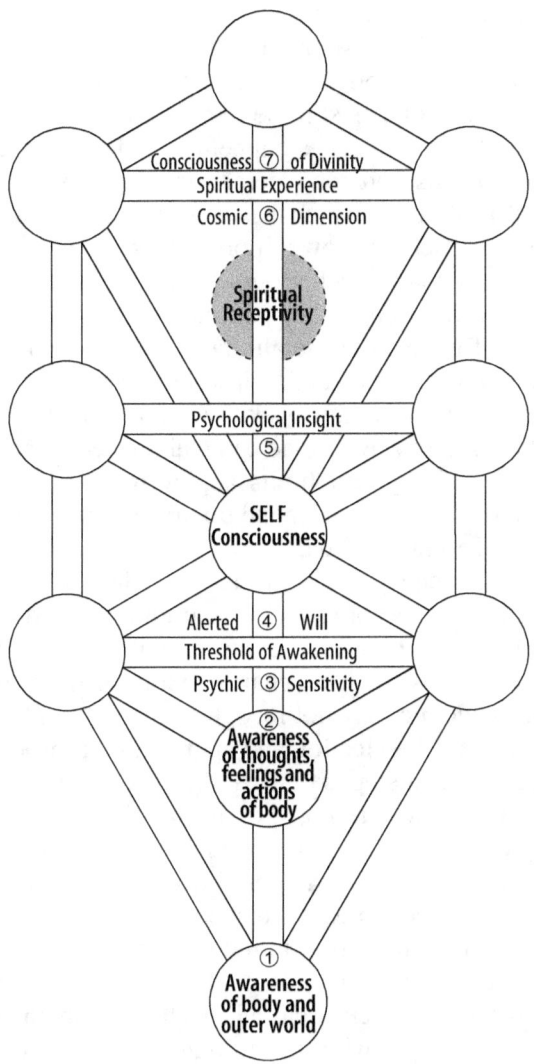

Figure 24 — THRESHOLD

As an individual evolves so they move up through different stages. These at first are experienced as flashes of consciousness at each new level. In time they become semi-permanent when required. For example, one becomes increasingly watchful of the body's state and the ego's performance. Likewise, when the will is applied, insight into one's own and others' souls is enhanced while cosmic consciousness can be obtained from time to time. Only when the Divine level is well established can the lower levels be permanent. This completion can only occur with great inner effort over one or many lifetimes. (Halevi.)

supper at the tutor's home or, by prearranged plan, in a seemingly accidental encounter in a restaurant where the student is observed and even questioned in an offhand way about life. If candidates are as astute as they are supposed to be they might suspect or realise that something out of the ordinary is happening and will act accordingly.

The reason for this apparent secrecy is that Kabbalah has always been a discreet Tradition in which the chain of connection is not obvious lest a structure generates power politics, as happens in any open organisation. In Kabbalah each group is considered autonomous, even though it be in affiliation with a particular school. Moreover, every tutor is master of his own house although they may confer with each other. In this way there are no high priests or popes. It is also a Tradition in which a student may not always know who is the tutor of his or her own instructor. In this way no one can claim direct descent from this or that teacher. This system limits achievement to personal merit. Thus every generation has to depend upon itself to be worthy enough to transmit the Teaching. Having a great teacher sometimes creates big problems in identity for a group, as it has in certain esoteric schools which have become living museums of how the master worked centuries ago in distant countries. Kabbalah is alive and well today because it does, in fact, change with the times although the orthodox and academic may not recognise the present form.

When the process of selection and approval by prospective peers is accomplished, the next step is to mark the candidates' coming change of status by a formal ceremony of declaration in which they are invited to accept the responsibilities of being members of the inner core of the school. This is carried out in secret in order to hold to the reality that it is, indeed, an esoteric society. There are many methods by which a student becomes initiated into the inner court of a Tradition. Some schools make a complex formality of the ceremony while others execute apparently casual enactments which, nevertheless, deeply affect the people who go through them. An example of one such method is for the candidate, who does not know as yet that he has been selected, to receive a letter of invitation. In this are stated the conditions for acceptance into a communion of those who are totally committed to the transmission of the Teaching and service to God. These conditions vary according to time and place but their essence is the same, that is:

'To acknowledge God. To aid the Divine to behold the Divine. To help in the work of unification. To speak only for oneself but to serve the Tradition in every way so as to perpetuate the Teaching for future generations.'

If the conditions are accepted by the candidates, they are then invited to be at a certain place at a particular time. This may be in a situation well known to the candidates or it could be in a strange location at an awkward hour. This is to put off anyone who, at the last moment, does not consider it important enough to make the effort. On arrival at the place the candidates might find one or two others from the group there and maybe someone else from another group utterly unknown to them. All would have been instructed in the invitation not to mention the arrangement to anyone, even intimates. Such discretion inevitably heightens the consciousness of the moment. This is intentional because the event is designed to be remembered in great depth.

The place where they meet might be a public building or a private house vacated for the purpose. There they wait until an often quite unfamiliar person arrives to conduct the ceremony before the members of the school conclave who are to act as witnesses. They are then taken, by a master of ceremonies, through the process of declaration of acceptance and ordination into the Tradition. This varies according to the Line and its customs. Some keep the ritual plain but terse in content, others spend some considerable time in building up to the moment when the candidates are asked if they will declare their acceptance of the responsibilities set out in the invitation before the witnesses. This moment is profoundly enhanced by a kabbalistic invocation so that there is no doubt that such a promise is as binding as a sacred marriage service. When the declarations are said and heard and the company is brought down again into the level of the mundane by the descending invocation, then the witnesses and the master of ceremonies retire but not before presenting each newly ordained individual with the symbolic present that should remind them of their promise. Sometimes, as said, it can be obvious like a seven-branched candlestick but occasionally it might be an object that catches the peculiar character of that particular person. There is great humour in Kabbalah.

The effect of such an ordination is profound and very often new initiates spend the following days pondering what happened and its implications. In some cases, it changes the course of individuals' lives as they realise to what they have committed themselves. Indeed, for some it means that they must go off on their own and begin again but at a different level. Occasionally, certain individuals take fright and do nothing for years, terrified of obligations they have taken on, until they are forced by circumstances to meet their promise. This can happen in the home, at leisure or in a profession. It does not always mean taking a new group.

To have a core of such initiates made up of people from various groups is a sign that a new phase of the school's Work has begun. This inner faculty is the basis of a different kind of operation. It is the spiritual triad of the School Tree and forms the contact point between the groups and the Line of the Tradition.

44. Schools

As an individual is held within a group and a group is part of a school, so a school fits into the wider field of a society. However, as people differ in character so do schools, although their essential objectives are the same. This is because each school must meet the need of a particular situation. Thus one may have, in New York, a school of traditional Kabbalah to match the criteria of the ultra-orthodox and a school of contemporary Kabbalah designed for people who have a modern western education. Moreover, there are schools in various parts of the same city that serve different Ashkenazi and Sefardi communities. The Hassidim, for example, have a *Chabad* form of teaching with its emphasis on intellect while the Rabbi Nachman school uses the mode of fables to transmit the Torah. This situation is found all round the world.

Besides the purely Jewish Lines there are Kabbalistic schools that have a blend of other cultural backgrounds. An example of this was the Medici Academy in Florence where an important Renaissance School used to meet. The Florentine Pico della Mirandola, the Christian Kabbalist, and Dante, who wrote the *Divine Comedy*, were both influenced deeply by rabbis and *conversos* fleeing from Spain who were delighted to transmit the Teaching to genuine seekers. The schools of Italy, France, England and Germany were profoundly grateful for this influx of Kabbalah. Robert Fludd, the 17th century English mystic, learnt much from his rabbinical acquaintances, and the Cambridge Neo-Platonists who met at Lady Anne Conway's house in Warwickshire obviously had access to kabbalistic ideas coming from Holland where there was a school. The kabbalistic symbols seen in the literature and churches of Germany indicate that schools of Kabbalah existed there, as they did in the Austrian and Ottoman Empires.

Some of these schools have continued as living Lines and others have decayed and gone leaving only a trace, like the Tarot, that eloquent Hermetic-Kabbalistic pack of cards originally designed for esoteric contemplation but now, alas, mostly used for personal divination. The same degeneration of the Teaching has occurred within the Lines of mainstream Kabbalah in that many Jews think of it as being only concerned with magic. Fortunately, schools are not just composed of individuals but an ever-moving generation of seekers, and so schools blossom and fade and blossom again over several centuries before finally withering. Much of what happens in a school is largely unseen by the outside world which is why there is so little evidence for scholars. One has to have been through a school to know what really goes on. However, sometimes one gains an insight into their workings if one goes to the sites of schools that still exist.

Take, for example, Gerona. If one spends some time in the ancient part of the town, it soon becomes clear to the perceptive that it was a cultural and spiritual hotbed in the Middle Ages. None of the Kabbalists who lived there could have avoided the influence of the University and Cathedral over-shadowing the Juderia. To meditate in the hidden garden of Rabbi Nachmanides and sit in the upper room of the old synagogue reveals much about the Gerona school and its attitudes. No French or German Kabbalists could have accomplished what those Catalans did. The cultural climate was just right for what had to be done. Not even the sophisticated Toledans could produce such metaphysics. The Gerona scheme was the one that changed the face of Kabbalah.

Something of a school's particular approach can be detected in the kind of literature it produces. Some, for instance, used the visionary method which generated the Merkabah accounts. Others used the Hebrew alphabet for meditation and contemplation while some worked within the context of the scriptures. Many worked through the mode of the parable, some through poetry and others legal jargon, depending on the situation. Not everyone used the Tree or metaphysical speculation.

When Safed was a great kabbalistic centre in the sixteenth century there were schools that were quite open and used everyday activity as a kabbalistic way of life from birth to death. This was a unique situation in that the locals were aware of the Tradition and accepted it. Some schools have a door onto the street which acts as a two-way connection, like the Yoshevei ha Klaus Centre in Poland, whose sages were consulted by the community. The Sufis had the same system. The Konya school in Turkey was not only the home of Dervish turning but a centre of considerable influence on the city. The Buddhist and

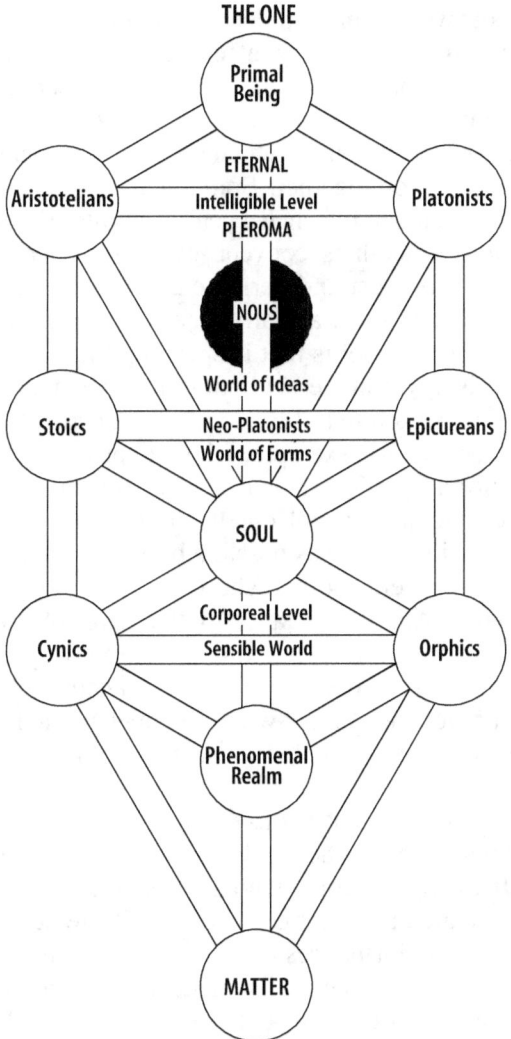

Figure 25—TRADITION
Here the various ancient Hellenic schools are set out on the Tree according to their characteristics and classical cosmology. At the top come the inspirational Platonists, with the reason-based Aristotelians as their complement. Below, Epicureans speak of how to enjoy pleasure while the Stoics learn to endure the pain of life on Earth. Beneath them come the degenerates who sneered at whatever came their way or exploited every instinct. The Neo-Platonists are an amalgam of the four upper lines and were the culmination of Greek revelation and reason. Here is also seen the Hellenic version of the four Worlds in the Eternal, the Worlds of Ideas, Forms and the Sensible realm. (Halevi.)

Christian schools worked in a similar way in their localities. In modern times the circumstances are very different. Today the monasteries are gone but we find esoteric schools operating in renovated mansions deep in the country where people retreat for six months' intense work; and schools in old town houses which are used as a centre for groups to gather separately or together. Some schools meet each week in different places but assemble once a year in a building especially hired for the occasion. Yet others convene every five years, maintaining individual contact by post and periodic councils of senior members. More than one school never actually meets in the physical World.

The function of a school is that it opens up the transpersonal scale of operation. It is a cosmic vessel both to receive and transmit higher influences and be sensitive to the moods and needs of the country in which it exists. Thus, for example, when a spiritual teacher came to Europe without any particular plan except to project his meditation and technique it took a school quietly to set up an organisation to manage the operation. This was possible because of applied discipline, a communication system and knowhow in presenting the teacher to a Western audience. Another instance of this level of operation is the worldwide network that holds a noon meditation for peace as the Sun touches the meridian in each country. This keeps up a twenty-four hour cycle of prayer and contact with the upper Worlds, thus allowing no break in the flow of Divine Light and spiritual influence into global consciousness.

Some schools publish translations of classic spiritual texts for seekers that are distributed round the world while others set up colleges in various countries where people who are not committed members can study subjects related to esoterica. The Rudolf Steiner School, which has many kabbalistic influences in its teaching, is an example of this. They also have educational establishments for children where the soul and spirit are nurtured as well as the mind, heart and body. Purely kabbalistic schools are less conspicuous in this field but their effects can be seen in the cultural backgrounds of Gabirol, Spinoza, Freud and Einstein, all of whom brought the dimension of the other Worlds into their areas of work.

A school takes a long time to gestate and mature. It will have its trials, crises and rebellions, as well as creative and dull periods. There will be times when groups, like individuals, break away for both good and bad reasons and there will be moments when the ever-lurking Lucific element seeks to destroy it through people seeking power and glory in a way they cannot gain in the world. This occurred in one school in which the leader saw himself as a Renaissance Duke with his court of philosophers, poets and artists. This charade was maintained by ranks of devotees who served obediently until, one by one, they realised they were being trapped and not freed. A similar thing happened in nineteenth century Russia when certain rabbis became elevated to sainthood by virtue of birth and projection on the part of their congregations. To avoid these dangers requires discrimination from everyone in a school. Nothing should be accepted just because it comes via a chain of instruction. This does not mean everything should be opposed because it emanates from authority but that spiritual commonsense should be applied at every level so as to prevent a school from becoming a party machine, as happened to the Holy Office during the Inquisition period in Spain.

On a practical level a school can have a direct effect on society. Some schools, for example, publish books and magazines, others through their members have influenced the media, government, law and medicine. Study groups have affected religious institutions, produced papers on economics and altered academic thinking. Some schools have changed education, introduced new concepts into psychology and even astronomy. Certain schools have built up libraries and helped scholars while others have aided in the drafting of state constitutions. More than one school has created a style in architecture by constructing buildings based upon esoteric ideas. Schools have been known to provide special scholarships and, in medieval times, start universities. The great cathedrals were conceived by people who belonged to schools and, without doubt, many of the clerks involved in the design were acquainted with Jewish Kabbalists of the time. Indeed, it is interesting to note that the Juderias of Chartres and Béziers, the Cathar city, are close to their cathedrals. It is also significant that the most creative spiritual period in Spain, which brought forth a new form of Sufism and Kabbalah, was at a time when Jewish and Arabian schools met and exchanged their views via the medium of philosophy. Moreover, the dissemination of these new esoteric interpretations of the Bible and Koran could not have occurred so rapidly throughout the West and the Middle East if it had not been for the spiritual highways guarded by the Templars and the various schools of translators, like the ones in Toledo and Lunel that acted as literary exchanges.

The life of a school extends far beyond the span of an individual and so we are unlikely to perceive the effect of a contemporary school upon the global society in which we now live. Times have changed and schools are no longer confined to one city or country. Kabbalah is now studied where there were once only Red Indians; it is practised in busy Manchester as well as in Brussels, in the seclusion of a Canadian backwater and off a smart street in Mexico City. Books on Kabbalah are written in Hebrew, English, Latin, Aramaic, Yiddish and Ladino and they are no longer confined to the learnèd or the orthodox. There is a need being met today that allows those who seek that mode of spirituality to pursue the same path as the Kabbalists of old did in the Temple, synagogue and study house. Moreover, the division between religions is slowly narrowing so that Jew, Muslim and Christian, all of whom stem from the same root, are ceasing to regard each other as unbelievers. It is now possible for educated people to study openly the same sacred Teaching that is embodied in the traditions of Kabbalah, Sufism and esoteric Christianity without loss of cultural integrity.

All the foregoing gives perhaps a sense of the scale of a school. It is of an order above the experience of the personal because it relates not to one life but to history. Beyond this lies the Line of a school which is yet another measure in time wherein the continuity of a school carries, over the centuries, a particular mode of presentation, like the rituals of the Masons or the alphabetical meditations of the Abulafian Line.

45. Introductory Course

Let us assume that perhaps a decade has passed and that our school has grown into a well-integrated organisation of about five hundred core members with a periphery element of about thirty people coming into or passing out of its orbit. By this time the general efficiency would have reached its peak as the school resolves into its optimum level of operation. Three hundred to five hundred members is about the right scale for a school in which everybody can be acquainted with everyone else. Above this size, the personal element begins to be lost and a school breaks up into segments that never meet. Organisations of a larger order do exist but they tend to become institutional if they are over-governed by a central council; and this can lead to esoteric politics which, being more potent than the secular kind, can and often do destroy a school from the inside. The decadent periods of Hasmonean and Byzantine religious history illustrate this principle well in the orthodox Jewish and Christian Traditions.

When our imaginary school reaches its fully operational phase it will probably have its own house or, at least, a place which it hires for communal activities if the groups still meet in private homes. It would almost certainly have a beginner's group, where people can learn the theory and techniques of Kabbalah, and several special study units besides the general meetings that happen each week. The structure of each group would be governed by the experience and circumstances of its members and tutor. There would also be a senior group taken by the head tutor who may or may not be the original instructor 'X'. Sometimes the old leader is removed. This can be for either good or bad reasons. In this Work there is no guarantee that one will see a project through to its conclusion. One may be needed elsewhere. Centred at the heart of the school would be the conclave of advisors constituting an inner council. These might be formally elected or secretly initiated elders, according to whether the school was run as a democracy or by a now-experienced master.

The programme of the school at this point should have been well worked out. There would be the regular activities of meetings, meditations and ritual practices and the ongoing specialist study and working that explore and develop esoteric themes in terms of perhaps science and art. For example, the periodic table of chemical elements may have been related to the ten sefirot and the unit studying esoteric design may have produced a kabbalistic mandala for meditation. During the Golden Age of Moorish Spain the schools of the various traditions conceived and created poetry and prayers based upon selected lines from scripture which are clearly metaphysical in construction. Ibn Gabirol's poem *Keter-Malkhut* is a fine example of this with its image of Jacob's Ladder built up in verse. While most of these activities are not usually seen in public, there is a very important point of contact where a school presents the Tradition to the world. This is the open introductory course that develops out of the occasional public lecture, if there is a clear response for further information.

Such a course might be organised in the following way. First a decision is come to by the chief tutor or council that such a policy should be initiated. This follows the rule that a school should provide the Teaching for those who seek it. Next, it must be decided how it should be done. Some schools use the hard sell technique, like certain Hassidim who operate as zealous missionaries. Other schools will do just the opposite so that only those who are in earnest will seek them out. Or there is the balance between these extremes in the operation that sets up a weekend workshop for those who might be interested in Kabbalah. This might be done within the context of an already existing organisation that handles educational courses, ranging from yoga classes to talks on the mystery religions. Kabbalah might be just one item on their international programme. Or the school might advertise in its own right by mail or through journals concerned with esoteric-religious matters. Out of this might come forty or fifty responses to a residential weekend to be held in the country or a one day course in town.

The venue may or may not be owned by the school, and it might or might not be staffed by them, apart from those needed to monitor it. The residential type of operation would require a house, crew and people to see things run smoothly, so that the tutor taking the course is not bothered by the booking-in process, payments and a dozen other administration problems, like managing the small bookstall that is always called for at such introductory courses. The tutor might be the head of the school but it is usually someone who has the gift of public presenting. An otherwise excellent group taker is not always the best person to introduce Kabbalah to the public which needs to be entertained as well as informed. The Hassidic rabbis were masters of this art with their penetrating stories and jokes.

The course may begin on Friday evening when everyone can get to know each other over dinner. After coffee the company would then gather in the lecture hall where the tutor initiates the course with a silent meditation and then an open invocation for the Holy Spirit to come down and watch over the proceedings. This ritual precedes every session with the repetition of the names of the sefirot going up from Malkhut to Keter. The evening is then continued, perhaps with an introductory slide lecture on the general history of the Tradition and its principles. In this the relationship between man, the universe and the Divine are shown in images drawn from every source to show the variations of the Teaching down the ages. Such themes as the Tree of Life, the purpose of Existence and the many levels of correspondence can be developed as the diagram of Jacob's Ladder illustrates how mankind aids God to behold God. After the slides can come questions with answers that whet the soul's appetite for the following day.

The first session of Saturday, or the Jewish Sabbath, might be devoted to prayer, silent or otherwise. This could be optional. The second session, starting at 9.30 am after breakfast, would be a detailed account of the theory of the macrocosm of the universe followed, after coffee at 11.00 am, with a similar exposition on the composition of a human being—the microcosm.

These sessions are extremely useful as questions of particular interest emerge which help the tutor to assess at what level the group can operate. This session should finish at 1.00 pm sharp for lunch, after which the group should take the afternoon off so that people can digest the theory and rest, as one should on the Sabbath after studying the Torah. It also gives people time to get to know one another better as they go out for walks or talk in their rooms. Tea should be ready by 4.00 pm and the next session start at 4.30 pm with the lecture hall cleared for the Way of Action.

In this session the emphasis is entirely physical with the students following the tutor's directions as they stand about the room. Such techniques, as working the Tree in terms of the head, trunk and limbs should generate a practical awareness of kabbalistic principles[2]. As the exercises become more complex, so should a consciousness of

---

2. See Chapter 29

symbolic gesture deepen until it is seen that certain bodily configurations create the capacity to carry a charge of inner power. This process will begin to separate out the mineral, vegetable and animal levels of the body from the human so that, when the group goes through the procedure of sitting in the Tree made up of chairs, they will experience the potency of each sefirah as they literally move up the Tree in a procession led by the tutor from Malkhut to Keter. The session should culminate with a moment of physical stillness and silence before breaking for supper at 6.00 pm.

The session beginning at 8.30 pm that evening is the one working on the Way of the Heart. Here again, we use the techniques we described earlier[3], such as forming a heart of chairs and slowly working up the feeling triad by making it beat as the group alternates each side in active and passive states. Then emotion can be evoked by recalling important moments and relationships in one's life and considering their pleasures and pains. Deep questioning of unsolved issues then leads to prayers of petition which might reveal the answer to this or that problem. Here, as in the previous session, there should be a periodic pause for students to make observations on their experience. As a rule the tutor might comment or question but never criticise the material that emerges. The session should gradually resolve into a silent meditation led by the tutor in which any questions formulated as a result of the work done are asked inwardly while in a state of quiet or highly active inner emotion depending on what arises in individuals. As the tutor brings the company into contact with the Heart of Hearts, they should experience what ought to be felt in a truly religious service before the tutor slowly brings them down into the mundane by 9.30 pm with the invocation used in the school to end the day. The group should then silently disperse and relax for the rest of the evening elsewhere in the building.

The Sunday morning meditation, before breakfast, should be optional. The session beginning at 9.30 am is concerned with the Way of Contemplation. Here the room should be arranged facing the two diagrams of the single Tree and Jacob's Ladder. After the tutor has begun the day with the invocation, the question should be asked, 'What is the difference between the soul and the spirit?' After a brief account of the relationship between the four Worlds, the tutor should then ask the students to carry on by deduction from the diagram and observation based on experience and begin to differentiate between

---
3. See Chapter 28

the psychological and the cosmic aspects of the universe and a human being. Out of the ensuing discussion much will arise that will clarify, with the gentle guidance of the tutor, what exactly is the soul which most people assume is the same as the spirit. Many new facts will emerge, such as the soul being a filter, a place of focus and a part of the psyche that is concerned with the personal, as against the transpersonal aspect of the spirit. The session should be terminated by the group drawing some conclusions never considered before and break for coffee at 11 am sharp, after coming down the Tree. Punctuality is part of the discipline. One can easily miss one's moment.

After coffee the group should be taken on an interior journey by the tutor while they sit in a circle. In this they ascend, in imagination, out of the physical and psychological Worlds, via a series of steps that takes them from the familiarity of their home into a strange country where they sleep and dream a precognitive dream. They then go on to cross the psychological sea to a yet stranger land where the Wise One lives. This being takes each individual on up the Holy Mountain, through the clouds of the spirit and into the Golden City at its peak, where they go to the great Temple and through its courts to stand before the veil of the Holy of Holies. From here the tutor brings them slowly down the same route and back into the room. Now the people reflect on what they have been shown as the tutor explains the kabbalistic structure of the journey, which has been punctuated by periodic pauses to give observations on what was seen for the others to share, before earthing for lunch at 1.00 pm.[4]

After lunch there should be an hour's debriefing and feedback session in which comments and questions are made. The company should then disperse after tea, some with the address of a school's contact point in their pockets if they wish to follow up the weekend. More important is that the operation was well done and that the Work has come into the public domain. In this way, the school gives out to and keeps in touch with the world. Having seen one external operation, let us now examine some others that are occasionally mounted when the time is right.

---

4. See author's *The Kabbalist at Work* (Kabbalah Society) for a detailed account.

46. Production

Taking the mode of Action at the level of a kabbalistic school, there are two ways in which this might be applied to creative and spiritual work. The first is the static approach on the pillar of form and the second the dynamic on the pillar of force, as they are sometimes called. The equilibrium of the middle pillar would be manifest in the consciousness used in either case. All spiritual Traditions have their equivalents to these modes of Action. The great cathedrals and mosques are examples of the static with church music and Dervish dancing corresponding to the dynamic. The difference between these and their secular parallel is that they are based upon esoteric principles and therefore resonate and transmit the presence of higher Worlds when they are entered or witnessed. Anyone walking into Chartres Cathedral or the Blue Mosque in Istanbul, hearing Allegri's celestial music sung by King's College choir or seeing the Dervishes spin on an axis of stillness will experience that other-worldliness in manifestation on Earth as it is in Heaven.

Schools, being made in the same image of God as people, contain higher consciousness which seeks to be expressed in all the Worlds. The most immediate level is that of the concrete and so naturally something which involves the physical elements is an obvious example of a spiritual monument. Before there were sophisticated temples, certain areas were set aside and marked out as holy spaces. There is good reason to believe, for example, that the original Stonehenge was just a circle of small markers, the great sarsens and their lintels being added later as masonry techniques developed. Thus, the simplest form of an esoteric site is a space that has been separated and ordered according to a spiritual notion. We see this concept at perfection in the Zen garden which is a miniature model of the universe. All over the world, in every culture there is the equivalent, as far apart as Tibet or Morocco, Mexico or Australia. Such places are designed to make a sanctuary in the midst of the activity of Nature, which is conducive to meditation upon interior matters or the contemplation of exterior concerns related to the cosmos. Here we have our design brief for a kabbalistic garden.

The site of such a place would probably be within the grounds of the school's house. It might be behind the walls of a property in a big city or part of the land attached to a place in the country. The reason for its construction would be a mixture of a working exercise and the desire to create, form and make a holy space outside the house where people could directly observe Heaven and Earth in operation. This gives us the criterion for the ground plan. Firstly, the garden must have a directional axis, as well as a series of ascending levels. Here we have the interaction of two major concepts setting their mark upon the design. If it is decided to raise one end of the garden, rather than a central elevation, the other elements would have to be adapted accordingly so that the pillars and the sefirot are eloquently interwoven within the layout of earth, water, air and light. All this has to be worked out in the drawing board phase, before a blade of grass is pulled out or a stone moved. There may be modifications later but these will be minor alterations after the plan has been evolved to its most refined stage by much discussion.

Once the design is approved the construction can begin. Then a working party, composed of those with special skills, would be chosen, supported by a rota of students from every group (in a great cycle of shifts to get everything right), because it is not just an ordinary job but a labour of Love in which every stone is selected and the soil carefully sifted. The digging of water channels, perhaps to represent the paths or triads, is a construction and geometric problem that will require intense concentration; so too will the building up of the garden levels that express, by their character of bushes and flowers, the qualities of various senses or states of being. An elaborate pond might, for instance, represent the Yesodic ego with a deep well for Daat, the place of Knowledge, while a beautiful fountain at the centre of the design, made of three distinct materials, could symbolise the Self of Tiferet. The layout of the garden should indicate which side is the Merciful by it being placed on the south perimeter, as opposed to a shaded north for Severity. There could be seats for each sefirah or particular triads with an altar at the Crown position of Keter at the eastern head of the garden.

Over the years, certain plants could be cultivated to detail the qualities of different parts of the Tree with seasonal colours expressing the nature of the triads and sefirot. In time the garden will reach its peak of perfection. People will enter it to restore or improve the balance in themselves by working there or just sitting and walking. Such a place will eventually acquire an extraordinary atmosphere so that individuals coming in from a hectic working day will seek its Grace in which to quieten down before attending meetings. Some will come just to sit and watch the heavens move or seasons turn in utter silence, even though outside the walls the noise and movement of the workaday world continues unabated. Such gardens give an access to Paradise and many rare and deep moments will be experienced in the stillness and beauty of the place. It will be like no ordinary garden, however well kept and elegant, because it was dedicated, at its inception, as a place where the Holy Spirit can come down and meet the Companions of the Light as they refresh themselves there in an earthly Eden.

The dynamic opposite to such a garden would be a kabbalistic miracle play. In this project the design phase would be a script, perhaps based upon an existing story or fable. It might be from the Bible or an entirely original plot thought up by a member or creative group within the school. Its ingredients should be a balance of strong story and spiritual content. In other words it should follow the dramatic sequence of: 1) a normal situation, 2) intrusion of a disturbing factor, 3) conflict, 4) development, 5) crisis and 6) resolution—the result being an inward evolution rather than the usual 'happy ever after' or 'everyone dead' of conventional drama. Having designed the general plot, the rôles should represent various principles, either as individual personifications, such as angels and demons, or characters that contain opposing elements struggling within themselves like Dr. Jekyll and Mr. Hyde.

Seen in kabbalistic terms a play or mime could set out, in dramatic form, the interaction of the four Worlds or the relationship between the sefirot. Likewise a ballet might illustrate, in costume, set, light and dance, the journey of a person up the Tree and the various phases to be met. Similarly, a carefully written script could, with deep acting, develop a crisis of consciousness between just two protagonists, each of whom represents a pillar, with a third character bringing about a resolution. A pantomime, bringing in all the levels of mineral, plant, animal, human, angelic and demonic, could be not only much fun for the school drama society but an extremely powerful expression of the Work at the end of a yearly session. Fables like Cinderella, which contain many esoteric ideas, can easily be adapted for kabbalistic work. If Cinderella is the soul, then the step mother could be ego with the ugly sisters acting as the wilful and willess aspects of Hod and Nezah. The prince is clearly the spirit with the king as Keter. The rest of the story could be very amusingly adapted with the pumpkin as the vegetable level and the mice that pull it as the animal level. The setting of the kitchen as the lower part of the World of Action and the ball at the palace as Paradise is a designer's dream where soul and spirit meet and unite in a mystic marriage.

In an esoteric school the actual production process of drama lends itself to kabbalistic work. Thus, instead of the usual displays of temperament and ego associated with such theatrical operations, discipline and attention would be a vital part of the action. The various areas of construction, management and acting are ideal for the creative use of skills and for developing self-knowledge. The inevitable crises during rehearsals, when costumes are not quite right and the lighting is not on cue, are perfect situations for self-observation and learning how to relate to something bigger than one's own desires. The very delicate operation of directing the actors' moves and the liaison between the technicians and the cast will reveal much to everyone involved. For example, the greatest performers are invariably the most modest and courteous to members of the stage staff and the most professional of stage managers understand the working principles of every practical discipline from the electronics to painting, from the printing of programmes to the making of a prop suit of armour. The exercise of being aware of timing is most useful, not only on stage but in the sequence in which different departments must produce and integrate their contributions.

The director, of course, like a tutor is a key person in the operation. It does not matter if it is a dance routine, a mime, a complex operetta or play, the essential problems are the same. The director has to hold constantly the pivotal idea and maintain the inner connection while everybody else only sees his own aspect of the production. The director might be severe or merciful in dealing with people but the sight of the essential objective should never be lost; that is, to make people aware that they are expressing spiritual principles. There may be moments when the dialogue between two characters is flat or two dancers are over assertive, when the music does not create the right mood and the setting is too dull. All these things can disturb the director's equilibrium. However, he or she must never become identified with the notion that it is his/her production. It is dedicated to God. In this way an entirely different spirit can pervade the production as the influence coming down from the Keter of the Company is held by the Tiferet position of the director.

During the production several kabbalistic principles can be observed. First the will to do it emulates the conceptual level of Creation. Then the design of the form emerges in the style of the play, setting and costumes. Having been earthed, the Asiyyatic aspect is manifested in the construction of the scenery and props with the Yeziratic level emerging in the gradual cohesion of the rehearsals as the company integrates. There is always a certain point in any production when the spirit of the play manifests and something is indeed breathed into what is going on. Suddenly it has a life of its own. In this case the object is to take it still further, so that everyone is as truly conscious as she can be as she performs her various tasks. As the rehearsals come up to the night of presentation, everything should integrate at all levels as each person seeks to perfect and serve what is being transmitted through whatever this particular task is. If the audience is the rest of the school, then they, too, will participate in the performance and raise it far beyond any experience felt in an ordinary theatre. If the production is public, then the audience should be in a state like those who have just witnessed a deeply religious ceremony, even though what they saw might have been a pantomime or a modern version of Shakespeare's *The Tempest*, which is a fine example of an esoteric miracle play. If a performance is carried out consciously, then the whole dimension is different and people are profoundly affected as they resonate with what has been presented. This was how the ancient Greek schools transmitted their teaching. In our times, spiritual adepts make miracle movies like the *Star Wars* series or a TV series such as *Kung Fu*.

47. Retreat

In accordance with the Way of Devotion, some schools are able to provide special places of retreat. These, in principle, are designed to isolate the person physically from the distractions of ordinary life, so that they may devote their attention completely to the interior work of the heart. In ancient times people who were inclined to this method retired into the desert or deep into the forest so as not to be caught up in the trivia of city living. Moreover, they often became ascetics in order not to be involved in the trials and pleasures of personal relationships that, to them, obscured the clear view of the Divine which they sought. Some people who could not retire from life, because of family or professional commitments, created similar spaces for retirement in their homes with special rooms in which they were not to be disturbed during certain hours. Others, who could not even manage this, were instructed by their spiritual mentors to make a separated space within themselves as they lived amidst the hurly burly of life. This was known by the Greco-Egyptian Tradition of Hermes Trismegistus as being 'Hermetically Sealed', which gave rise to the term 'Hermit' being used for the early desert fathers of Christianity and those strange holy men in the forests of the King Arthur legends. In Hebrew the words *Kodesh, Kaddish,* and *Kaddashah,* meaning 'sacred', have their source in the root idea 'to be separated'.

In the Judaic and Kabbalistic Tradition complete retirement from the world was discouraged, not only because the Bible stated that marriage and family were part of creation but that ordinary life had to be raised to the level of the sacred. Therefore, while there were prophets and sages who lived in the desert, groups like the monastic order of the Essenes were the exception and were reactions, like those of the desert fathers, to the corruption of the cities and a decadent priesthood.

There has always been a strong devotional element in Judaism which is apparent in the psalms and the vast array of prayers to be found in the Jewish liturgy. In Kabbalah prayers were especially designed to take the devotee up the Tree and hold them in what was called *devekut* or close affiliation with the Holy One. This, however, required a certain training that could only be received from an adept in Kabbalah who taught one not just to pray with the mouth and heart, but with conscious intention which was called *kavvanah*. A kabbalistic school, therefore, would not only provide a building or a room especially set aside for such meditations but teach the art of meditation. Such a course might be taught over a weekend, during a week or over a fortnight of concentrated effort. The mode might be the form of the daily cycle of prayers, as in a monastery, or special sets of prayers and inner exercises in the work of the heart. These we will outline in a moment because first we must see how a school can provide the facilities for such things to happen. The place where these disciplines can be practised clearly needs quiet and so a room in a town house far from the noise of the street would be a prerequisite. For a school with a house in the country this is no problem, indeed certain hours, days or weeks could be devoted exclusively to meditation. Perhaps a school that could afford it would convert for this purpose a small outbuilding like those found on old farms. Schools have been known to provide huts for solitary meditation as well as to refurbish barns adapted for large gatherings of meditators. These may be simple white-washed spaces or carefully set out areas with centres of focus like a kabbalistic mandala or a desk for the scrolls of the Torah. It depends on the inclination of that particular branch of the Tradition.

Those in need of deep solitude at certain points could be provided for by a school, inasmuch as someone takes the responsibility of meeting their practical requirements during their retreat so as to leave them completely free for their devotions. This may be at a crucial period in that person's development when, for example, an over-worked businessman needs to be in total silence away from outward activity for a time in order to regain his equilibrium and make contact with the Divine. People in this state should have discreet supervision through a tutor, skilled in the art of meditation, who visits them from time to time in their seclusion. This will keep their meditations from wandering into fantasy or preoccupations with their current problem. To learn how to petition the Divine from the place of the self and not the ego is not easy and requires guided practice. This and many other solitary exercises can be carried out under the unique conditions a school can supply.

A meditation group could be composed of outsiders who come for specific instruction or a composite of members from different groups throughout the school who are either learning or carrying out a particular operation. An obvious example of this is the Sabbath Day service in which the meditation group meet and endeavour to celebrate with the highest level of conscious participation. Such a phenomenon is very rarely found in the ordinary conditions of a synagogue, church or mosque where it is usually a social rather than a spiritual occasion. Under the auspices of a school, the level of meditation reached should be as deep as that found in any genuine religious order. The synagogue of the Bet El school in the Old City of Jerusalem was a place of this order. Here, the atmosphere was famous for its serene spirituality and melody; which brings us on to the various modes of meditation that can be taught.

Besides the performance of an orthodox service in the state of *devekut*, there is the collective practice of forming a vessel to catch the Dew of Heaven. This is done by a group that is used to this way of working under the direction of a leader. The purpose of such an exercise may be simply to give the experience to those not yet familiar with excursions into the higher Worlds and to collect and then discharge the spiritual substance accumulated in the group vessel for healing or general good use. Such an art takes time to master and the group in question might be in training for some specific task later. The effect of such experiences is to saturate the place and people present with the influx of the Heavens so that they know what it is like to exist in that state of consciousness for a sustained period, as very few individuals can maintain that level by themselves when surrounded by distractions.

Another course in meditation might be to work on the various levels of will in the body and psyche. Here, the tutor takes the group up from the desire for inertia in the elemental body, through the appetitive hunger of the vegetable soul and into the restlessness of the animal level. From here the group is confronted with the wilfulness of the right pillar and the willessness of the left pillar as they pass through the stage of willingness into the awakening triad of self-will before entering the soul triad of 'not my will, but Thine'. When this state is attained then real meditation can begin as the group moves up into the triad of the spirit and beyond to experience contact with the Divine. After a period in deepest communion, the group is then led back down to spend the rest of the time in the particular form of prayer agreed for that session.

The foregoing is, in fact, a preparation for meditation and this might take the mode of a silent session in which each person does her private devotion or a communal effort that uses a specific technique. This might be a kabbalistic mantra, such as one of the Names of God which the group repeats in an endless chain, or the recitation of the sefirotic cycle in which the group goes up and down the Tree. The holy title 'I AM THAT I AM' is one which, over a period of time, becomes a transcendental sound of pure being as the group chants its implication in a song of praise and affirmation. Such a prayer is not to be taken lightly as one must not speak the Name of the Lord in vain; and so the atmosphere of the room must be made sacred by the invocation of the Tree and the asking for Divine permission.

Some schools organise meditation centres throughout a large area, even nationally. They may, moreover, invite prominent teachers of their Tradition to come and talk about prayer, either to invited audiences of school members or to the public, thus enabling people not involved in direct self-development to come to hear about meditation and even to go on courses held at the school or a place hired for the purpose. In this way a school passes on into the world in a very practical way what Grace it has received. For example, in every school there will be people with a particular inclination to the devotional method; and these people act as tutors to classes outside the school who want to learn the art of prayer; for prayer must be practised consciously if it is to have any effect on the person or the Worlds above. The initial exercises of how to hold the attention of the mind on one word at a time and ask, 'Lord, teach me to be receptive' are not to be found in the standard prayer books of religion. A course on prayer enables many people to return to their religious roots with a new dimension added that could not have occurred without the help of people from an esoteric school.

The large scale effect of such operations is seen in the rise of the local synagogue in ancient Jewish communities, far from the Temple in Jerusalem. The Christian monastic system and its civilising effect on the countryside of pagan Europe is another example, as are the Sufi Tekkes of Turkey which allowed ordinary folk to taste something of the mystical side of Islam. The Hassidic movement is a classic esoteric operation which taught a desolated community how to pray with joy, overcome grief and restore faith amid the most awful conditions of persecution. Here kabbalistic ideas were given out to the people and, though most of them did not know the inner details of the prayers, their performance transformed the collective attitude, so that they saw life as a process of redeeming the Divine sparks hidden in the darkness of their desperate situation. Direct contact with the higher Worlds had been the exclusive domain of learned rabbis up to that point but, from that time on, a devout peasant could experience the ecstasy of *devekut* by practising prayer in a certain way. This had not been the case for centuries.

Access to higher knowledge is the essence of Kabbalah. For some it comes through action and for others through devotion. Now we look at the method of contemplation for those with the temperament of intellect when applied at the level of a school.

48. Conference

One of the tasks of an esoteric school, of whatever Tradition, is to transmit the Teaching about the relationship between man, the universe and God to the contemporary generation in its own terms. Work at the individual and group levels is a simple and direct operation, in that the people are actually in intimate contact with the Tradition and wish to learn about the higher Worlds. In the case of the general public there are a myriad of preoccupations and diversions, ranging from the need to survive to the latest fashion in ideas. This applies to the social, political, scientific, artistic and religious communities which, on the whole, cling to past ways of looking at the world about them; even the most radical concepts often being no more than an unconsidered reaction against conditions. To change means that something quite new has to occur, not just a swing of the pendulum. Such a transformation is possible in the moment of equilibrium between two extremes but only if there is a conscious element that can inject a new dimension. This injection is the historic rôle of esoteric schools.

An example of this process was seen in the Renaissance, when the opposing forces of chaos and order manifested in terrible religious wars and persecution on one side and great works of art and scientific discovery on the other. The latter was stimulated by the influence of Neo-Platonic and Kabbalistic ideas. This may not be apparent to most people because such injections often came in at a high and discreet level through essentially obscure men, such as Dr. John Dee, the occult adviser to Queen Elizabeth, or Francis Bacon who, although outwardly a political lawyer, nevertheless had great influence upon the ways of government, science and art. Shakespeare, for example, undoubtedly belonged to this esoterically-oriented circle. His work is full of ideas that no countryman from Stratford-on-Avon could have encountered. The scene in which Portia speaks of Justice being tempered with Mercy, and how Mercy is an attribute of God, certainly indicates a knowledge of Kabbalah. This 'Invisible College', as it was later called, was behind the transformation of England from an offshore kingdom to a cultivated world power that projected respect for law and democracy to many parts of the globe.

However, times have changed and esoteric ideas are no longer directed so much at governments and legal establishments as they are towards scientific discovery which is, to our age, what creative art was to the Renaissance. Therefore, let us look at a school operation of today and how it might be handled with this objective in mind.

Let us suppose that the scientific study group of the school has made some important correlations and discoveries about kabbalistic theory in relation to modern physiology and psychology. It could produce a paper that is read at the Annual General Meeting of the whole school and even publish it, with copies going to prominent people in the scientific fraternity who probably would not read it. This, clearly, is not a very satisfactory method of disseminating higher knowledge into the outer world. A way has to be devised to draw attention to what is offered and attract the right people. Therefore those with experience in such matters in the school are consulted. They might be academics, advertising experts and journalists. The conclusion might be to set up an open conference because this is the acceptable mode of gathering interested people. It will be designed to draw both the scientifically-minded and those concerned with esoterica. This could be achieved by inviting some well known and respected person who is prepared to talk about the relationship between ancient knowledge and modern discovery. When such a figure consents to talk at the conference, plans can then go ahead in which two members of the science study group can present their findings to illustrate what the leading speaker is saying in the light of the two disciplines.

Having obtained permission from the school's council, a conference unit is formed composed of people with the talents and connections to organise it, to hire a hall and to set in motion the publicity so that on the day perhaps five hundred people will arrive for a conference, officially sponsored by a 'Society for the Propagation of Ancient and New Ideas'. The publicity for the 'SPAN' will have to be designed to catch the attention of seriously-minded people who are prepared to step outside their professional framework or rôles, if only for a weekend, and share their interest in things of the Spirit. To add an enticement, the brochure might say, as an incentive: 'Here is an unusual opportunity to meet others in different disciplines who are intrigued by the similarities between scientific metaphysics and spiritual philosophy.' The school may choose not to use the word 'Kabbalah' in the handout, in case people thought it was concerned with magic, as many do. Once the audience is involved it is a different matter.

The conference might take the form of a general introduction, given by a chairperson, on the relationship between the esoteric view of the body and psyche and the scientific approach, after which the main speaker would deliver his lecture according to his experience and findings in the related fields. This might be a talk on a particular aspect such as the working of the brain and consciousness, the body and the chakra centres of energy or, if the speaker were privy to what is to follow, an exposition according to his understanding of the esoteric and scientific methods. This would prepare the audience for the talks on specific topics of interest, such as how the upper level of the body corresponds in energy and matter to the lower part of the psyche or how there is a clear resonance between the same triads of the psychological and physical Trees giving rise to activity, lethargy and disease. A detailed example of this might be the direct relationship between the feeling triad of Hod, Nezah and Yesod and the complementary triad of the organs in the body Tree. Out of this can come more detailed expositions of the four elemental levels of Earth or the mechanical and practical, Water or the chemical and emotional, Air or the electrical and intellectual and Fire or awareness and will; and further, the interaction of the pillars of psychological and physical energy, matter and consciousness.

In the questions that might follow much could be transmitted to an intelligent audience. Such ideas as the Self and the central nervous system being the same principle but in different anatomies; and the notion that the soul is the psychological equivalent of the synthesising processes of metabolism could stimulate much thought in people who recognise facts or have intuitions but cannot see the connections. Kabbalah has a scheme that covers all aspects and relates them very precisely which is what a scientist wants. It has actually happened, in a conference that was arranged on these lines, that some of the audience have suddenly been shown a missing link in their work, because the sefirotic Tree revealed the complementary aspect or factor needed, such as the recognition that all processes have an active, passive and controlling principle. The idea that there are four interpenetrating Worlds often has a profound effect on those who have never seen the diagram of Jacob's Ladder. It explains how and why certain phenomena do or do not relate. The distinction, for instance, between the vegetable and animal levels and the human aspect of the psyche

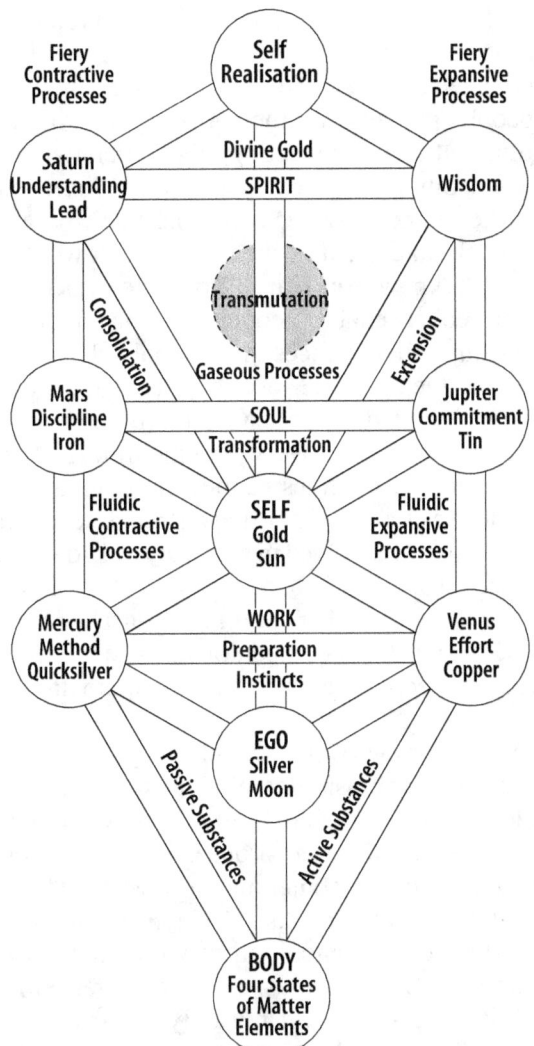

Figure 26—SECRETS

During the terrible war between the Catholics and Protestants around the time of the Reformation, schools of the soul had to conceal themselves. Out of this problem came Alchemy, in which esoteric ideas were cast in chemical terms. This was designed to allow people of good will on both sides to communicate without their respective authorities knowing what they were really doing. When set on the Tree the metals, processes and aim to make Divine Gold make esoteric sense. It is all about transformation of gross matter into a more refined configuration. For example, the soul has to have the strength of Iron and the softness of Tin, or Justice and Mercy, while Air is clearly Spirit with Fire as the Divine transforming element. (Halevi.)

places the work of the behaviourists, and of Freud, and Jung, in perspective.

The effect of such a conference can be quite dramatic. Not only are there many people, perhaps half the gathering, hearing esoteric ideas for the first time but they are meeting others there whom they would not normally encounter in their profession. Some will be quite surprised by who attends, not realising that this or that professor or co-worker is deeply interested in such matters but would never let his or her colleagues know for fear of ridicule. Encounters at such conferences, moreover, enable people working in isolation to meet and form friendships and alliances that not only change their lives but alter the course of their work. Most new discoveries come about by the cross-fertilisation of different and often unrelated factors. Many occur by accident, like the discovery of penicillin. Here, the conscious connecting of various disciplines enables more creative possibilities because, if one looks closely, very often a strange set of circumstances brings people not directly involved in spiritual work to such conferences. It might happen through the chance seeing of an advertisement, a decision to come because another option was cancelled for that weekend or because a friend wanted a companion at the conference. Whatever the reason, it often becomes apparent that it was vital that they were present.

From the point of view of the school, the job is done once it has acted as a catalyst and transmitter. Kabbalistic ideas have gone out into the world in an acceptable form. If the conference has been successful, then there is clearly an aroused interest in those unfamiliar with the Tradition. This is sometimes assessed by the numbers of esoteric books bought at the bookstall which should be provided and staffed by members of the school, all of whom have been instructed to hold their attention in consciousness so as to raise the level of the conference. This collective effort not only creates a clear and lucid atmosphere but eliminates the hidden element of petty competition that is seen at many scientific gatherings where people try to discredit each other's theories. This presence of conscious intention allows the influence of the upper Worlds to permeate the conference, so that people draw closer and become more open to each other as the hours pass in listening to lectures or in private conversation. This attention is held right up to the end of the conference when it is earthed by everyone taking some conscious substance home or back into their profession. After all have gone except school members, there should be a ceremony of thanksgiving, even as there was one of dedication before the conference began in the place in which it was held.

An historic precedent for this type of gathering was the Royal Society in England whose roots lay in the previously mentioned 'Invisible College'. Its members included people like Harvey, who discovered the blood circulation pattern, and Sir Isaac Newton who was much more of a mystic than a scientist with his deep preoccupation with the Bible. Indeed, it might be said that if Newton had not had an esoteric outlook, he would never have thought in terms of universal laws when he saw the apple fall. Only a person who considered the interaction of everything in Existence could break out of the mundane logic of the senses. Such a view is particularly kabbalistic. In our own time, Taoist metaphysics have had much impact on thoughtful physicists. This school's influence came from the Orient via the west coast of America. Much has yet to be done in this same area with Kabbalah, which is of the Occidental Tradition, and so such events as those described in this chapter are designed to act as a stimulus. Having set out an external situation, let us now look in exactly the opposite direction and see how an interior mystical operation is set up by a school.

49. Building the Temple

Every true and living school has an inner core of those who are fully committed to Kabbalah and know its purpose as a living reality. These people are those who operate at the level of the soul triad of each group and give conscientious service to it for its own sake and not for what can be got out of it, even for personal development. Such people know how to receive and impart and have reached the point of 'not my will, but Thy Will be done'. In a group of thirty, perhaps five or six individuals may have reached this level of psychological maturity and spiritual responsibility. There will be others who can enter the soul triad but cannot, as yet, sustain themselves in it long enough with any reliability. Something will always distract them and they forget or go off on personal side trips.

This inner core of deeply involved people is the collective soul of the school. They may not meet often but the quality of the school and its spiritual capacity depend on them as much as on the calibre of its tutors and the inner connection of its leader. This senior section of elders, together with the main body of students and beginners, makes up the Tree of the organisation. Now while there may be a tutors' group taken by the head of the school, there may not be a group composed only of elders. They are usually distributed equally throughout the organisation, so as to maintain a good level in each group. If they were concentrated into an exclusive group, this would leave people in a less aware state without any contact with advanced individuals. However, there are occasions when the different levels in the school come together to carry out special tasks, such as 'Building the Temple', which require experience, knowledge and psychological and spiritual resolution.

Such operations might be convened to take place at certain times of the year, such as at Passover and Easter, the spring festivals of Resurrection and Salvation. They might be arranged to take place in the school building or somewhere else far from the centre of the Work; they could even occur on a sacred site. The people invited would be those each tutor knew to be members of the inner core of his or her group. The organisation of the operation would be discreet in the truly esoteric sense, in that it is hidden and people would be required to say nothing outside of what was to be done. This is not just a matter of tact and discipline but conserves and seals the force, form and consciousness of the operation. A particular day would be selected for its celestial auspiciousness, to be the time focus on the place. People would arrive the day before and go through the procedure of preparation, such as a solitary or group meditation, and instruction in what is intended on the morrow. Participants would then make their bodies and psyches ready for the event.

The plan in this case is to construct a sacred building in the Worlds of Formation and Creation which are the homes of the soul and spirit respectively. This should be done by the company, which might be about forty or fifty in number, forming and creating a Temple, based upon the kabbalistic model set out in the Bible, in a location dedicated to holiness. The construction should be directed by the leader of the school with the most senior elders watching over the site from the four quarters to guard against intrusion and to take care of anyone who might require help. The process should be started with a dedication and a statement of intent, after the usual invocation of the Tree and Holy Names. Having done this, participants then visualise the art of disrobing and taking a *mikvah* or ritual bath. This is done by the leader creating and forming an image of a sweet-watered cistern into which people step and bathe themselves. Having thus been cleansed in form, the company now visualise themselves robed in white, blue and purple. These colours are the traditional hues specified in *Exodus* for the Divine, spiritual and soul levels of a human being. Having completed this phase the company is ready for *avodah* or Sacred Work.

After seating themselves in a circle, the leader then describes the Holy Mountain within the space they contain. It is not of this world and so its dimensions are of a different scale. Once the visionary setting has been established, those present are asked to make observations on what they perceive so that a collective image forms the base of what they are about to experience. These pauses for reports on what is seen and felt are vital in the build-up of the power and substance of what the group is to construct. The leader then designates the four quarters of the circle to begin preparing the site by clearing and levelling it, in the mind's eye, and reporting back periodically to the group on the progress and problems encountered. These difficulties, of course, are generated by individual imperfections for they are, in fact, preparing the site for the Temple within themselves. Particular imbalances might be overcome by direction from the leader or suggestions of the tutor in charge of that section of the site. The work is carried out until the imaginary area is quite level, flat and ready to receive the first stage of the outer court.

The outer court, representing the human as against the natural level of the World of Asiyyah, is begun after a break for coffee; for one must never lose contact with the Earth. This is constructed in the group imagination by the leader who describes the stages of laying down a tiled floor and building up the outer walls with their four gates. The centre area is left bare for what is to come. Again, the problems encountered during the building are examined during the periodic pauses. For example, getting a door lintel just right would reveal as much to the company as to the person working on it. Some people might find the effort to imagine labour easy, others more difficult; some people's attention might be distracted or they might become obsessed with what they are doing. All is noted and corrected as the outer court is slowly brought to a point of completion and decorated with simple motifs based on natural forms, to represent the lowest of the four Worlds. Rest comes in the form of lunch.

The design of the inner court is more elaborate. It should have flowing forms and many colours. The leader might describe symbols related to the growth of the soul, the levels of the psyche, the planetary influences in fate and the patterns in individual types. The company would interpret these instructions, each according to his understanding and yet, in the reports, many common factors should emerge in the communal image each is building. The inner court should, according to the Work put in, gradually take on a quality that is quite different from the outer court in that it has a more fluid character in which everything seems to be on the move in rhythms of brightening and darkening, blooming and fading. Some people can be disturbed by the endless movement and they should be prevented from panicking, either by being held steady or retiring from the Work to the outer court where they can recover in its earthy stability. When the court is finished, people should give their impressions of it so as to complete a composite picture. The break for tea should act as a touchdown for a while. By the time Work is begun on the sanctuary, the company should be deep into the experience. For example, by now people will be able to enter the imaginary construction area with ease because it will have a reality of its own. This should be so strong that when the

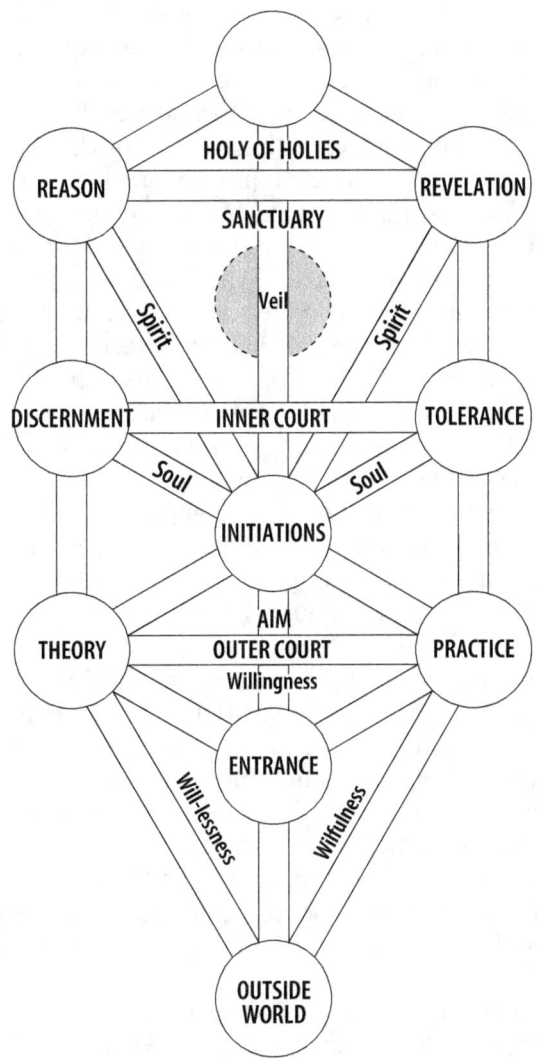

Figure 27—TEMPLE
Any school constructing a sacred place should follow the principles of the Tree. For example, an esoteric space must have an upper and lower area. Here the Biblical Temple sets out the basic plan in which different activities can occur. A design can be horizontal or vertical, round or square, outside or inside and be simple or elaborate in symbolism. It does not matter. This is a question of choice or culture. Whatever it is, it must be dedicated to the aim of the school or it will remain a secular structure. Some buildings, in time, become great monuments to civilisations, like the Temple Mount in Jerusalem. (Halevi.)

leader gives out the directions for the assembly of the Sanctuary, individuals will instantly know exactly what is required of them and go where they are needed. As a matter of interest, some people are quite surprised at the tasks they find themselves doing. Once, during such an operation an architect, with what he thought were great ideas, found himself inwardly directed just to making the pillars. This labourer's task was a significant experience. As the sanctuary rises, it should evoke a sense of the Heavens, the walls and furniture reflecting celestial space and its inhabitants. Symbols of the stellar regions and archangels may emerge in the collective imagination as it builds on a sacred site that no fleshly eye or hand has seen or touched. As the Sanctuary is brought to completion, the company will become awed that the space is indeed a sacred vestibule for the Holy of Holies. The operation should be terminated at this point for supper before the company peaks in the construction process.

After an early and light supper the company should return to their sacred circle to finish building the Temple. This is done by the measured instruction of the leader in setting up the altar at the centre of the Holy of Holies and enclosing it within a white cube that has a single door facing east which is veiled. Much time can be spent on getting it as near perfection as humanly possible, in imagination, by working on the ceiling, each wall and the floor. After this is done the altar, which is a cube of pure black, is set in the middle of the chamber. This represents the Nothingness amidst the pure white of Divinity. The curtain at the door should be of the deepest blue in colour and have the design of the Sefirotic Tree on it embroidered in gold. This should radiate a scintillating light while concealing the total darkness within the Holy of Holies. When the company has completed the Work everyone should retire from the building to rest before meeting for Divine service, later in the evening.

At the appointed hour, everyone should assemble in the place of the circle in silence. At the moment when all are ready, the leader should begin with the invocation and dedicate the Temple before them to the service of the Holy One. To most, if not all present, the Temple will be as real, if not more so, than any earthly construction. It will have a quality of profound beauty and stability that no elemental decay in Nature can touch. When the company is aware that the Spirit is flowing down to enter the edifice, the leader should take them up the Holy Mountain and in through the door of the outer court. Here they should pause to reflect in silence as they slowly progress, stage by stage, around the court before entering the inner court. After circling this in a slow progression, the leader should gather the company opposite the gate to the Sanctuary. Here they should wait and meditate upon what has happened since they began building the Temple. When they have shifted from the psyche to spirituality they should enter the Sanctuary singly and stand in prayer before the veil of the Holy of Holies. Here they may become conscious of the Presence which now resides behind the veil as the leader dedicates the Temple for the school as the House of the Holy One. After each person has made his or her personal dedication, the company should then withdraw and return to earth under the direction of the leader who brings them, slowly, back into the original physical space before retiring for the night. On the following morning all should return home to the world knowing that from this time on, the school has its own invisible place of worship that may be reached from anywhere—for it is not on the earthly plane.

Such an inner Temple may exist in another reality but it is there and can be entered each time the inner core of the school meet. People can go to it as individuals or in a group. It will exist as a usable entity for as long as the school continues and, indeed, even centuries after the school has gone it can be contacted by the perceptive as a memorial of that particular school. Such a building can only come into being by intense effort. However, it has to be maintained, like any sacred building, or it will decay and be deserted by the Holy Spirit, only to be taken over and inhabited by who or whatever can gain access. Therefore, the school Temple should be carefully nurtured by the constant use and dedication of the members who know of its existence. Here is the connection with the Heavenly Temple in the Celestial Jerusalem that is the model and the focus of a sacred building, whether in this World or the next.

50. Networking

In ancient and medieval times Kabbalah operated at both an individual and a collective level. Kabbalists were scattered all over the known world, from Persia to the Yemen, from Mesopotamia and Palestine to North Africa, Asia Minor, Eastern Europe and as far north as England, Germany and Poland as well as Spain, Portugal and Morocco. Most of these Kabbalists worked in small groups attached to the local synagogue. They studied Kabbalah as an additional practice to the usual Talmudic curricula and religious cycle. Some people working in isolation had minimal contact with the chain of Teaching but they were always deeply immersed in the culture of the Jewish world. This sense of culture embraced not only Jewish religious values and the sense of being a nation dispersed throughout the world but of being part of an extensive Jewish communication system. This was based upon the trading connections set up by ever-migrating families with relatives in different countries. Thus it was possible, not only to know what was going on politically and commercially throughout world Jewry, but to hear about the latest preoccupations of scholars for it must be remembered that all adult males could read, if not speak, Hebrew which was the *lingua franca* of Jews. This gave rise to a kabbalistic network throughout the Middle Eastern and Greco-Roman empires, and later Europe, with nodal points in different cities at various times, like Gerona in medieval Spain and Kracow in sixteenth-century Poland.

Some time in the ninth century of the common era a certain Rabbi Aaron ben Samuel, who belonged to a family of mystics, travelled from the School at Baghdad along the trade routes west to the great sea and to Italy. From here his teaching was transmitted up through Italy to Provence but not before crossing the Alps and being picked up by groups in learned communities that had been in Germany since Roman times. The westbound flow, meanwhile, moved into Languedoc and passed into Spain to meet another flow that had travelled along the North African coast and into Moorish Spain. When the two streams met there began a Golden Age of Kabbalah with schools arising throughout the Peninsula. The most significant of these were in Toledo, Gerona and Burgos which were intercultural centres drawing upon influences coming from Islam and Christendom as well as the old Greco-Roman civilisation. Here we get the sense of the importance of time and place. However, without the networking of Kabbalists over the centuries, this creative period of Spanish Kabbalah that formulated the diagram of the Sefirotic Tree could never have happened.

An individual example is the travels of Abraham Ibn Ezra, a Kabbalist from Toledo. He not only wrote a number of important learned and esoteric books but visited various schools in France, Italy and England in the twelfth century. It is recorded that the new formulation of the Teaching that he brought had a great effect on the groups he contacted, sometimes upsetting the more conservative members. However, what he had to transmit was so important that he was invited to England and lived in London for a year or two where he wrote a book on astrology. He no doubt visited the communities at York and Oxford where there were certainly groups of learned, if not esoterically inclined people. Such connections were crucial to the Tradition, not only to keep it alive but in touch with what was going on in the larger scale of things. Thus innovation or conservation, depending on the need of the time, was disseminated throughout the network of the known world from the various centres to its periphery. Here we have another level of esoteric organisation.

In our time Kabbalah is no longer exclusively Jewish but the principle of networking is the same. Throughout the modern world there are many schools based upon either Kabbalah or a parallel Teaching which, in essence, is identical. This does not mean that there are no differences—these are right and necessary in order that the needs and conditions of that place should be met; however, the spiritually-oriented community is in closer contact now with the Tradition than it has ever been. The old concept of infidel or gentile cannot apply to people on the Path. Cultures may differ but the pursuit of right action, true devotion and the contemplation of reality bridges what differences there may be in detail. Kabbalah, when presented to the committed Hindu or Buddhist, is quite recognisable to them as the same esoteric scheme, as are the Sufi or Native American Indian Teachings about the relationship between man, the universe and the Divine.

In the case of Kabbalah, the cross-connection begins between the groups within a school. Here the natural differences of style and character are used to open out the scale of Kabbalah so that the groups that work primarily through action can see the value of contemplation and devotion and *vice versa*. This gives a school a richness that no one working method could supply. A meeting once or twice a year of all the groups is an excellent way of communicating developments. Besides lectures on ideas, there can be demonstrations of meditative techniques and special rituals. Private conversation and public discussion will add to the varied mixture from which, perhaps, could be generated a new and original impulse as certain discoveries are cross-fertilised to produce a Kabbalah that is intelligible to the next generation. This, in fact, is what happened in medieval Spain where Kabbalists had to meet the menace of philosophy based on pure logic, that had infatuated the intelligentsia of their time. The schools there took Kabbalah out of its old allegorical and Biblical vocabulary and cast it in the form of an esoteric philosophy which caught the imagination of many seekers who had turned away from the orthodox presentation of the Teaching because they had been educated in the 'New Learning' that was fashionable then.

Today we face a similar situation but on a global scale. However, the process of networking still functions through people, so that when two schools in different countries link, it will be by means of the connection made between individuals. Such contacts may come through so-called 'accidents' (the hand of Providence) or by conscious effort. Meetings can occur in a bookshop in Jerusalem or during a dinner party in London. They can come about by an invitation of one school to another to send someone to speak on their Tradition or at an ecumenical conference of faiths where members of different schools liaise with one another.

Now, while such encounters are part of the present day work of schools, there is a definite etiquette that must be respected. No member should try to convert someone from another Line. Nor should there be any pressure, if a person is unsure of his present position, although he may be permitted to come to a meeting of another group as a visitor. It is only after an individual has finally and independently decided to leave his current school that he can be considered as a prospective member. Within meetings of different groups and schools there must not be contentious debate about the merits of the different systems and working methods. Such conflicts usually arise from the ego and its sense of superiority which, when threatened, can destroy much goodwill between individuals, groups and schools. Respect for different ways of working is vital. The ability to perceive beyond the outer form of another Tradition is a sign of psychological maturity. Indeed, the hallmark of spiritual development is inclusiveness and not exclusivity. A Tradition cannot be universal when it accepts only its own view, whatever that may be.

In practical terms, networking means people travelling; that is, individuals going out and being aware of others on the Path, wherever they may be, in a village temple in India or a meditation centre in San Francisco. The spiritually-oriented always recognise each other because they are alert at that level, so that the awakened Westerner will know and be known by the Oriental equivalent. The Kabbalist walking in the streets of Tokyo will instantly recognise the student of Zen, not just by the clothes worn but by the eyes. Indeed, the less obtrusive the dress the better because it is the sign of true interior values. The Kabbalists climbing the Mount of Olives will acknowledge, and be acknowledged by, the Sufi who passes by, although neither will reveal by an outer indication that each knows the other to be a brother in God. These encounters are part of a general situation that is emerging throughout a world where cultures are intermixing. Initiates of every tradition are constantly meeting in business and social situations. The old racial barriers are dissolving and with that the inter-penetration and contact of esoteric systems deepens. A Buddhist monk might be found sitting next to a Hassid on the same flight; or a Zoroastrian working in the same office as a Rosicrucian. There is no end to the possibilities that Providence might organise. From our point of view they are all opportunities to make connections and bring about an increasing number of interlinking threads that make up the network that is being woven at the present time around the world.

The purpose of the network is not just to make friendly relations between various Traditions but to manifest what already exists on a higher level. In the upper Worlds there is little or no form of the Teaching and the problem of separation and competition, such as was seen between Islam and Christianity during the Crusades, does not exist; although different Lines and Traditions may be there. Here on Earth and in life, the lower levels of vegetable and animal drives, working through the ego, divide people into tribal units. Schools help individuals to become human and so the networking between Traditions brings about a greater sense of union and affects mankind as a whole. As one can perceive, this is part of the Divine Plan to bring the unity that exists above into a reality below. Such an operation can only be carried out by individuals who have reached a certain inner integration in themselves and who belong to a group which, in turn, relates to a school and Spiritual Line. This interconnection of levels enables influences to flow down from the upper realm and out into the world at every level from the Tradition to the individual who relates, as a cell of Adam Kadmon, to the whole human race.

Networking is a very wide and subtle operation. It cannot be encompassed by any one school, Line or Tradition. It is global in scale and works within the sphere of spirituality which, like the atmosphere and biosphere, provides an envelope of life around the planet. The *noosphere*, as Teilhard de Chardin called it, is the intermediary zone of consciousness between Heaven and Earth which enables Grace to flow down and nourish evolution. Networking is a crucial part of this process and schools are there to aid the connections between spiritually aware people who are part of a worldwide system for receiving and transmitting higher energy, substance and consciousness to the rest of the human species. Within this global scheme there is a vertical differentiation that disseminates the Divine influx to every level. This is the spiritual hierarchy found in every tradition.

51. Hierarchy

Besides the horizontal connections that a school may have, there is the spiritual hierarchy to which it is related. This is the factor that makes a group and school more than just a collection of people joined in a common purpose, like a business organisation or social club. It is this vertical dimension that gives a school not only its meaning but the power to function as an agent between the Worlds. Every relatively normal incarnate human being has a physical body and a psyche. They may not have a very well-developed spiritual organism but he or she will certainly possess a connection with the Divine; so it is with a school. Thus its buildings and the bodies of its members constitute the natural level with the psychological level interleaving with it through the elemental, vegetable, and animal strata of physical and social action. The truly human factor begins with the group meetings at the awakening triad. The soul level is the place where the inner core of the school resides and communicates with the World of the Spirit. Here is where the upper celestial academies contact the lower schools in the physical World and where they work together.

Above this area of contact lies a hierarchy of supervision, previously spoken of as the 'Academies on High'. These, as we have said, are concerned with the different levels and operations of spiritual work and relationship to various schools on earth, according to their capacity and quality. Some schools, for example, might be very small and in places remote from centres of civilisation, such as the one in the Outback of Australia where the light has just been lit and has to be nurtured until the time comes to meet the spiritual need of a growing community. Another might be equally small, like the tiny circle of masters in the Himalayas who have an enormous influence upon the spiritual atmosphere of the Earth. Such a school does not need the same kind of supervision as the flickering light in the Australian Outback; their brilliant flame may be thousands of years old. In contrast, a school in a large industrial city like Manchester will need quite a different sort of attention, as would the monthly meeting taking place in a farmhouse which serves as the local focus of esoteric work in Quebec, Canada. Likewise, schools at different stages of development clearly have to be taken into account, as each phase requires a particular kind of monitoring. This is carried out by those whose presence is sometimes felt in group work but rarely seen.

One way of perceiving a glimpse of this hierarchy is for a group to go into a deep state of receptive meditation. When everyone is tuned in, the tutor takes the group up out of the room they are in and into the 'upper chamber' that occupies the same space but not the same time scale. This is done by gradually loosening the sensual connection with the body and shifting consciousness from the elemental, vegetable and animal levels to the state of being alert and then awake in the triad of the soul, as has been previously described for other exercises. The difference here is that the tutor directs the attention of the group into a specific focus, as they visualise themselves seated in a circle round the chamber. Here they sit for a period observing each other and the architecture of the room as they establish the reality of the Yeziratic dimension. This chamber is the inner meeting place that has been built by the collective effort of the group over years of work. It will become, to some members, extraordinarily familiar and to others more substantial than any room on Earth. When the group has stabilised the image held in their communal consciousness, the tutor should ask whether there are any other people present. To their surprise, students sometimes perceive the presence of past members and even one or two who are absent that night. They may even become aware of entities who do not belong there and who might be friendly or hostile, according to the quality of the group. These, however, will not be so noteworthy as the other-worldly elder figures placed strategically round the chamber and the obvious leader of the inner meeting.

Some people see these beings quite clearly and others hardly at all. Many individuals only feel their presence while certain students are aware of red or blue colours. Occasionally, somebody will actually

---

Figure 28 (Right)— SITUATION
This Jacob's Ladder sets out a progress report on the current state of humanity. It is said that there is a limit to the number of sparks that make up Adam Kadmon and that many of them are now on the first journey of being incarnated. These are the young souls. Below them come those who have, for this life, destroyed their possibility of growth by being too wilful or willess. The vegetable masses are, on the whole, dominated by the animal level while those seeking to individuate, on the second journey, come under the guidance of those who choose to make the third journey to aid humanity to develop. At the End of Time, all will return to Adam Kadmon when God has beheld God through our SELF-realisation. (Halevi).

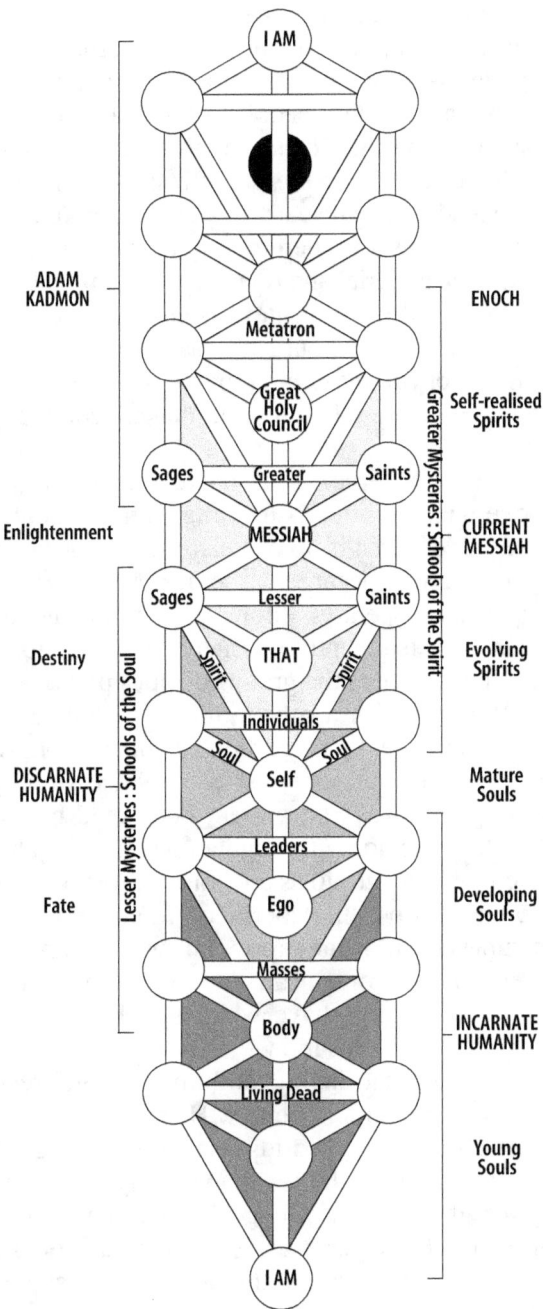

see a face or hear a voice and it has even been known for laughter to be heard during these interior meetings, which usually take the form of questions being asked by the tutor, for the group, or by individuals in a silent session, after which people report back on what has been heard. It is easy to see that such exercises are open to vivid imagination and great trouble must be taken to sift out what is projection and what is objective. The tendency to discard all such communication is as bad as accepting everything said. Therefore, much practice must be given to sorting through the material and rejecting what might be unwelcome intrusion from the hostile or mischievous entities that are attracted to such sessions. Conclusions should be based on reasoned reflection and a co-ordination of findings common to all members of the group. Nothing should be accepted unless it makes good practical and kabbalistic sense.

The purpose of this exercise is to make people aware of what is happening above while a group is meeting. A tutor should always be conscious of this level, even if no one else is. As a group develops so more of its members will became conscious of the *Maggid* or 'Inner Teacher' who usually operates through the tutor and occasionally through a student who is receptive. When enough members are tuned into the 'upper' meeting then the group becomes part of a great ladder of instruction. In the case of a school, the scale is larger and higher. This implies that there are distinct orders of supervision. A group, for example, will have several supervisors to watch over individuals. Such beings may not always be present but would be around when their particular charge is going through a crucial time. Then there are those who watch over the group as a whole to protect it from external intrusion or to check a psychic aberration in some member present. The manifest supervision of the group will work mainly through the tutor, whose personal mentor is nearly always present at the meetings. On the larger scale, schools have what is called a 'Watcher' who guards the spirit of the organisation.

Here it must be said that there is an important difference between human and angelic or demonic beings. Humanity has experience of the physical and all the other Worlds, including the highest, whereas the angelic and demonic entities know only their own realms, although they may be very knowledgeable and powerful within their context. Nearly all the supervisors encountered would have been incarnated human beings at some time and may, in some cases, still be in the flesh. The job of these supervisors is to observe and instruct at a particular level, for their own as well as our benefit. One does not automatically know everything on becoming discarnate. Supervisors in charge of specific groups have a particular task and might be seen as non-commissioned officers but of a very high order compared to the average member.

Supervisors concerned with schools are of higher rank. They will advise on tactics to meet the various phases and crises within the organisation. They might, for example, in an issue over delegating new tutors, influence a decision towards a more Gevuric or Hesedic approach or indicate that an increased emphasis on theory or activity is needed. This class of supervisors would be officers up to the rank of Colonel who are responsible for a regiment. Schools, like regiments, are specialists and perform in the field according to a wider plan. This strategic level is governed by what might be called the 'Keeper of a Line' who is responsible for the continuity of a particular brand of Teaching over a period of time. The rank of Brigadier might be applicable here, in that this level of operation means holding a section of an advance or defence of a Tradition which is watched over by the equivalent of a General or Master. The military parallel is not without reason as, indeed, a war between order and chaos, ignorance and enlightenment, is the constant battle going on in Heaven as well as on Earth. Indeed, the analogue of military ranks is reflected by the celestial army of angels and archangels commanded by Great Michael who is traditionally called 'Captain of the Hosts'. The Field Marshal might be likened to Metatron, the transfigured Enoch, who bears the Name of the Holy One and oversees the whole campaign of mankind's evolution, including its protection.

As we can see from the foregoing there is a whole chain of command, stretching from the seventh heaven where Metatron resides down to the individual in a group. Here it is remarkable to note that, while a person may occupy this or that rank which is merely a function in the hierarchy, he still has access to the highest, as many mystics have reported. Thus people have been shown the total scheme of the Worlds, like Rabbi Ismael in the Hebrew *Book of Enoch* whilst going through a personal initiation. This has also happened to a suburban housewife during a period of great crisis.

From the point of view of this chapter we should see how the vertical dimension is a crucial factor in whether or not a group or school is able to contribute anything above or below. A company of people with goodwill may have innumerable connections round the world but may be no more than an information dispenser, as indeed are many so-called esoteric schools. There has to be the upper connection which some people see as the spiritual core of humanity. In Kabbalah this is called the 'House of Israel', although it may also be known as the 'Isle of the Blessed' to some and 'The Assembly of Saints' to others. It has been named 'Inner Circle' and 'The White Lodge' but these are merely appellations to what is far above any sectarian or racial understanding of the holy hierarchy of human beings who have attained the greatest degrees of spirituality. These people, for that is what they are, form the upper links of the human chain of evolution. Sometimes they come down and walk on the Earth with us as incarnates although we do not always recognise them at the time.

Like great Teachers, schools have a destiny. Because the element of free will is a factor in human affairs, even a school can miss its moment in history. Therefore, those in charge of such operations have to be acutely aware of current conditions so that a school may fulfil the purpose for which it was brought into existence. This requires a deep comprehension of the past, present and future and the art of timing.

52. Timing

In the Jewish Tradition, history is the instrument of the Divine. Indeed the whole of Existence and its purpose is confined between the beginning and the end of time, there being nothing but God beyond either extreme. Manifestation is the mirror by which the Holy One beholds the Divine Reflection; the creative outgoing and the evolutionary return are all part of the process and cycle of becoming that perfect image of God. Kabbalah states, in its Teaching, that Manifestation is an unfoldment which passes through four distinct stages of Emanation, Creation, Formation and Materialisation. This descending sequence is a setting for the upward evolutionary impulse, begun in the production of matter and energy apparently out of nothing in the physical universe as consciousness crystallises at the Malkhut of Malkhuts. The subsequent rising up of the four elemental states to form the stars in turn gives birth to the more complex planets. Here we have the re-entry of the returning impulse into the World of Forms but in the concrete.

The differentiation of the various mineral elements reveals a refinement within that solid, liquid, gaseous and radiating level; and the emergence of living molecules from the earth's early ocean again shows a continuing progression. So does the separation of plant and animal into lower and upper strata in the organic state of existence. Here we have yet greater complexity and sensitivity allowing for higher consciousness, even if it is only to be aware of the seasons or friend or foe. With the superior vertebrates comes the maximum the animal kingdom can obtain until the coming of mankind; which is a quantum jump in consciousness because human beings can be aware of things not of the Earth. This added dimension not only increases the Earth's capacity for consciousness but marks the beginning of history where the interactions between the upper and lower Worlds are worked out in the fates of individuals and the destiny of peoples.

The Bible, like many other ancient texts, describes in myth the struggle and survival, the tests and their results on the ancestors of the human race. The essence of many stories is how one or two individuals raised themselves above the vegetable and animal levels of mankind and, with the help of angelic beings or the Divine, made direct contact with the higher regions of Existence and lived lives of quite a different order. Some of these heroes, as they are sometimes called, are good and some evil, according to how they utilised their knowledge in relation to their fellow human beings. Enoch, in the Biblical tradition, was the first to attain full development as an individual and teach what he had been taught by his contact with the unseen realms. The rest of the Bible is concerned with the transmission of this Teaching when applied to a particular nation which was chosen to demonstrate what and what not to do. The detailed record of the Children of Israel from Abraham, their first initiate, right up to the death of Joshua ben Miriam of Nazareth, illustrates very precisely the evolutionary process from the individual up through tribal to national to the universal, in the light of inner and outer development. However, the death of Jesus and the destruction of the Temple did not end the progression. This has been going on in the refinement of Judaism, the expansion of Christianity and the emergence of Islam, not to mention the many other Traditions.

The history of mankind, since it has been recorded, is outwardly the struggle for survival and domination, the evolution of physical techniques and the development of civilisation. The inward aspect of evolution is the same as in ancient Egyptian times. Individuals seeking to evolve have sought out 'those who know' as the gnostic mystics were called. Groups and schools to teach and train these seekers have operated in the Temple of Luxor as well as at Stonehenge or by the side of the Ganges. The monuments, diagrams and texts found in Mexico, Africa and Australia demonstrate over and over again the ever present spiritual work of aiding people to mature inwardly. Kabbalah is one of many such Traditions and occupies a particular position in Western civilisation as the source of many Lines that now seem very remote from their roots in Kabbalah. The Freemasons are one example, as are many of the ideas behind the occult school of the Golden Dawn. These branches and leaves are the products of schools which sent out specialists to meet the need of that moment in history.

One of the tasks of a school is to hold the purity of its Line and yet adapt its position, so as to be able to communicate with the current generation. This is not easy for, besides the conservative elements that always oppose innovation, a school has to be well prepared and finely tuned in order to carry out such an operation successfully. Some inexperienced groups, for example, will misjudge the moment, start an impulse too early or too late and miss the opportunity. An instance of this was a certain religious sect who, in their zeal to convert, got exactly the reverse of the reaction they wanted because they had not, to use a commercial phrase, 'studied the market'. To catch the mood of a time is a great art and, indeed, that is what Art is about. This is seen in the fact that music, drama, sculpture and painting evoke so poignantly a given epoch. From a school's point of view, it is the same process but in reverse in that its influence percolates through a community to help the natural structure and dynamics at work move in the direction of truth, love and right action. This is seen in the history of Europe during the seventeenth century when society was just beginning to emerge from an age of religious competition. Because of an esoteric input, science and art underwent a major change as people became more aware of the world, by European exploration of the globe Earth and the discoveries made by the microscope and telescope. Newton who, it will be recalled, belonged to The Invisible College, introduced the notion of a universal law in which everything affected everything else. This was possible because he and others, like Spinoza and Pascal, understood the mood of their time and spoke in terms that shifted the West out of the medieval beliefs into the Age of Reason although this epoch, like all others, eventually became decadent and turned into its very opposite.

A school can be the generator of such an impulse. If it is a fully developed organisation, it will have the infrastructure and external connections to do the job. For example, members will be dispersed throughout society and it will have access to the hierarchy of the upper Worlds. The question is 'What and when to transmit?' Some schools may have only one statement to make, such as 'meditate'; another might have the continuous task of training people to evolve as individuals. Yet another may be commissioned to put on a one-shot operation, for example to draw people's attention to some social problem such as economic slavery or an important reform in education. All these topics and many more have been influenced over the millennia by esoteric schools. Indeed, the *Book of Exodus* is all about an operation in which an unruly collection of tribes was turned into a nation modelled upon Divine Law. So too was the Church which transformed the Roman Empire into a spiritually-oriented civilisation. The fact that both the Israelites and the Church periodically fell from Grace illustrates how schools have to adapt to meet the changing conditions of their age, so as to keep the original impulse going.

Closer to our time we see the growth of a large number of movements that seek to replace the traditional sources of spiritual knowledge. This is because the more conservative circles of religious life have not moved with circumstances and still seek to retain old, established forms which were once a revolutionary solution to the same problem in its day. The synagogue was the answer to the destruction of the Temple and the litany of Christendom the replacement for pagan rites. For many people today these modes still hold but, for others, they do not and so many sects and preliminary training groups have arisen to meet their needs. Some of these operations are not genuine because they are based on motivations described earlier in this book[5]. The art of imitation is more to do with style than content. One must judge by the result. Does a group free or bind? Does the tutor live his or her Teaching or not? True teachers take care of the individual, even if they may seem to be very strict. False teachers seek to make everyone conform to their exclusive outlook and regard all other ways as heretical. This is exactly the reverse of spiritual work. Those who are part of a genuine Tradition which is carrying out an 'Impulse' operation proceed with enormous caution. Prudence prevents energy and knowledge from being wasted, so that the right moment for outward manifestation is recognised. When Joshua ben Miriam of Nazareth went down to the Jordan to be baptised by his cousin John, both had arrived at a point in their development when the Holy Spirit could fuse their respective tasks. At this juncture they met and their destinies entered history.

History is the instrument of the Divine. Everything that happens is planned, although it is the choice of individuals to react this or that way to the situation. Europe acquired a global empire because the balance of forces in the world, between 1500 and 1900, was such that large areas of the Earth would inevitably fall under her economic and military influence. It appears to have been a piecemeal operation. However, a deeper look reveals the hand of Providence working through the European experience to set up a model for a social and technical civilisation that would eventually free people from heavy and mechanical labour. This inevitably creates unemployment and the problem of how to use the released time positively in order to help the nations of the world develop physically, psychologically and spiritually.

The work of a school is to be in touch with the state of the society <u>in which it exists</u>, so that the esoteric movements in Russia are quite

---

5. See *Pseudo Groups*, Chapter 8

different from those in North America or South Africa. However, their task is always to bring the spiritual dimension into their midst by training individuals and creating a nodal point of higher reality, even as the monasteries did in the Dark Ages of Europe. Some schools may be required to do no more than this but others are brought into existence for a particular purpose, so that all the Work is but a preparation for a specific time. This could be the culmination of decades, the flowering of that school as it performed its part in the cosmic drama on Earth. Let us look at such a moment of destiny.

53. Moment of Destiny

Most people perceive history as something remote when in fact the everyday events of life make up the fabric of it. Wars and mass immigrations are made up of individuals caught up in a vast flow of cosmic forces. They are seen through events that happened to people personally, like the man who spent the First World War in the trenches or the woman who crossed the prairies in a wagon train. Millions of such incidents help to change the political map of the world or shift a whole population across a continent. We read of revolutions in Russia or gold rushes to Australia and see them in the lives that were carried along by a vast unseen impulse. It is only after the event that historians sort out what was really happening behind all the clamour, activity, mythology and reality of an epoch; and even then it is likely to be biased according to their nationality and level of comprehension.

People who perceive history from a spiritual point of view do not only see the physical reflexes of large masses and the reactions of the collective souls of nations but the cosmic implications of what is happening. They consider not only the economic and social factors of the time, such as a recession, but the very long-term view and the inner dimension of human affairs. They grasp what is coming, long before the learned pundits, even as the prophets of old time foresaw centuries ahead and knew why and what would happen if a certain course of action was not taken. These considerations are not based on a political frame of reference, which is concerned only with the obvious, but rather the understanding of the celestial climate that will favour this or that situation. In order to offset or encourage certain trends, such as a moral crisis in the West, a high level of spirituality is needed as well as a mature and efficient organisation to carry out the designs of the Watchers over the welfare of mankind. Here is where the destiny of a school comes in.

The prerequisite for such perceptions is that seeds have been sown many years before a crisis is due to happen and that as a tendency towards, say, barbarity or greater civilisation grows into a swell, so there are schools created to meet the challenge and convert it positively.

Moment of Destiny

The story of the Children of Israel going down into Egypt illustrates the point. Here there was a long-term plan to prepare the Israelites for a return to the Promised Land as a mature people, just as the Canaanites had reached their lowest point of degradation. The exercise of creating a nation, based upon Divine Law, could not have been carried out by one single individual. The training of Moses in Egypt and Midian was only the beginning of a group that was to develop out of the Israelite Elders. Later, this group became the school of the priesthood. The prophets took over when the priests lost the light and then the rabbis were given the job. Out of this Tradition arose the schools of Islam and Christianity. All was foreshadowed in the Divine remark to Abraham about becoming father to many nations. This is the scale of the Holy Spirit.

Taking a later example, when Joshua ben Miriam came down from Galilee to start his mission, much had been done already to prepare for the moment. At that time things were coming to a head in the Western world's religious life. The tension between God and Caesar was at a climax in Palestine. The old order was about to be ended. When the Romans destroyed Jerusalem, not only did they terminate the Temple services but exiled many thousands of people. This precipitated an outward movement as the Spirit manifested in the rabbinical schools outside Judea and in the Christian sect that was later to convert the whole Roman Empire.

The life of Jesus and the work of his school is a prime example of perfect timing. He matured at just the right moment and many of the connections with groups at home and abroad were open to receive the spiritual impulses that were to come out of the Holy Land. Thus both the Jews and the Gentiles of the ancient world were ready for a new lease of spiritual life, although it took several centuries for the general population to discard their old gods and worship a single Deity. It was a quantum jump in religious consciousness. On a smaller scale, the same thing happened in sixteenth century Safed when it became a centre of Kabbalah. For a few decades the town was the focus of enormous esoteric creativity as, with the aid of the newly invented printing press, schools sent out a shock wave of spirit that was still potent up to the last century. In the middle of this setting, the charismatic teacher, Isaac Luria, said to his disciples one day, 'Let us go to Jerusalem to greet the Messiah'. One pupil replied that he must first go home, another that he had things to do and another that he must make ready. Luria, we are told, shook his head and said that the moment had been lost; for to hesitate meant to miss the instant when a certain thing is possible and so the Messiah would not come that day. The moment had gone. The message here is that there is a precise instant when all the Worlds are aligned and an operation can begin. However, this moment can only be met if there has been preparation and if there is a readiness to take it.

Generally speaking it is probably correct to assume that a school is founded by 'those who know' many years before a certain expected event. The majority of the school may not be aware of this future moment, nor may many tutors who have spent their whole lives training others in self-development. It might be only a handful of elders who know what the purpose of that particular branch of the Work is. This is not strange because very few people reach this level of vision. Indeed, it is not uncommon for many hundreds of members to attend groups for years without having any real ideas, beyond perpetuating the Teaching, until someone comes with a message and a movement is begun to start a new religion or stop the slave trade or translate and publish some esoteric texts, because now the time is right. A school in Asia Minor was, no doubt, behind the great library at Pergamon which duplicated those books lost in the burning of Alexandria. That was their task. Another school influenced the drafting of the United States Constitution which emerged at a crucial point in history. Indeed, the moment was so critical that they timed the official signing to take place at the most propitious astrological minute.

At such a moment all the factors have to be in the right place. The people at the centre of the operation must be in line with what is coming down from the upper Worlds and those at the periphery must be correctly co-ordinated. If a school is not ready at the time, it will not be able to receive the influences flowing towards it. The slightest collective tremor will lose the focus and the misalignment will not allow the flow through. Unfortunately, earthly conditions are not always ideal to receive the influx because the psychological climate may be the exact reverse of what is needed. Thus, if things are not skilfully handled, the manifestation generated can become either fanatical or stillborn in its response to political conflict, social laxity or bad economic conditions. Not every great sage or saint is fortunate to have favourable circumstances. Confucius wandered for many years from court to court seeking a wise patron. The time was not right for his Teaching to earth. When the great Kabbalist, Nachmanides, was expelled from Spain and went to Jerusalem in the thirteenth century, he found the religious life of the Jewish quarter all but dead. He laid the seeds of a school that was to revive the Holy City as a spiritual centre in readiness for those who were to come *en masse* from Spain in the great exile three hundred years later. Little did he know, or perhaps he did know, that when he was banished from his beloved Spain he was making ready a home to which future Kabbalists would come.

A moment of destiny for a school, as for an individual, is concerned with the spiritual life; that is, it relates to a cosmic dimension that takes into account a scale of many lifetimes. Here we have an insight into the precision of Heaven, in how it manages to arrange so many elements to mature at the right moment. That moment might be conspicuous, such as that during the siege of Jerusalem when Rabbi ben Zakkai had himself carried out across the Roman lines as a corpse in order to preserve the Torah for future generations; or it might be very undramatic, like the unrecorded debate about where a certain key diagram should be released into the public domain, in order to clarify and unify the Teaching for its particular epoch. The answer came from Heaven, in that the argument was resolved when someone else, who had left the school, published the diagram without permission. This was seen as a sign that it was correct to publish it by those who originally opposed the motion. From this time on kabbalistic ideas underwent a transformation into contemporary terms.

The contribution of each school is made according to its particular character and era. Thus the Cordovero school in Safed added new prayers to the liturgy while the school of Provence introduced some novel and far reaching terms for the Absolute, like *En Sof* which means 'without end'. The Essenes developed a unique social system that became the model of many monasteries and the Merkabah Riders of the Talmudic period worked out their own peculiar mode of penetrating the veils of reality. Each of these schools was, at some point, the bright beacon of that moment. At one time the lamp shone in Pumbedita, at another in Alexandria, at another Lunel and in Toledo. Many years of preparation are needed to meet such a responsibility. Everyone involved has to be placed in the correct position by fate, coincidence or conscious effort. Fate is needed to get those who are unaware of what their life is about, as yet, into the right place in order to serve Heaven. 'Those who know' make a fine focus of their lives and tune it into the space and time designated to perform whatever needs to be done. For instance, when two members of a particular school were forced to leave their country, only the elder knew what was to happen and what needed to be done. It was only many years later that the junior, by then a tutor, realised what his teacher's instructions were. This was to bring an esoteric system to the West that was to affect many thousands of people in their development. Both men are now dead but the movement they founded still continues. In time, this school will fulfil the prophecy of its founder and go, according to cosmic law, into reverse. Once it has completed its task it will, like every bloom, begin to wither. The most sensitive and intelligent will leave first as the groups die inwardly and the school becomes a spiritless shell, like so many religious institutions. Let us examine the phenomenon and see how it is part of the process of death and resurrection.

54. Blossom and Decline

After a seed has gone through the processes of rooting, sprouting and leafing, it culminates in a flower. The flower unfolds at the most favourable time of the year for its pollination when the earth, water, air and light can bring it to its most perfect realisation. Then Creation converts matter into form by means of a rising impulse of consciousness that reaches its peak when the flower extends to its maximum experience of vitality and beauty. Such a moment may only last a day. At this point every fibre is firm and full and the colour fresh and sharp, as its scent is released into the atmosphere to attract the pollinating insects as well as decorating whatever place in which the flower is set. The same laws of development apply to a school when, like a human being, its prime is reached and everything seems to be in its place as it performs the work it was destined for, long ago, in the time and space of the upper Worlds.

To be present at such a point in a school's existence is a great privilege. It may last only a generation or even a year. Its quality is like being in a Golden Age. Nothing seems impossible. People are full of love and yet disciplined. The Work goes easily after, perhaps, decades of struggle. There is a sense of breakthrough and flow and one knows, without doubt, that somewhere there is a connection with the Academies on High for the Knowledge and Grace that pours down and through the school is of no ordinary human order. People who may be brilliant by ordinary standards are seen to know nothing in relation to the wisdom that can be imparted by quite mediocre tutors who are in tune with the harmonic of the school. Individuals blossom and groups grow in depth of understanding over months that, normally, years of labour could never obtain. Creation abounds. Houses are renovated and converted into temples with rooms filled with the sweet, silent Presence of the Holy Spirit that pervades all that is done there. Workshops produce masterpieces of calligraphy, cooking, scientific papers and plays or whatever speciality is being studied and practised. There seems no end to the possibilities the school might become in a flowering of creation and spiritual manifestation.

Such a phenomenon was witnessed around the Neo-Platonic and Kabbalistic Academy of Marsilio Ficino in Medici Florence. This esoteric school was at the centre of the Italian Renaissance and stimulated the impulse of development and creation amid the countermotion of war and destruction prevalent at the time. This was a case of a school acting as the ordering focus to the great energy present in Italy during that period. Elsewhere the cosmic dynamic was used to power the Reformation and Counter-Reformation which provoked the gruesome wars of religion and the terrible institution of the Inquisition. If Spain had not exiled its cultured and industrious Jews and Moors, the Spanish Empire might have been more liberal to its European provinces and less cruel to the American natives. England was fortunate to have a school at work in the late sixteenth century. Religious persecution was minimised during the Elizabethan reign; and Bacon's, Dee's and Shakespeare's work encouraged Arts and Sciences that were to make that country one of the leading lights in Christendom. The school which contained members at court probably had connections, via Erasmus, with a Flemish branch of the Society of the Common Life which was and still is a Line of the Kabbalistic Tradition.

In mainstream Kabbalah, such golden epochs are seen in the highly creative period of Gerona in Catalonia and at an earlier time with the school of Andalucia which produced the remarkable poet Ibn Gabirol who was also an original in philosophical thought. The period of the schools of Karo, Cordovero and Luria in Safed is the classic example of a golden era. Indeed, Cordovero's group method is regarded by many as the ideal mode of spiritual living. This group dedicated itself to a set of rules that were designed to evince the maximum spiritual purity. Alas, even this illustrious company, on reaching a peak of perfection, could not maintain the bloom of the flower once its zenith had been passed. Time changes every situation, at first imperceptibly, as the cosmic balance shifts and the flower begins, at its very tips, to fade. Difficulties between members of the brotherhood are recorded as the forces that had brought them to the possibility of living in true righteousness altered and created the first tensions of the next phase of the process, once the objective of the operation had been reached. This process stops psychological crystallisation and spiritual atrophy.

All esoteric traditions recognise that the moment of attainment cannot be sustained at the earthly level. It is not in the nature of the elemental World to remain still. The circumstance changes and those who recognise the reality move on with what the ancient Chinese called the Tao. In Kabbalah it is called the Way of the Lord or the Procession of Days from the beginning to the end of time. Those who see or perceive the beginning of the next cycle in the midst of manifestation adjust and do not hold on to what is but shall be no more lest they, too, become what has gone. They move on. Those who do not recognise this unfoldment of cosmic law miss the minute alterations that change a situation moment by moment. At first those who see it as something wrong try to correct it and, indeed, succeed in holding the process back for a while; but gradually any attempt to preserve cannot impede the inevitable transformation that goes on as time passes. The flower must wither and no amount of effort can restore its fading glory.

An example of the early stage of this phase is seen in a blind faith in the school, a little over-confidence and a certain amount of arrogance. People start to assume many things, take every rule and rôle for granted. The creative tension is no longer present and tutors start to become dogmatic. Students quote without thought and act according to instruction. The element of bureaucracy creeps in and principles become regulations. People start to think of the school as more important than the individual and, while this is true in one sense, it should never deny a person the right to be true to themselves. No one must ever become just a party member. To the perceptive, perhaps the most noticeable thing is the change of atmosphere in the organisation. It is less charged and lacks a certain clarity. Things are taken as fixed and less and less original reflection occurs. All these signs indicate the decline of a school that has done its job and is being phased out before it becomes a psychological prison of rigid forms instead of a place where people learn about spiritual freedom.

An example of a later stage of the process of decline is when a school no longer teaches but merely repeats what was once taught consciously. Many erstwhile esoteric schools are still to be observed doing this. The same material is used as in medieval times and so are the techniques. The language is archaic and the methods no longer efficacious, unless the students enter into the spirit of that long past epoch to preserve the illusion. Some ageing institutions don the dress of their founder's period and act out the modes and manners of that time in order to recapture what once was alive. Near the Old City of Jerusalem one can see college-educated Westerners dressed in the costume of the Hassidim which is a copy of that which the Polish aristocracy wore at the time of their founder, the Baal Shem Tov. For those born and bred into this lifestyle, within the closed compound of the Mier Sherim district, this may be a living reality but it is not the same for someone with the values of the late twentieth century unless they are trying to move backwards in the flow of manifestation. Spirituality is not generated by wearing the costume of another time or place. This can be escapism or the pursuit of a cultural identity. The cut of a coat may remain but Kabbalah always moves with the present. The Baal Shem Tov himself brought the Teaching up to date and spoke about it in the vernacular of his epoch. Alas, many of the schools which he started are now no more than dried out blossoms preserved between the pages of old customs.

The most recognisable sign of change is when the head of a school dies. If that person is indeed the link connection between Heaven and Earth for the school, some provision is usually made for someone to take over the position of leader. This is often planned for years ahead and several candidates are considered for the job. Sometimes the most obvious person is not the one chosen, because of some fatal flaw or because another individual is in fact better suited to the task. Occasionally a total stranger is brought in from somewhere else, in order to have an objective view of the situation, as the long and deep involvement of the school's members sometimes blinds them from seeing what should be done. This can be an elegant solution to an internal political problem. People in schools are still human and have ambitions, even though for the highest reasons. Indeed, well-meaning individuals can sometimes be the most dangerous block to a school's progress. They might, for example, seek to preserve all as it was in the leader's time right down to his pipe in the study or, conversely, desire to change everything and alter the character of the school so that many members rebel or leave. While such a transformation might be useful on occasions, it can destroy the viability of the organisation so that only those who agree with the new leader will stay. This is not such an uncommon occurrence and usually marks the end of that school's Work.

The fading of the bloom from its perfection is a perfectly natural phenomenon. The wise see it as progress and look to what might emerge out of the seed that must fall from the withering flower. Alas, few ever note what new thing sprouts at the foot of the dying plant or is taking root far away from its parent. As time passes only those with eyes to see will perceive the new because all the others will be looking back towards the old. The declining process can take hundreds of years. Decaying buildings and archaic forms are the hallmark as the rôles and power of the school become increasingly orthodox and political in orientation. Fortunately, the Line will go on elsewhere in a different manifestation until it, too, becomes redundant and gives way to the next cosmic phase as mankind shifts to the New Age.

55. Death and Rebirth

Once the central connection between Heaven and Earth has been broken, in the form of a departed leader, or the atmosphere of the school gradually becomes more social, so it begins to lose the Spirit. It was once noted by a visitor to several schools in a certain area that only about one in ten still retained the spirit of its founder. The rest were imitations of varying degrees, ranging from a perfectly maintained machine to a grossly incompetently run rabble. The former was governed by cold and dead intellect and the latter by animal magnetism and superstition. In between these two extremes could be found schools of muddled thinking, mixed disciplines, mindless copy and playacting. How, one may ask, can a school degenerate into these states which, incidentally, are quite recognisable in every spiritual Tradition? The answer is that the *Tiferet* of the school has been lost and with it its truth, beauty and integrity.

How does this come about? Firstly, the reason for the school coming into existence has been fulfilled. If this is acknowledged by the leader or senior members, then an adjustment can occur and a new aim set because there is always plenty of work to do, even if it is not as dramatic or spectacular as founding a movement or bringing about some innovation in society. There is always the perpetuation of the Teaching that must go on for each generation. It is like a woman who, having gone through the drama of courtship, marriage and bearing children, must take up the rôle of grandmother and operate off-stage and not at its centre. The ancient schools that acknowledged this stage of their life survived for many centuries doing just this. However, if a school does not perceive that its moment has come and gone, then its view of itself becomes a Yesodic image which is more concerned with its past than its present or future.

The image of a school that is influential draws not only those who seek to learn from the best esoteric situation of their time and place but those who want power of a different order from ordinary life. These people, as mentioned before, are either incapable of competing in the mundane World and therefore seek some occult advantage or they are individuals who wish to take over an existing situation they could never generate themselves. The former type usually emerges from the lower ranks of a school to take over the lesser but key positions in the organisation, leading to an inevitable increase in rules that are designed to control the members, because these people lack the being and knowledge to inspire authority in themselves. The latter type are usually more intelligent and manoeuvre their way through the unsuspecting hierarchy of the organisation into a position where they can affect the leadership directly. This is now possible because the check of the original teacher has gone and the person in charge is often a compromise between the two extremes that invariably arise within a dying school when the master has gone. The replacement person, if a candidate has not been nominated by the departed teacher, is frequently a nice but weak personality whom each faction will try to use as a front for their views. This figurehead is often displaced by our usurper who stages a crisis that sometimes splits a school down the middle, with the result that the power comes to them as the individual to meet the moment, like a Churchill or Napoleon.

Now while the foregoing may seem totally alien to esoteric schools, it happens over and over again because members are not prepared for it. While a school is under the direction of the Spirit, all will go relatively well. However, remove its cosmic purpose and it soon becomes like any other organisation into which social and even demonic forces will move in order to possess the reservoir of energy and substance that has been built up. A prime example of this was the dynastic struggle within the Hassidic movement where people sided with this or that relative of the founder rabbi. The Church has no better record, nor has Islam, when they became political. Among the Hindus there was a case in which a disciple actually took another to court because he felt he had been passed over in the succession. His master's judgement was quite correct. Every school has this problem once the inner connection is lost.

The realisation that the Spirit has departed may not be apparent for many years. Some schools can run on the momentum of their former glory for decades. People who travelled in the Middle East during the late 1800s found Sufi and Kabbalistic groups in Turkey and Palestine that were no more than faithful but quite empty shells of once deeply spiritual schools. However, before this state of affairs is reached, several stages have to be passed through. These can be roughly calibrated as the peak period, reflected glory, repeating momentum, declining energy, decaying form, decadence and death. Such a descent can occur over a year in the case of a small organisation or several centuries in the situation of a well-established academy with buildings and a hierarchy of tutors and administrators. In the case of the Second Temple in Jerusalem, the decline was cut short by the destruction which left only the rabbinic line to carry on the Tradition. This was called in Kabbalah 'The Remnant of the House of Israel'.

The remnant in a school are those members who still have an inner connection with the Teaching. This core may not have any organised form but, as long as each individual is committed to the school, so it will live on, hidden deep with the organisation, until they move on. Many of these persons may not be aware of what they are carrying except that they are somehow still carrying on the Work, despite the fact that they see the school drifting away from its original objective and into social politics and petty regulations. Such people might recognise each other in the groups that make up the school, if only by eye contact, in as much as they are awake to what is happening and are not taken in by the imitation of approved actions and ideas. Some will try to alter the course of the school from within the organisation but that will involve them in a power game which is not the point of the operation. Others will bide their time, hoping for something to happen; for some master to come and solve the problem that only they see. Yet others will simply leave, to vanish back into life and be lost, or join other similar schools at perhaps a more creative stage of their cycle.

The most committed will wait to see if anything can be done with the existing situation. Some might even try a palace revolution at an inner council meeting. These usually fail, because they are implemented at the same level at which the establishment works to preserve its authority; and the non-conformists are either edged out or isolated into a group especially created for such dissidents where their protest is spent on a tutor who is no more than a jailer. Here we see the decay of the spiritual into temporal power. The more wise and prudent might defer, for a very long time, before taking any action. Meanwhile they might operate as individuals within groups who question the interpretation of accepted working methods and ideas that are outmoded. Such people will draw to them those who may not be aware of what is happening at a deeper level but, nevertheless, recognise an honest enquiry in response to official dogma from a tutor who speaks not from him or herself but the party line. Such individuals can cause much havoc in a group and, very often, before they are removed by pressure or confrontation with a senior they are offered a bribe to conform, such as a tutorship. Some fall for this ploy, believing that something can be done from this position, and some soon forget why they became tutors as privileges accrue to them and their self-esteem. The Lucific principle can enter at any stage in the game, even into those who believe they act with the best of intentions.

Those who do not succumb to these and many other temptations, such as being a revolutionary or innovator as a means to notoriety or individuality, may move on to the next stage. This stage is the realisation that nothing can be done, that the school must go down and perhaps the quicker the better, as it draws inexperienced seekers into a World that is neither of the Earth nor Heaven but a self-contained illusion of a cult ghetto. A short walk through the religious centre of any country soon reveals how people can come to believe that they are elite and separate from the human race. This state can occur amid the most urban and educated societies. Having recognised the situation those alert to it can form, if only through meeting privately, an independent group. Such an operation clearly will meet with fierce opposition from authority and so very discreet gatherings have to be arranged through the informal grapevine system that arises in these kind of organisations. Sometimes out of these unofficial meetings comes the seed of the next stage of the Line.

As a school begins to disintegrate, so it loses the quality of its Teaching and practices. This means an increase in the number of people who do not understand what it is all about and a decrease in those who do, resulting in a further degradation of the Tradition into a mere shell. With the open politicising of the institution comes fragmentation in which various factions go their own way, each declaring that they have the authority to take the school's reputation and continue its task. Meanwhile, the soul of the school may be moving on, unbeknown to those who take up the official positions of preservers of the Tradition. This new movement could be the continuation of the Line but in a different form, although it might not surface for many years. As time passes, the original organisation will shrivel to become perhaps a tiny circle upholding an ancient candle that may not be lit, according to the rules, if fewer than seven members are present. When fewer than three meet then that school is dead, although the Line may now be carried on far from that place or in the next street.

Fig 29 WORK
The task of the trained Kabbalist is to be able to unify all the Worlds and levels within and relate them to the Macrocosm. Such a person can then make a connection between the higher and lower Worlds. Here the Kabbalist operates in harmony with the mineral, vegetable and animal kingdoms, the works of Nature and humanity, the realm of the elements and Solar system, as well as the angels and archangels. Here Great Michael and Metatron co-operate with the mystic, sage and saint so that the Divine can execute the plan of the Absolute. (Graphic, Halevi.)

56. Epilogue

We have seen, during the course of this study, how the Teaching comes out from the Holy One, through the great scribe Metatron and the Academy on High, down into the lower Worlds to reach one individual who becomes the agent by which the Teaching manifests in the physical World. We have been shown how a group is formed, its problems and the temptations of those responsible for its running. We have gained insight into the structure and dynamics of a group as it grows and how the various levels begin to differentiate. We have observed the crises that face a group from time to time and its gradual development into an instrument for more than just self-development.

We have glimpsed how, when the time is right and the people are ready, a quantum leap occurs as the group expands and divides in order to become a school and how this is quite a different scale of operation. In being shown the increased capacity to receive and impart and communicate with similar organisations, we perceive the wider and subtler networks of schools that span both space and time. This has given us an overview of the World of the Spirit as it manifests on the Earth and how all traditions relate, although they may be operating in quite different ways, according to their cultural and temporal setting. We also begin to see how each school is brought into being in order to carry out some particular spiritual task and that, once this is accomplished, it begins to fade so as to make space for the next school in the Line of its Tradition.

A Tradition is the broad way of a particular religion. It is the exoteric aspect of a mass cultural entity and serves as the gateway out of the mundane level of the festival cycle into the inner dimension of that religion. As we may now realise, it is all part of the process of return or *Teshuvah*, as it is called in Kabbalah. This is seen in the various levels of the chain of Teaching upon the Earth and how they bring individuals, groups and schools into direct contact with the celestial academies of the soul and spirit above. Those who have passed through a school of Kabbalah will recognise the stages and will know that these Lines of esoteric transmission are as real as any university, even though there is little trace of their existence beyond hearsay and a few fragments of literature such as the Zohar or, indeed, the Bible.

A Line may, at some point, be just one person and, at another, a mass of people concentrated in a city or dispersed among the nations. A Line is an ever-moving light that can illuminate briefly a large and sophisticated community like Philo's Alexandria or be preserved by tiny groups over the centuries like the Sephardi Kabbalists in Morocco. A Line can manifest openly as it did in Toledo or remain hidden within the great Talmudic colleges in Babylonia. It can be carried by the most orthodox fundamentalist in the backwoods of Podolia or transmitted by a university professor in New York City. The Teaching has no special conditions other than that Truth should manifest in the presence of an honest seeker. A school of Kabbalah is there to provide the follow-up, take those who wish to serve the Holy One and teach them how to become receptive to both the inner and outer Worlds and thus be able to act as imparters, whether as individuals or in concert with others on the Path.

The image of a school is a precise analogue, for it illustrates the various degrees of experience in consciousness, growth and capacity in a recognisable order. Through its gradation we learn how to come to terms with fate and to meet our spiritual destiny. Within the context of a group we can recognise our unique identity and relate the gifts we have been given to others' skills, not in the competitive way of the world but as each person fits into his own particular place in the school which is part of a whole that, in turn, is an element in a larger scheme and so on, until we see how everything is interconnected in time and manifestation.

Existence is the unfolding of the Holy Name I AM THAT I AM. Adam Kadmon is the as-yet incomplete reflection and we the spark cells of this Image of the Divine. Our task is to realise, in each of our lives, the God Consciousness that lies at the root of our being and pervades the universe. Schools of Kabbalah are brought into being to aid this process and place it in the widest and deepest context, so that we may gaze, in our moment of enlightenment, upon the countenance of the inner and outer Worlds and realise WHO beholds WHO.

Index

A

Aaron 40
Abraham 30, 34
Academies 277, 293, 300
Accidents 274
Active and passive rôles 187
Adam 27
Adam Kadmon 29, 49
Advice 99, 220
Ambition 209
Appointed hour 124
Architecture 243
Art 285
Ascetics 255
Astrology 67, 123
Authority 86, 243, 300
Avodah 229, 232, 267

B

Babylonia 30
Bacon 260, 294
Barakah 31, 40, 233
Bath 179, 267
Beating heart ritual 187
Beelzebub 207
Bible 30, 283
Binah type 69, 72
Blake 41
Body 163-165
Boehme 23, 29
Books 23, 244
Breakdown 150

C

Cathedral 243
Chain of connections 236
Chair ceremony 166, 248
Chariot 198
Charisma 56, 149
Charlatans 117
Choice 87, 194
Cinderella 252
Civilisation 25, 286
Colours 182
Commitment 171, 173
Communities 20, 24
Companions 21, 170
Competition 137, 170
Confusion 133
Conscious endeavour 255
Consent 171
Cordovero's group 294
Cosmic 127
Crisis 108, 193, 225
Cult 117
Cycles 225

D

Dark ones 78, 215
Dark night of soul 108
Dead 202
Dead schools 227
Debt 229
Deduction 248
Dee Dr. 260, 294

Devekut 256
Dew of Heaven 257
Discipline 133, 253
Disorder 227
Dissidents 225
Drama, sacred 183, 230, 252
Dress 56
Drugs 65
Duality 153

E

Ecstasy 132, 157, 188, 197, 259
Ego 50, 154
Elders 46, 47
Enoch 27, 29, 38, 147, 161, 229, 284
Entities 203
Epileptics 204
Essenes 35, 255
Eternal student 143
Euphoria 139
Europe 286
Evil 78, 91
Evolution 284
Exercises 158–167, 187
Existence 27
Experience 168, 174

F

Families 20, 21, 24
Fantasy 56, 197, 210, 256
Fate 170, 262
Ficino 294
Florence 239, 294
Fludd 32, 239
Free will 192

G

Gabirol 242, 246, 294
Gadlut 47
Games 143
Garden 250
Gerona 240
Gevuric type 69, 72
Glamour 139
Gnostics 284
Golden Age 293
Grace 77, 98, 276, 293
Groups 24, 31, 33, 47–53
Group Tree 59
Growth 73
Guru 56

H

Hassidim 56, 111, 119, 258
Heart exercises 186, 248
Heavenly Dew 232
Hermit 255
Hesedic type 69, 72
Hierarchy 77
History 244, 247, 283–287
Hod 154
Hodian type 68, 72
Hokhmah type 69, 72
Holy of Holies 270
Holy Space 178, 250–265
House of Israel 282, 300
Hubris 84
Hysterics 204

I

I AM THAT I AM 19
Ibn Ezra 273
Identification 173

Ignorance 97
Individual 21
Individuation 81, 173
Inflation 149, 175, 220
Initiation 86, 107
Inner circle 282
Inner conclave 234
Inner core 171, 173, 245, 266,
Inner Teacher 198
Innocence 97
Integrity 57, 175, 192, 211
Intercession 99, 232
Invisible College 260
Invocation 179, 248
Israelites 289

J

Jacob 38
Jacob's Ladder 154
Jerusalem 30, 31
Jesus 289
Joseph 38

K

Kabal 86
Karma 194
Katnut 47
Kavvanah 256
Keeper of Line 281
Konya 240

L

Language 72, 132, 168, 186
Leadership 53–56, 101, 245, 296
Leaving school 215
Lectures 222
Levels 20, 73, 126

Levi 40
Line 24, 42, 300, 304
Lord's Prayer 161
Love 138
Love affairs 169
Lucifer 139, 147, 174, 207, 211, 227, 242, 301
Luria 289

M

Macro-microcosm 247
Maggidim 41, 198, 280
Magic 134, 141, 204
Mantra 159, 258
Meditation 160, 231, 256
Melchizedek 30, 34, 38, 43
Merit 77
Merkabah 198
Merlin 139
Metatron 40, 147, 229, 281
Mikvah 267
Miraculous 117
Miriam 68
Modesty 173
Moment 290
Moon 67, 123, 183
Moses 25, 34
Mottos 126
Movement 231

N

Nachmanides 290
Nations 20, 24
Neurosis 143
Nezah 154
Nezah type 68
Noah 20
Noon fellowship 121, 242

Noosphere 276

O

Observations 153, 248
Opposition 78, 91, 171, 179, 188
Ordination 38, 42, 104, 233
Orthodox Line 216

P

Paradise 252
Partnership 51, 73
Path 21, 22, 201
Planets 67, 183
Possession 175, 206
Power 209
Power politics 236, 245
Prayer 258
Pride 149, 175
Priesthood 40
Projection 57, 73, 116, 137
Prophets 40
Providence 110, 113, 123, 172, 200, 227, 286
Prudence 286
Psychic powers 141
Psychodrama 184
Psychosis 93, 206
Psychotherapy 231
Public domain 220, 247, 260

Q

Quaternity 153
Question 190

R

Race 20

Raziel 27
Rebellion 175, 209
Recognition 116
Religion 25, 115, 244, 258
Remnant 300
Rôles 57, 117, 129, 139, 174, 230
Roots, rot of 228
Routine 209
Royal Society 265

S

Sabbath 247, 257
Safed 31, 36, 38, 41, 113, 122, 180, 218, 240, 289
Salt of the Earth 22
Satan 134, 147, 151
Scale 244
Scholars 141
Schools 24, 239
Seat of Disciple 198
Seat of Solomon 138, 151, 156, 166
Seduction 139, 234
Seeker 51
Sefirot 61, 154
Self 67, 98, 184
Self-consciousness 156
Self-deception 211
Sexes 187
Shadow 174, 207
Shakespeare 260, 294
Shem 38
Shema 158
Sickness 143, 231
Siege Perilous 74
Silence 156, 190, 258, 267
Soul 74, 249
Spinoza 32
Stairway 197

Steiner 242
Students 65
Sun sign 66
Super effort 225
Supernatural 202
Supervision of Heaven 86, 109, 200
Supervisors 280

T

Tact 171
Takeover 209, 228
Teachers 42
Teaching 17, 23, 24, 29, 30, 32, 111, 130, 216, 224
Templars 243
Temple 188, 199, 249
Temptation 139, 175
Three, group of 51
Threshold 156
Timing 88, 253
Toledo 35, 243
Tradition 24, 25, 51, 275
Tree of Life 59, 124, 154, 182
Tree within each Sefirah 184
Triads 184
Trinity 153
Trust 175
Tutors 71
Types 65

U

Unexpected, the 108
Unity 152
Upper room 62, 79, 144, 191, 199, 278
Usurpers 299

V

Veil of Heaven 98
Vessel 47, 52, 178, 180, 198, 232, 257

W

Wanderers 141
Watchers 280, 288
Weekend meetings 220, 246
Will 257
Wise One 249
Work 23, 33, 126, 173, 229
Workshops 246

Y

Yeshivah 17
Yezirah 74

Z

Zen 250, 275
Zodiac 65

www.ingramcontent.com/pod-product-compliance
Lightning Source LLC
Chambersburg PA
CBHW072046110526
44590CB00018B/3055